THE
VAVILOV
AFFAIR

THE
VAVILOV
AFFAIR

Mark Popovsky
with a Foreword by Andrei Sakharov

ARCHON BOOKS
1984

© 1984 Mark Popovsky   All rights reserved
First published 1984 as an Archon Book,
an imprint of The Shoe String Press, Inc.
Hamden, Connecticut 06514

Printed in the United States of America

The paper in this book meets the guidelines for performance and
durability of the Committee on Production Guidelines for Book
Longevity of the Council on Library Resources.

Library of Congress Cataloging in Publication Data
Popovskiĭ, Mark Aleksandrovich.
   The Vavilov affair.

   Includes bibliographical references and index.
   1. Vavilov, N. I. (Nikolaĭ Ivanovich), 1887-1943.
2. Plant breeders—Soviet Union—Biography. 3. Plant
geneticists—Soviet Union—Biography. 4. Plant-breeding—
Soviet Union—History. 5. Plant genetics—Soviet Union—
History. 6. Science and state—Soviet Union—History.
7. Political purges—Soviet Union—History. I. Title.
SB63.V38P66   1984   581.1'5'0947   84-9342
ISBN 0-208-02035-7 (alk. paper)

Contents

Foreword

The Vavilov affair, which took place some forty years ago and was one of hundreds of thousands of trumped-up and unsubstantiated cases that were fabricated in those frightful years, is for a number of reasons of great interest today both in the Soviet Union and in the West. One reason is to be found in the personality of the book's central figure, Academician Nikolai Vavilov, and in the tremendous services he rendered to science. Another reason is the special place that the Vavilov affair occupies in the tragedy associated with the name of the notorious Lysenko—probably the ugliest episode in the history of contemporary science. But perhaps the most important feature of the book is that it typifies the deep-seated processes and relationships operating in Soviet society at that time, no matter where the events were taking place: in a scientific institute, in a police investigator's torture chamber, in a death cell, or in the dissecting room of a prison hospital. Mark Popovsky's book is bitter but truthful. With good reason he says that, though Vavilov remained subjectively totally honest and utterly devoted to science and his country's interests, by some of his actions he did, in a certain sense, himself dig the hole into which he fell at the end of his life. At the same time the book reveals the true stature of Nikolai Vavilov, undistorted by the lies, embellishments, and half-truths of official publications.

Popovsky has succeeded in performing a great feat of journalism: by his persistence and at times his cunning he managed to extract from the hands of vigilant and highly placed officials (who were not quite so sure of themselves in October 1964) a "top secret" document from the secret police archives—file no. 1,500 on Academician Vavilov—preserving the notes he took on it in apparently harmless school notebooks and making them available to us. This is probably the only police file of such importance to be exposed in this way. From it we learn how the zealous investigator Aleksei

Grigorievich Khvat conducted his innumerable interrogations, and we realize that at the same time tens of thousands of interrogators were performing the very same task and demonstrating the truth of the saying "Just give us the man; we'll find a case against him." We are able to read reports by informers' and statements by "experts" that played a fateful role in the affair; we learn the names of the informers and are told about their later successes and entirely respectable fates in the society that replaced the Stalin system but that inherited too much from it.

I regret not having come across this book when Mark Popovsky was still in the Soviet Union. These lines are intended as a mark of my esteem for the author.

ANDREI SAKHAROV, ACADEMICIAN

Prologue
The Search for Nikolai Vavilov

Truth will come to light; murder cannot be hid long.
Shakespeare, The Merchant of Venice

It took me thirteen years—from 1964 until 1977, when I left the Soviet Union for good—to complete a draft of this book. The idea of writing it first came to me when I was on a visit to a town in southern Russia in the mid 1950s.

During my visit I took the opportunity of calling on an elderly scholar, a geneticist of some repute, who had been exiled to the town before the Second World War and was still living there. I expected the encounter to amount to no more than an exchange of pleasantries, with me doing most of the talking. It turned out quite differently.

Before I sat down to tea, my attention was caught by a picture hanging on the wall of the dining room. It was a photograph of a man of about forty, thickset, good-looking, and with a happy, self-confident smile on his face. Noticing my interest, my host said, "That was my teacher, Academician Nikolai Vavilov, the great biologist and explorer."

"A biologist?" I said, surprised. I had written many articles about distinguished Soviet biologists, but this was the first time I had heard of Nikolai Vavilov. "Don't you mean a physicist?" I suggested. "A physicist called Vavilov was president of the Academy of Science at one time."

"No, not him," my host said sadly. "The physicist Sergei Vavilov was Nikolai's younger brother. It's not surprising that you've not heard of Nikolai; no one has dared mention his name since he was arrested."

At this point the scientist's wife, a small gray-haired woman, broke into the conversation: "I have told you Nikolai Ivanovich's picture shouldn't be there. If you want to keep it, put it in a drawer in your desk. We have enough problems. I'm surprised they still leave you your job. . . . And all because of Vavilov. You know very well how many enemies Vavilov has and the sort of people they are!" The professor's wife delivered her monologue in a whisper, glancing continually at the windows and doors. "I have nothing to fear," her husband countered. "I haven't stolen anything and I haven't murdered anybody. And I'm not taking Nikolai Ivanovich off the wall. He hung there while Stalin was alive." The elderly couple fell silent, obviously cross with each other. I felt that I had touched off a long-standing family quarrel.

But they did not remain cross with each other for long. At first hesitatingly, with one eye on his wife, and then more boldly, the old scientist began to tell me all about the teacher he held in such high esteem. Yes, he said, Nikolai Ivanovich had been arrested. And he had been in prison, though nobody knew where. Some said he had been seen in Siberia, but most of his colleagues believed that he had been executed in Moscow at the very beginning of the war. The professor's wife pursed her lips tightly and rattled the dishes in anger; although Stalin was dead and people were talking disapprovingly of the "cult of Stalin's personality," she disliked talk of prisons and executions in her house. You never knew what might happen. . . . "You'd better tell him what a remarkable man Vavilov was," she said. "After all, the whole world knew of him."

That is how I first learned of the fame Nikolai Vavilov had enjoyed in the 1920s and 1930s. The professor gave me an outline of Vavilov's career: as a botanist, geneticist, agronomist, geographer, and explorer, he had visited more than fifty countries in search of plant specimens. In 1924 he became the first European to lead a caravan across Kafiristan (now Nuristan), the mountainous province of Afghanistan; two years later Vavilov's expedition had crossed Ethiopia. Later he traveled extensively in South and Central America, Canada, the United States, and Europe, visited Japan, Korea, and western China, and explored the Soviet Union from one end to the other.

His adventures brought him international fame and his name appeared regularly in the pages of the world's press as well as those of his native land: "Vavilov crosses the Andes!" wrote *Izvestia* triumphantly; "Vavilov visits Japanese scientists," reported *Pravda*. On his travels, he met with the future emperor of Ethiopia and with ministers of the British and French governments. The publication of his book *The Geographic Origins of Cultivated Plants* in 1926 was a major event in international scientific circles. In the same year Vavilov was awarded the highest Soviet decoration for science—the Lenin Prize—and was made a member of the highest state body, the All-Russian Central Executive Committee

His achievements were recognized by the scientific community: at the age of thirty-six Vavilov was elected a corresponding member of the Soviet Academy of Science, and five years later he became the youngest full member of the academy. At about this time he was also made a member of the Ukrainian Academy of Science, the British Society of Horticulturists, the British Association of Biologists, the Academy of Science in Halle (Germany), and the Czechoslovak Academy of Agricultural Sciences, and he lectured at international congresses in Italy, Britain, Germany, and the United States.

Carried away by their recollections of Vavilov, the professor and his wife painted for me a vivid picture of an extraordinary man. He had obviously been a scholar of exceptional talents, bursting with energy and enthusiasm for his subject, and admired equally by his students and colleagues, as well as by scholars the world over.

"But what happened?" I asked, interrupting the flow of words. "What was his crime? Surely such a man could not simply be seized and thrown into prison?" The elderly couple eyed me sympathetically: I was too young to understand. I belonged to the age group that had not suffered in Stalin's terror of 1937, had managed to survive the war, and had not landed in a prison camp during Stalin's postwar "purge." My view of the world was very different from that of these two people.

My curiosity was now aroused, but the professor and his wife could do little to satisfy it. They were still too frightened to talk about Vavilov's fate, beyond recounting some wild rumors— according to one account, after Vavilov was shot, his body had been dissolved in sulfuric acid in the prison. It was then that I decided that I would tell the story of Nikolai Vavilov and try to fill in the gaps in the professor's story. (When, some years later, I succeeded in establishing the truth about Vavilov's end, it turned out to be even more terrible than the rumors had suggested.)

The time was propitious for revealing the crimes committed in the Stalinist period. In 1956 Khrushchev had exposed some of the dictator's worst crimes and there was a noticeable thaw in intellectual life. But I knew I would have to move quickly: Vavilov's contemporaries were dying, records were disappearing, and memories were fading. The next day I called on the professor at his institute and told him I was going to write Vavilov's biography. "There must be a simpler way of committing suicide," he said.

"Why do you say that?"

"Remember what my wife told you about Vavilov's enemies?"

"Yes, but you also spoke about his friends."

"The difference is that while Vavilov's friends are learned and decent people, his enemies are powerful and utterly unscrupulous. In any case, his friends are not likely to talk very frankly to you."

The professor turned out to be right: it was nineteen years before my book was finished. After meeting with the professor, I began to seek out Vavilov's former pupils and colleagues to get them to talk about him; most of them fobbed me off with a promise to talk when they had some spare time. It was only at the end of 1964, when Khrushchev fell from power and there was another brief thaw in the intellectual atmosphere, that I managed to collect a number of stories dealing with the Vavilov affair. In the end I interviewed about a hundred people.

The first documents I managed to get my hands on were the records of the All-Union Institute of Plant Breeding, which Vavilov had established in Petrograd (now Leningrad) in 1921 as the first section of a future Academy of Agricultural Science. Later I examined the records of the Geographical Society of the USSR, which Vavilov headed from 1932 to 1940, the Soviet Academy of Science, and Academy of Agricultural Science (often called the Lenin Academy).

Slowly the story of Vavilov's life began to emerge; even in papers relating to the 1920s I began to come across hints of the tragedy of 1940. What had at first seemed to be disconnected halves of Vavilov's biography—the brilliant biologist and the condemned prisoner—started to make sense. With each new bundle of files that

I examined, I saw with increasing clarity the process that had finally landed this great scientist in a prison cell and the reasons why a man with a frank face and a boyish smile should have acquired such dangerous and powerful enemies.

Even with my access to these records, however, everything that had happened within the prison walls following Vavilov's arrest remained secret. The Soviet authorities had never permitted any historian to have access to documents relating to what took place in the cells where prisoners were interrogated or in the courtyards where they were executed. But at the beginning of 1965 I sent the Secretariat of the Soviet Union of Writers (of which I was a member) an official letter, as required by the regulations. I said I was working on a biography of the great Soviet scientist Vavilov, Lenin Prizewinner, and so on, but I had come up against a problem: at the end of his life Vavilov had had some difficulties with the "competent organs," though he had since been "rehabilitated." Would it not be possible for me to have access to the police file on his case—not, of course, in order to describe the methods of the secret police, but purely and simply to establish the reason for Vavilov's arrest. Was he arrested because of scientific arguments with his opponents, or was it a genuine political affair? The letter was addressed to a certain Voronkov, secretary of the writers' union for "organizational questions," a position usually occupied by a colonel or general in the KGB who keeps an eye on writers from inside the organization. Voronkov received my letter in the midst of the thaw period, made some inquiries, and found out that I wrote the right kind of books and that my political loyalty was not in question. He forwarded my request to the deputy procurator general of the USSR with a note to say that I was completely reliable and suggesting that, if possible, I should be allowed to see what I needed for my work. Both Voronkov and the officials in the Procuratura knew perfectly well that no description of the punitive actions of the KGB could ever find its way into print in the Soviet Union; the censorship office, which happens to be one of the departments of the KGB would prevent such a publication. Therefore they had no cause to worry about me on that account: whatever I might write, the censors could always strike it out.

Eventually I was invited to call on the deputy procuratura general, Malyarov, and after a brief questioning (during which I continued to affirm that I needed Vavilov's file only for the purpose of general orientation), I was granted permission to see the secret papers.

It was not only the post-Khrushchev political thaw that enabled me to gain access to these documents. It was also the result of a rather complicated game I had been playing with the authorities for more than ten years. Although I was trying to obtain documents exposing the nature of the Soviet system, I was still officially approved as a writer and was regarded by the authorities as one of their own people. In the strict social stratification of Soviet society, a writer or journalist occupies a privileged position. If he is a member of the Union of Writers—that is, if he is officially recognized as a writer—he can travel freely around the country and approach anybody he wishes. From him the authorities demand loyalty, but that loyalty is well rewarded.

In April 1965, at the office of the procurator general in Moscow, I was handed ten thick files, each labeled "To be preserved indefinitely." They referred to case no. 1,500, N. I. Vavilov, charged with "crimes against the State." They contained a full account of how and why Nikolai Vavilov was arrested, what documents were seized when his apartment and office were searched, how he was interrogated, who informed on him, what sentence he received, and how he died.

I was issued with a pass and started going to the Procuratura every day as if it were my regular place of work. I would take with me every day a blank school notebook, go to the office of a top official in the judiciary, and sit down at a desk opposite his. The official would solemnly remove one of the Vavilov files from his personal safe and place it silently in front of me. He was obviously not particularly pleased to have me in his office and made his contempt for me apparent in every way; but since the situation in the days following the fall of Khrushchev was uncertain, to say the least, he did not dare question the instruction from his superior that for some reason allowed a writer not only to see secret papers but also to make notes on them. And so we sat there each day, facing each other in silence, radiating mutual antipathy.

I had little time for constructive thought during this period. Each day, as soon as I got my hands on the next set of papers, I feverishly set about the task of copying the more important documents into my notebook. This process continued until I reached the ninth volume. With a deeply suspicious look on his face, the official placed that file in front of me and, for the first time, spoke—to warn me that I was allowed access to only the *first half* of the volume and that I was not permitted to examine anything else. To make it quite clear, he folded the volume back in two. I nodded my head, arranged myself more comfortably at my desk, and immediately delved into the second half of the volume.

Such were the contents that I completely forgot about the man sitting opposite me. When I looked up from the file fifteen minutes later and glanced across at him, I was surprised at his reaction to my disobedience: he was watching me with an almost servile respect and seemed even to smile, though rather uncertainly. Instead of ringing every alarm in the building and marching me away, he seemed to have assessed my impudence as a sign that a higher authority (perhaps the highest) had given me the right not to obey anyone; if that were the case, he knew that he would have to tread very carefully. The simplest course of action would have been for him to establish the extent of my authority by asking his superiors, but he obviously felt that might be construed as obstruction. And so we continued to sit together for several days in a new relationship: the humble writer, every inch Gogol's inspector general, evoking fear and concern in the all-powerful legal official.

It was not surprising that I was supposed to have been denied access to the second half of the volume, for it contained the reports made by agents of the secret police, which had been sent daily in the 1930s and 1940s from the offices of the Soviet Academy of Science to the appropriate department of the NKVD (predecessor of the KGB). What shocked me most was the fact that the reports had been written not by regular NKVD employees, but by professors and academicians recruited by the secret police. I copied down as fast as I could what the informers had written about Vavilov (for example, a report of what Academician Luzin, a mathematician, had said to Academician Komarov, a botanist, about the arrest of Academician Vavilov, a geneticist). It was this information that was later to be responsible for the beginning of my problems with the KGB.

When I returned home each evening from the Procuratura I would immediately make copies of my notebooks, remove the original from my apartment, and hide it with friends. It was only six months later that the officials realized the mistake they had made in giving me access to the Vavilov papers, when, during lectures that I gave on Vavilov's persecution, I referred occasionally to the documents in the KGB file. One lecture, at the All-Union Institute of Plant Breeding in Leningrad, where there were dozens of people who had known Vavilov, had a particularly dramatic effect. Facts that I quoted from file no. 1,500 evoked considerable emotion among the audience: I saw people in tears, and informers whom I mentioned by name jumped up and left the hall to the hissing and jeers of their colleagues. The KGB soon heard about it, and I was summoned to the office of the procurator general, where a general in the judiciary gave me a "fatherly reprimand": "Really, Mark Alexandrovich, behaving like that. . . . We showed you the documents as a writer; we knew that even if you wrote about them, the censors could keep an eye on you. But you have gotten around us, you have betrayed our trust, giving public lectures about secret papers. That's not at all the way to behave, Mark Alexandrovich." Such was the extent of the "liberalism" permitted by the procurator general in 1965.

I was lucky: I remained at liberty. But the following year I was punished for publishing an article entitled "A Thousand Days in the Life of Academician Nikolai Vavilov" in a provincial magazine.[1] There was not a word in the article about either prison or interrogation (the article dealt only with the three years before Vavilov's arrest, 1937–40); but a few details of the forthcoming tragedy nevertheless crept into the story. Orchestrated tragedies are forbidden in the Soviet Union. The Central Committee of the Soviet Communist party gave orders to prevent the publication of my works anywhere in the country.

"A Thousand Days" ends with Vavilov's arrest, which I had learned about from those directly involved in it; the censors struck out the details. But the most significant part of the article was that, on the basis of the facts at my disposal, I was able to show who had *organized* the arrest and murder of Vavilov, and how these events were carried out. Though the secret police had actually killed Nikolai Vavilov, the gun had been loaded by someone from a different department, a respectable civilian with an international reputation. Trofim Denisovich Lysenko, an academician and the winner of several Stalin prizes, features frequently in the pages of KGB file no. 1,500.

Even without reference to legal documents, I was well acquainted with Lysenko's name, as were my contemporaries. We read about him in the newspapers and heard about him on the radio; the views of Academician Lysenko were set out in schools and college textbooks and expounded on television. We were told that he was a great scholar and man of the people who had given our country such harvests as had never before been seen. Moreover, it was claimed that his achievements were based not on the questionable discoveries of "bourgeois" science but on the remarkable experience of ordinary Soviet people, collective farmers. His discoveries always had a practical value and were the result of a dialectic Marxist-Leninist approach to biology and agriculture. Lysenko, deputy to the Supreme Soviet and Hero of Socialist Labor, was the favorite of both Party and the people, and in 1939 he was elected to the Soviet Academy of Science along with Stalin and Molotov.

After Stalin's death Lysenko's star appeared to be waning slightly, and for a time he lost the presidency of the Academy of Agricultural Sciences; but he soon found favor with Khrushchev and was restored to the presidency. Articles by Lysenko and his associates laying down the law on agriculture began to appear once again in the pages of *Pravda*. By the 1960s, however, I had collected enough material to bring Lysenko to court, had circumstances been otherwise. I—and I was not alone—had sufficient documentary evidence to prove that it was Lysenko who prepared the ground for Vavilov's arrest, suppressed his scientific school, and so deprived Soviet society of priceless scientific and practical achievements. As long as Khrushchev was alive, however, not a single magazine dared to publish any of the evidence; only a few academicians (Kedrov, Semenov) were permitted to question the *scientific foundations* of Lysenko's teachings.

My article "A Thousand Days," however, made it clear that Lysenko's actions ought to be judged not in a scientific forum but in a criminal court. I cited dozens of examples of his amoral behavior, which often came very close to being, and sometimes *was*, criminal. At the Central Committee I was shown a couple of dozen complaints, allegedly from "working people"; doctors of science, professors, and heads of institutes, all supporters of Lysenko, were indignant at my article and urged the Central Committee to punish me. The ban on my works lasted for two years.

During this period I remained silent and kept a low profile. In secret I continued to write Vavilov's biography. Following the Soviet invasion of Czechoslovakia in 1968, several Western newspapers paid belated attention to "A Thousand Days," to my great discomfiture. Summaries and reviews of it appeared in Austrian, Swiss, and Yugoslav newspapers and finally in the London *Times,* thus increasing the danger that I and my manuscript might fall into the hands of the KGB. In the end a KGB agent visited my apartment and warned me, in not so paternal a manner as before, that I should not contemplate communicating, either in conversations with foreigners or in published works, the secret information I had obtained. After this visit I realized that I no longer enjoyed the state protection guaranteed to an "official" writer: I was not trusted.

In 1969 I completed the first version of the Vavilov biography, and from 1970 onward the manuscript began to circulate in intellectual circles in Moscow and Leningrad. I did not let it sink in the vast sea of *Samizdat* material but ensured that several copies of the work were constantly circulating around the country: trusted friends picked them up and took them to Central Asia, Kiev, Voronezh, and the Far East. I estimate that five or six thousand people must have read my account of the Vavilov tragedy at that time. The manuscript did not, of course, bear my name.

In the meantime I continued to add to the work. The second version, published in 1971, was followed by a third in 1974. To carry out a thorough revision of the whole biography, I found it necessary to recover my notes on the Vavilov file from their hiding place and bring them home, where they remained, in an old leather file-cover among other papers on a bookshelf. On more than one occasion I reproached myself for my carelessness with my notes, especially after the Moscow Procuratura accused me in 1976 of having stolen Academician Vavilov's diaries of his adolescent years. Like most charges concocted by the KGB, it was quite ridiculous: Vavilov did not keep a diary during his adolescence (he began making daily notes only when he was on expeditions). But facts were irrelevant—the KGB needed a criminal charge to dispatch an uncooperative writer into prison, and the Procuratura duly produced it.

On the morning of June 3, 1977, a number of policemen burst into my apartment in Moscow. They were accompanied by several people in civilian dress: a woman police official, the statutory civilian witnesses, and a smartly dressed young man, who turned out to be the most important of them all. He was Captain Bogachev of the KGB, who handed me the search warrant.

The warrant gave him authority to search my apartment for the fictitious Vavilov diaries, which I was supposed to have stolen ten years previously from a private source. Captain Bogachev, however, knew the real reason for his visit.

The search lasted four hours. The officers sitting at the door dozed off, the two neighbors whom the police had enlisted as witnesses mooched dejectedly around the apartment, and eventually even the lively Bogachev began to tire. He leafed through some papers on a shelf, came across the old leather file, and asked me in a weary voice, "And what's this?"

"Things I don't need, waste paper," I replied in a deliberately casual tone. And Bogachev put the file down, the very file he had come for, the one containing seven blue school notebooks with extracts from KGB file no. 1,500. As I bade him goodbye, I felt like saying, "Poor old Bogachev, your superiors won't be very happy about this."

But even if Bogachev had found the file, he and his superiors could have done nothing to alter the fate of the Vavilov manuscript. The manuscript, together with copies of the documents in file no. 1,500, and even photographs of myself and Professor Bakhteyev looking for Vavilov's grave in a Saratov cemetery in the winter of 1967—everything had long since been smuggled to the West by trustworthy people and was awaiting my consent for publication.

For the next five months I waited to learn what the KGB would do with me: would they arrest me, or would they abandon the idea of yet another show trial and allow me to emigrate? They finally decided on emigration. On the eve of my departure, in my last little game to outwit the authorities, I took a whole sackful of manuscripts for inspection: I laid out before the KGB agents manuscripts that had no political significance at all, while all the really important papers had already been photographed and sent abroad. With these other manuscripts I simply wanted to establish a precedent: permission for a writer to export legally his own works. But the KGB was not to be moved and my attempt failed. Twenty-four hours later, however, the importance of that point of principle had receded: on the evening of November 6, 1977, my wife and I were strolling around the streets of Vienna and enjoying our newfound freedom.

1   The Making of a Scientist

Halfway through my journey upon the road of life
I found myself in a dense forest . . .
      Dante Alighieri, La Divina Commedia: Inferno

On his father's side, Nikolai Vavilov descended from a long line of *muzhiki* (Russian peasants) from a village called Ivankovo, which lies on the old trade route near the town of Volokolamsk, not far from Moscow. Vavilov's grandfather and great-grandfather were both serfs, but his father, Ivan Ilich, lived in better times: at the age of ten he was sent to Moscow to train as a choirboy, and he remained in the Russian capital, first as a member of a church choir and later as an errand boy in a merchant's store. A clever and enthusiastic employee, he was soon promoted to shop assistant, and eventually, though still a young man, he became manager of a shop belonging to a famous Moscow textile firm. On the eve of the First World War Ivan Vavilov was already one of the directors of the firm; government orders during the war made him a millionaire and he became leader of the Moscow City Council.

Ivan Vavilov's younger son, the physicist Sergei Vavilov, later said of his father, "He was a clever man, entirely self-taught, but who read and wrote a great deal. He was by all accounts an excellent organizer, his affairs were always in good order, he was very daring and did not fear to embark on new undertakings. He was a public figure of liberal views and a genuine patriot. . . . He was liked and respected. In different circumstances he might well have become an engineer or a scientist."[1]

It is difficult to determine what is true in Sergei Vavilov's statement and what is said in self-defense, for it was made in Soviet times, when it was not wise to admit that one's father had been a wealthy factory-owner. Moreover, having lost his millions in the

1917 revolution, Ivan Vavilov fled the country and lived as an émigré in Bulgaria for ten years.

Ivan Vavilov married early, at the age of nineteen. His bride, Alexandra Mikhailovna, was the sixteen-year-old daughter of an engraver working in the factory. The marriage, which produced seven children (three of whom died in infancy), appears to have been successful. Little dark-eyed Alexandra turned out to be a good mother and housewife; though not, by all accounts, an outstanding personality, she was the real head of the household. She was small of build, quiet-spoken, wore her hair combed tightly back, and preferred plain black dresses. Alexandra would rise at dawn and with the help of her two daughters would be cleaning, washing, and looking after her large family until late at night. If her husband or either of her sons interfered in the housework, she would say with mock severity: "A man's place is at his work. I don't like men sitting at home, it's not their place." Nikolai took after his mother in appearance and character, and it was from her that he inherited his ability to manage on no more than four or five hours' sleep a night.

The Vavilovs' house in the Presnaya industrial district of Moscow contained a harmonious, closely knit family. Despite Ivan Vavilov's great wealth, his home reflected the modest tastes and peasant origins of the people living in it. The rooms contained nothing that was not absolutely necessary, with no decorations beyond a few reproductions of classical paintings. Their parents' habit of wearing unpretentious clothes and eating simple food remained with all four children for the rest of their lives. Moreover, it was a religious household, built on a sincere faith, free from ostentation. The Vavilovs strictly observed the fasts and the festivals of the Orthodox church calendar, and each day began and ended with a prayer. From their earliest years the children received a strict moral training in the virtues of modesty, hard work, and self-discipline. Sentimentality was not encouraged; members of the family were expected to keep their personal feelings to themselves. Parents and children addressed each other in the simplest way: "Sergei," "Nikolai," or "Father," "Mother." As years went by the young Vavilovs gradually lost their attachment to religion, but the moral principles obtained from a religious upbringing remained with them forever.

Despite its closely knit nature, however, the Vavilov family consisted of people with very different characters. Particularly noticeable was the difference between the two brothers. When they were young, Ivan Vavilov considered it perfectly legitimate to use the strap to further the children's education. Sergei would take his punishment without protest, although in later years he apparently would stuff a thick sheet of cardboard into his trousers to soften the effect of his father's wrath. But the reaction of Nikolai was quite different. At the age of thirteen, seeing his father with the strap in his hands, he jumped up on a windowsill and shouted: "Don't come near me or I'll throw myself out!" What made an impression upon his father was not simply the height but the realization that Nikolai would not allow himself to be beaten. His determination and desire for freedom were already becoming apparent.

This basic difference between Nikolai and Sergei was responsible for their estrangement in later years; both achieved positions of responsibility but cherished quite distinct concepts of honor, freedom, and justice. Forty years after this incident, in the darkest period of Stalin's terror, when his beloved science was under attack, Nikolai Vavilov declared publicly: "We will go to the stake, but we will not renounce our views." He spoke only of science, but in Stalin's day few were ready to defend even that. At the time Sergei advised his brother to give in. That attempt to live, as in childhood, by protecting his backside with a piece of cardboard, led in the end to Sergei helping Stalin to conceal the truth about his brother's murder.

Ivan Vavilov wanted his children to go into business, and he sent them to a commercial college, where they received a good all-round education in languages—English, French, and German—bookkeeping, statistics, history, literature, and natural science. But instead of commerce it was to science that all four Vavilov's turned: Alexandra eventually became a doctor, Lidia a bacteriologist, Sergei a physicist, and Nikolai a biologist.

It is difficult to say why the young Vavilov decided on biology not politics or commerce, as a career. Vavilov tended throughout his life to avoid political issues. As for commerce, he never seemed to strive after wealth. Perhaps his career choice can be understood only in the context of the philosophical ideas prevalent among the Russian intelligentsia in the late nineteenth and early twentieth centuries. If we leave aside the extreme positions adopted by the Bolsheviks and socialists, with their insistence on the need for a revolutionary solution to social problems, the most persistent idea of that period was a faith in a scientific evolution of society. The twentieth century began with a series of major scientific discoveries, and the more enlightened section of Russian society became firmly convinced that science was going to bring the world great blessings.

From the very beginning Russians conceived of science as a branch of social service, a field of activity primarily to benefit the peasant and all those who labored for scanty rewards. It was with the idea of science as a force for the advancement of society that the younger generation of Russians took up biology, geology, engineering, and medicine. It may well be that the young Vavilov was not himself aware of the reasons why, out of all the country's institutes of learning, he chose the Petrovsky Agricultural Institute on the outskirts of Moscow. The idea that there was a close link between science and justice, however strange it may seem to us, was generally accepted by his contemporaries. Biology, whether it was connected with agronomy or with medicine, was regarded as a department of science concerned with the feeding of the population, with bread, and with the people's health. It was regarded by the younger generation as a worthy, honorable, and socially useful occupation.

But Vavilov's decision to devote himself to the science of life was also a reflection of his own personality. Biology is a complex field of knowledge and living things are the summit of creation. Nikolai liked complicated problems; easy tasks did not interest him. Though he was quite without petty personal vanity and was self-effacing in his relations with people, Vavilov was nevertheless ambitious in the most important respect: he believed that it was his mission to discover something important, to penetrate the real secrets of life.

Fifteen years later, working in starving postrevolutionary Petrograd, Vavilov only smiled as he wrapped up his rationed piece of smoked fish in stock certificates and other documents belonging to the Vavilov family business. He did not regret in the slightest the confiscation of the money and property he had been due to inherit. He still believed then that, unlike his inheritance, the right to create and discover could never be taken from him.

For a long time I did not believe that I would be able to find people who knew Vavilov as a young man, because by the time I started writing this book Vavilov's contemporaries were already approaching their eighties. But after much searching I discovered, in the Moscow city archives, lists of university students for the years 1906–11. Further inquiries revealed that three of Vavilov's former classmates from the Petrovsky Agricultural Institute were living in Moscow. In fact Professor Lidia Petrovna Breslavets, a very close friend of Vavilov, was living just down the street from the archives.

Lidia Petrovna was only too pleased to talk about her friend Nikolai Vavilov. There was still a vigorous mind and a lively memory in her fragile body, wasted by illness and age. As she spoke, it seemed as though Vavilov himself was brought to life before me:

> I was standing one day in the canteen of the institute, to which I had just been admitted, and my companion said, 'Look, that's Vavilov over there, the man we've been telling you about.' I saw a student with a rather swarthy complexion and dark hair come into the canteen and begin a conversation with someone. I noticed with what concentration and attention he eyed the person he was speaking to—the same concentration and attention that I observed in him many years later at meetings, when he was discussing business matters or simply talking to friends.
>
> I was introduced to him and looked for the first time into those bright, intelligent eyes. With a quick handshake he rushed off to his lunch. He had no time to spare. Though still a student, he was already being pulled in all directions by his classmates, his teachers, and the professors. He had to dash off to an English lesson, to the library, or to take part in some scientific debate. But then suddenly he broke off eating, looked across at us, and smiled: he had realized that we were eating our main dish while he had absentmindedly started on his ice cream after his soup. He picked up his plate and came to sit at our table. We all laughed and immediately became friends, as happens with young people, friends for life.

We were researching the same subject—plant selection—and for that reason we came together on practical work. We went to the famous Poltava experimental station, the first to be set up in Russia for the purpose of providing the Russian peasant with better varieties of grain. My husband and I were already qualified agronomists, while Vavilov was still a student. But he was soon ahead of everybody by virtue of his diligence and learning. On one occasion an important official from the Department of Agriculture arrived at the station, and at an official lunch the head of the station, Tretyakov, introduced Vavilov as someone who conducted interesting experiments. The visitor got involved in a scientific discussion with him. Suddenly, in the midst of the conversation, a green lizard shot out of Vavilov's pocket and clambered up to his face. Everyone laughed, but Vavilov calmly tied the lizard up in a handkerchief and, quite unconcerned, continued the conversation. The lizard was forgotten and everybody was once again absorbed in the question of biology with which Vavilov was concerned. Since then I had many opportunities to observe that in his company the talk was never of everyday matters. He had a way of switching the conversation to general issues and of raising it to a discussion of principles.

What a worker he was! I remember that by the summer of 1913 he already had a good command of English and could read Linnaeus in Latin. But he did not know French very well, and so he asked me to translate for him a long article by a French botanist. I cheerfully agreed, thinking that I would work on it for a couple of hours the next day, the same the day after, and would finish the job on the third day. I started at seven in the evening, and at nine o'clock I stopped work with a clear conscience. But Vavilov looked at me with astonishment, and so I carried on. In short, I went home at two o'clock in the morning, but the translation was finished. There were many subsequent occasions when I was made to realize that Vavilov always completed anything he started on, and was quite capable of working eighteen hours a day.[2]

Professor Breslavets's account of Vavilov's capacity for work was confirmed by all who knew him as a youth and as an adult. After graduating from the agricultural institute he spent some time doing practical work at a plant selection station, where his diligence made a tremendous impression on his colleagues. Many years later Nikolai Khokhlov, a former employee at the station, commenting on later generations of research workers, said, "What sort of folk are they? Even while the sun's still in the sky they quit the fields. Whereas Nikolai Vavilov stayed working in the fields as long as it was light. Then he would go and sleep with the laborers in their barracks and would be up and about again even before the dawn."

Vavilov was lucky with the quality of the teaching he received, because the years 1906–11 were undoubtedly the best period in the Petrovsky Agricultural Institute. The students were hardworking, eager to learn. There were no vacations in those years: lectures began on September 15 and continued without a break to July 15. Then there were two months of practical work on the farms or at some experimental station, and then back to the lecture hall. In addition, there was a great deal of background reading to be done. Vavilov preferred to read original works by the great scholars of the past: there he hoped to find a suggestion as to which branch of biology he should devote himself.

He was much attracted at first to pure plant selection. Russia accounted for more than half the total grain exports of the world, while Russian peasants were gathering the poorest harvests in Europe. Their results were shameful. In 1908 Russia obtained on average 42 poods of grain per *desyatina* (about 7 quintals a hectare), while France averaged 90 poods of wheat, the United States 66, Germany 120, and tiny Holland 160. No self-respecting agronomist could tolerate such a situation. After all, it had been demonstrated that while about half the harvest depended on the quantity of fertilizer and a quarter on the method of cultivation, another quarter of every loaf of bread depended on the quality of the seed grain. The varieties of grain used had to be improved. Until then only the Germans, British, and Americans had concerned themselves with this matter. Now it was time for the Russians to set about it. A professor at the "Petrovka"—Dionisius Rudzinsky—had already set up the first plant selection station with a view to distinguishing the more productive varieties of wheat, barley, and oats. After graduating from the institute, Vavilov became Professor Rudzinsky's assistant.

Vavilov's enthusiasm for his subject is reflected in an account of a train journey he made from Moscow to Kharkov in January 1911. A large group of agronomists was on its way from Moscow to the first congress of people concerned with plant selection. The agronomists traveled in a special carriage, which they turned into a sort of debating club. Among them were skeptics who were not very sure of what plant selection might bring, as well as some enthusiasts. One of the people present described the occasion to me:

> Nikolai Ivanovich dominated the discussion despite his relative youth. He spoke not like a student but rather like a fully qualified and experienced professor. It was he who had the idea of organizing the debate in the form of a trial. One person assumed the role of the defendant, another acted as the defense counsel, and a third as the counsel for the prosecution in the case of plant selection. There were also witnesses, a detective, and a jury.
>
> Was plant selection a science or not? That was the question that "Judge" Rudzinsky invited the jury to consider. "It is not a science!" declared the counsel for the prosecution. He based his case on the fact that for thousands of years man had been selecting and improving the fruits of the earth, sowing the larger seeds, and cross-breeding the stronger, healthier, and more productive animals. In what way did we, scientists at the beginning of the twentieth century, differ from the untutored but highly experienced peasant sorting out his grain in his barn?
>
> "No, plant selection *is* a science!" came the heated reply from Vavilov, counsel for the defense. With someone's blanket thrown over his shoulders instead of a lawyer's gown, he delivered a passionate monologue. Of course farmers had been improving the quality of their

crops and herds for thousands of years, and such unenlightened selection had indeed produced results occasionally. But in ninety-five cases out of a hundred it did not produce a better variety, mainly because the peasant was not aware of the laws governing the inheritance of characteristics and had no idea which of the characteristics he was interested in were handed on and which ones disappeared or were suppressed in later generations. Science begins at the point where man can forecast the future of his experiment. Plant selection had already acquired the possibility of looking ahead.

Vavilov went on to cite the works of great scientists, including Gregor Mendel, in support of his argument. He pointed out that, as far back as the 1860s, Mendel, an amateur horticulturist, had conducted experiments with garden peas and revealed exactly how characteristics inherited from parents were distributed among descendants. He even expressed the process mathematically, as a result of which plant selection became a science.

The passionate speech by the twenty-four-year-old counsel for the defense evoked a ready response among his audience. The jury voted unanimously in favor of recognizing plant selection as a science and forecast for the young Vavilov a career as a great plant selector.[3] Though all Vavilov's later discoveries were of great service to the plant selectors, the agronomists traveling to 1911 congress could not have foreseen that their talented colleague's scientific future lay in an entirely new field, at the point where geography, botany, genetics, and history overlap.

Vavilov was not, however, a young man for whom no problems existed, and for whom everything always turned out for the best. Later, after achieving recognition as a great scholar and traveler, Vavilov consciously created the impression of fearless and feckless heroism. He brought back from America not just specimens, but also the expression "keep smiling." He often repeated these words and was always seen in public with a smile on his face; but the smile often concealed a surprising depth and bitterness of personal feeling. Such behavior was the result of his family milieu: in the Vavilov household it was not considered proper to reveal one's true emotions. The smile concealed a private person of greater complexity.

Vavilov's letters to his fiancée, Yekaterina Sakharova, are remarkable for their lack of determination and his lack of faith in his own powers. Only very rarely do the letters express any intimate emotion: the two young people seem almost without feelings. On the very eve of their marriage they were engaged in a detailed discussion of their scientific research, professional prospects, and social problems. But at one point, six months before their marriage, Vavilov opened up; the day after he had completed his last examination in the institute, he wrote to Katya:

> I do not have any more precise or clearer aim than has any agronomist. There are some lights shining vaguely in the mists (forgive the unaccustomed poetic turn) that are luring me on. I will not conceal from you the fact that I have very little confidence in myself or in my powers. Occasionally these doubts affect me very sharply, more powerfully than it appears to an outsider. . . . I have the rather ambitious desire to prepare myself for an academic career in scientific research. But I am well aware that I have too few gifts, and I know that disillusionment and reversals are possible. . . .
>
> In one of the Breslau reports, Rumker [a noted German selectionist] writes that if he had done anything of importance in his life, it was only because he had a constant goal in sight. Alas, my clear and concrete goal is shrouded in fog. But I'll go forth, come what may.

Even greater doubts arose in Vavilov over his pedagogic talents. He was assigned to teach at the Golitsyn Higher Agricultural Courses. The female students, who as a rule fell in love with their handsome lecturer, were poorly prepared in a scientific sense. Vavilov was irritated by all this, but he felt that the problems with teaching were more his fault, stemming from his lack of preparation.

> My failures in teaching put me in a foul mood and discourage me. . . . For some reason this is not apparent to others. And by some accident they overestimate any

trifling plus. And as a result Pryanishnikov [a professor of the Petrine Agricultural Institute] asks me to write the graduation address for the Golitsyn courses. . . . I, to tell the truth, was dumbfounded. I said that I felt uncomfortable, inexperienced, and so on, but by July first I am to think about it and give him my reply and my topic. Then there's the trip [a trip abroad, offered him as a future professor]. I'm not brave. And I have little confidence that I'll be able to do it. It's all too fast. It smacks of careerism, which God forbid. All these public appearances are nothing but trouble and dismay. . . . And worst of all, there's nothing to me. . . . I haven't even finished reading Johansen, or Lotz. I'm not even dreaming about *Mutation Theory.* Total ignorance in systematics and inability to experiment at all. And my language is horrible. I have to study and study.[4]

In his letters to his fiancée, the young man is quite obviously seeking her approval and support, and he found it. It is more natural for a man of twenty-four to seek a mistress, but sometimes he seeks a mother, and on the threshold of a brilliant career (in which, incidentally, very little room had been allotted to the opposite sex), Nikolai Vavilov found a mother in Katya Sakharova, and a rather strict one at that. On practically every issue her views differed from those of her future husband. They could not even agree on where to live after they were married. She wrote, "I really don't understand how there can be any question about where you will live. . . . At the Petrovka, where else? But where I shall be living, I really don't know. To be quite honest I would like to devote myself entirely to plant selection, biology, and mycology. But suppose I find I am not able to . . . . It seems as though the idea of doing socially useful work has become embedded in my brain cells."[5]

When public service is found to conflict with family happiness there are, of course, problems ahead. Only a complete lack of experience could have allowed Vavilov to choose such a woman as his companion for life, even though the bluestocking Katya loved him in her way. The marriage, which caused such wonderment among their contemporaries, actually held together for twelve years, though for the greater part of the time the couple lived in different towns. Six years after they were married, in 1918, apparently in an effort to salvage an impossible relationship, Katya gave birth to a son, Oleg. But even the birth of a child was not enough. The woman who had used all her great strength of will to support the young scientist at the beginning of his career could offer him nothing once he was standing on his own feet and had confidence in himself.

At the end of 1912, Vavilov began a two-year official trip abroad, visiting the principal biology laboratories in the Western world; it was the most important task he had ever undertaken. As a result of the outbreak of war in Europe, he had to return home in the autumn of 1914 without having completed the program of inquiries he had planned. But the months that he spent in England—in Cambridge and London—with the leading British geneticists Biffen and Pennet, and above all his acquaintance with William Bateson, the most brilliant geneticist of the beginning of the century, played a tremendous part in his life. Bateson's name occurs especially frequently in Vavilov's letters. When he came later to name his most revered teachers, Vavilov placed Bateson along with his two Moscow professors, Timiryazev and Pryanishnikov.

As the director of the John Innes Institute of Horticulture in London, William Bateson had decided that freedom of creative activity should be the institute's fundamental principle. Any serious biologist was free to work at the John Innes Institute on whatever subject he wished, could employ whatever methods he pleased, and could experiment on any biological subjects—from wheat to peacocks, from gillyflowers to guinea pigs. The only request the director made was that the scientists should research the processes of inheritance and evolution in the living world. To an outsider it might seem that, with such a lack of firm direction, the gardeners and farmers of Britain would be unlikely to obtain much of value from the scientists' efforts. But Bateson, a fellow of the Royal Society, believed that any honest and sufficiently able biologist who was provided with good conditions for experimentation would inevitably, sooner or later, contribute to the task of developing new varieties of plants and new breeds of animals. The director considered it his duty not to interfere with the scientists in their work. At the same time Bateson strongly defended the ideas of Gregor Mendel in his books and at international congresses.

Vavilov benefited greatly from Bateson's democratic ways. At the John Innes Institute he was allowed to continue the research into immunity in wheat that he had begun in Russia, and it was in Britain that Vavilov completed the postgraduate thesis that opened the way for him to become a professor. Many years later, when Vavilov was an academician and leader of a world-famous scientific school, his contemporaries found in his behavior the very same features: unlimited indulgence for anyone who was a genuine seeker after the truth and fearlessness when it came to combating untruth and juggling with facts. This European approach to his work won many friends for Vavilov in his own country but also earned him a fair number of sworn enemies.

Vavilov returned to Russia not with a new methodology, nor even with new ideas, but with something else—an interest in global research, an ambition to embrace with his research the plant world of our whole planet. It was then that he first became involved in the problems that later became his main life's work. Students at the "Petrovka" sang a ditty regretting that neither the artichoke nor the almond grew in Europe: Vavilov wanted to know *why* they did not grow there. Where did the cultivated plants growing in our fields come from? Where was their real home? Who were their ancestors? How did those plants—wheat, rye, flax, rice, and the other inhabitants of gardens and fields—manage to cross the barrier dividing wild plants from cultivated ones? It required more than a little audacity for someone who had only just graduated to turn his attention to problems of such vast scope.

In the summer of 1917 two university towns, Saratov and Voronezh, competed for Vavilov's services; each of them offered him a professional chair—an unusual honor for someone who had so recently obtained his doctorate. The battle ended in August, when Vavilov was able to write to a friend: "The fuss is over now, as you can see from the fact that I am now living in Saratov." And he added: "It's better living in Saratov than in Moscow." But Saratov, on the Volga, did not spoil the young professor with material blessings. He did not even have an apartment to live in, and for a long time had to sleep in his office at the university. But an apartment mattered little to Vavilov compared with the greatest luxury of all—the luxury of contact with colleagues. Saratov, capital of Russia's wheat-growing region, attracted in those years a considerable number of young, talented scientists—agronomists, agriculturists, plant physiologists, and botanists. Vavilov's reputation preceded him, and a group of young collaborators and students quickly grew up around him. In less than a year he had become one of the leading teachers at the university.

It is difficult to imagine a place or a time less suitable for scientific research than Saratov between 1917 and 1921. Riots, famine, typhus, and destruction abounded. First from the south and then from the north the fronts of the Civil War reached the city. But neither famine nor machine-gun fire on the streets could halt the process of daily concentrated thought that characterizes a scientific genius. None of Vavilov's contemporaries speak of his political views while the Civil War was raging. Did he want to see the monarchy restored, or did he support the Bolsheviks? He does not seem to have given the matter much thought himself. His mind was concerned with a revolution of its own. His contemporaries remember only his wonderful lectures; they recount how he cared for students exhausted by typhus and how, in the absence of a watchman, he drove the hungry rooks off the experimental seedbeds.

The *Saratov News* for June 21, 1920, was printed on one side of the paper, like the revolutionary proclamations and the frightening orders of the Civil War period; it was pasted up on fences and the walls of houses. This issue has a report in heavy type: "Professor Vavilov's Discovery." "Professor Nikolai Vavilov has succeeded in making a discovery of the greatest importance and of worldwide significance," the newspaper report began. The reporter did not exactly understand the discovery and described it in extremely confused terms, but he reported that the authorities of the Saratov region were so delighted that they had decided to publish Vavilov's work, to provide him with a well-equipped state farm for large-scale experiments, and even to equip a scientific expedition by Vavilov to other countries at government expense. (The authorities were, however, unable to carry out this last undertaking because the Bolshevik state was at the time enclosed not by state frontiers but by the fronts of the Civil War.)

Vavilov had, in fact, carried out a significant revolution in botanical science, about which he spoke at the Third All-Russian Plant Selection Congress, which opened in Saratov on June 4, 1920. One of Vavilov's students recalled:

> The large physics lecture hall in the university was packed full of people. There were not enough seats, and people were standing shoulder to shoulder in the gangways. There were well-known biologists from Moscow and the whole of the teaching staff of Saratov University was present, and even the lawyers and doctors came to hear Nikolai Ivanovich. When he had finished—and he did not speak very long—the hall remained hushed for a moment, and then there was a burst of applause, no, an ovation, a stormy ovation. I remember enthusiastic speeches which followed in which people spoke of a "revolution in biology." I still recall Professor Zalensky saying that in the person of Vavilov the congress was applauding a Mendeleyev in biology.

It was not purely by chance that the name of Dmitri Mendeleyev, the Russian chemist who formulated the periodic law of atomic weights in 1869, occurred to those who listened to Vavilov's lecture, which was entitled "The Law of Homologous Lines." Vavilov had in fact produced a law that made it possible to bring greater order into the variety of the Earth's vegetation.

In the first century A.D. the Greek Dioskorid had listed some six hundred plants, a number that did not increase significantly in the following millenium. But with the growth of exploration led by Columbus, Vasco da Gama, Magellan, and John Cabot, the botanical records expanded. The Spaniards brought from America the potato, maize, tobacco, sunflowers, tomato, and eggplant. Europeans learned for the first time of coffee and the cocoa plant; lilac imported from the Middle East began to blossom in Italian gardens; orange and mandarin orange trees brought from China began to bear fruit in Europe. From Ceylon came cloves and cinnamon, camphor and indigo. The Portuguese discovered the pineapple, agave, and green peppers. Explorers of the African continent came back with stories of gigantic species of trees—the baobab and the cabbage tree. It became increasingly difficult to distinguish particular plants: there were many cases of a flower being known by thirty or forty different names.

"If we don't split up this disorderly crowd into sections, like an army, everything will remain in a state of chaos and confusion," complained the sixteenth-century Italian botanist Cezalpin. But it was not until two hundred years later that order was established by the Swede Carolus Linnaeus, who introduced a new system of botanical classification. By then the number of known varieties of plant had risen to ten thousand. This green ocean had clearly overflowed the boundaries of human knowledge and threatened to drown botany as a science. Linnaeus's achievement was to divide the living world into distinct, immutable species and to give the species names suitable for botanists and agronomists to use. Linnaeus's classification remained unchallenged for many years.

But as time passed, scientists noticed that the species distinguished by Linnaeus were by no means immutable, as they had first appeared. Where the eighteenth-century naturalist had seen a single group of organisms of the same kind, his followers discovered hundreds of very important differences. Weaknesses began to appear in the Linnaean system. Botanists of the nineteenth and twentieth centuries began to divide plant species into subspecies, varieties, and races. By the beginning of the twentieth century Linnaeus's list, which had originally contained 10,000 species, had grown to include 130,000. Once again, the green ocean was threatening to burst the banks erected by the scientists.

At the age of thirty-three Nikolai Vavilov had the temerity to address himself to this problem, which had previously been the province of the great leaders of natural science. He explained his views by reference to a plant with which he was well acquainted, wheat—the genus *Triticum*. Wheat consists of eight species; one species, the so-called soft wheat, has a great number of varieties and races, but all seven other species of wheat have similar qualities. Both the spelt wheat, which provided food for the people of the Bronze Age in Europe, and the double-grain spelt, which was sown in earliest times on the banks of the Nile, reveal similar sets of qualities. This is no accidental repetition of characteristics. Vavilov checked his findings on two species of barley and found that the second species had exactly the same set of varieties as the first. He showed the same to be true of oats and rye. The larger the family of related species, the more clearly defined are the parallel—homologous—lines of characteristics.

The same parallels can be observed not only between different species but also between closely related genuses. Varieties of rye repeat characteristics found in a closely related genus of wheat; pumpkins have features similar to those found in melons and cucumbers; the vetch imitates the lentil. One the basis of his law of homologous lines, Vavilov was able to establish the existence in theory of varieties of plants that were later discovered in practice.

The tremendous significance of Vavilov's discovery—that wheat and rye, pumpkins and melons, vetches and lentils, developed different varieties according to a common, parallel system—was immediately apparent to Vavilov's audience in Saratov. It made possible a completely original, all-embracing classification of the plant life of the Earth, which would to a large extent supplement and to some extent replace Linnaeus's classification. Moreover, the law of homologous lines became from the very outset a compass for the botanist, agronomist, and plant breeder. "Instead of seeking to discover new forms simply by chance the researcher now has the task of establishing similarities between closely related species and genera and restoring the lines of the forms that are lacking," Vavilov announced in his Saratov lecture. "It is now possible to seek and to foretell with certainty the forms that are lacking in the system."[6]

Like Mendeleyev's law in chemistry, Vavilov's law revealed what had already been discovered or created in the world of cultivated plants and what had not yet been found but must inevitably be concealed somewhere in nature. The sixteen-page lecture included a whole program of action: to seek new plants with the most valuable economic qualities, and to seek them sure in the knowledge that such forms must exist somewhere.

The law of homologous lines has been known now for sixty years, and no one has disproved it. On the contrary, it has received repeated confirmation by botanists and plant breeders.

Vavilov did not rest on his laurels after announcing his discovery but started to think of ways of applying the law. In Saratov, then suffering from famine and cut off by the fighting from other parts of the country, he dreamed of organizing expeditions to distant lands. "I'd like to get away to Africa, to Abyssinia, the Sudan and Nubia. There's a lot to be found there," he confessed in a letter to a student.[7] In the end it was not for Africa that he left Saratov, but for Petrograd.

Why Petrograd, the former capital of Russia? In 1921 Petrograd was hardly a suitable place for scientific work or for any kind of normal life. In later years Soviet propaganda liked to describe the city as the "cradle of the Revolution." But for anyone who knows the true story of the October Revolution, Petrograd between 1918 and 1921 is associated more with the grave that with the cradle. Having given birth to the Revolution, Petrograd itself slowly died. The Bolsheviks destroyed the city's internal economic and social connections and created nothing as vital to take their place. Lacking raw materials, the factories came to a halt, the shops closed for lack of goods, and work stopped in schools and universities. Lenin's government moved out of the city in 1918, leaving it to its fate. The authorities did not concern themselves with even the most essential services—supplying water, generating electricity, or delivering foodstuffs. Those who could, fled from the starving city, but a large part of the intelligentsia, especially the professors, refused to flee. The professors and academicians simply died out. And with them, the librarians, actors, writers, teachers. All the best of Russia's spirit died of starvation in Petrograd in the years between 1919 and 1923.

Among the people who died in those days was the botanist Robert Eduardovich Regel, a close friend of Vavilov. Professor Regel had headed the Bureau of Applied Botany. It was a unique institution, founded in 1894 to introduce new varieties and to study the old ones. The institution was extremely poor and eked out a pathetic existence, even though Professor Regel himself was a serious scientist, a hard worker who gathered and studied almost three thousand samples of barley and undertook important research on Russian wheat and weeds. But the postrevolutionary shambles brought all his work to naught. In his letters to Vavilov from Saratov, the professor described the total destruction of his beloved work. The end of one of his letters carried a prophesy: "I don't know if we'll come out of this chaos alive. It is especially doubtful in my case, since I will not accept compromises."

Regel truly would not compromise with the Bolsheviks. He

tried to leave the condemned city and make his way to the provinces where his family was living, but he died of typhus on the train. Twenty years later, in 1940, a police officer interrogating Vavilov made him read lines from the obituary that Vavilov had written following Regel's death: "The ranks of Russian scholars are becoming thinner day by day and one trembles for the fate of Russian science."[8] These words were included in the indictment against Vavilov as evidence of his "anti-Soviet attitude." Neither Regel nor Vavilov survived the Soviet chaos: they both perished—Regel, who would not compromise his science or his politics, and Vavilov, who cared little for politics but died for his science.

In 1921, however, as a result of Vavilov's lack of interest in politics (which amounted in practice to making regular concessions to the authorities), he was offered Regel's position. He had to leave Saratov to take over the deserted Bureau of Applied Botany. It is true that nobody else was better suited for the job, but many people, equally worthy though less compliant, were not even offered positions in those years.

Vavilov certainly agreed to move to cold, starving Petrograd on the basis of careful calculation. But it was a scientific and not a selfish calculation. However agreeable it might be, a professorial chair in a provincial university had very limited resources for mounting expeditions. In Petrograd, at the head of the only scientific institution in the country dealing with problems of Russian agronomy, Vavilov could hope in time to obtain the funds necessary for the expeditions he had been dreaming about since his visit to Bateson. The transfer from Saratov in 1921 was a risky step, and possibly a dangerous one, but at the same time it offered some prospects. It was, after all, in Petersburg that Peter the Great had made his window onto Europe (and to Africa and America).

Vavilov had thought out his move to Petrograd in all its details. He did not leave Saratov simply as a person moving from the provinces to the center on promotion. He did not go laden with his own possessions, but took with him twenty-seven colleagues (a whole scientific school!), all the plant specimens collected over three years, and a huge library. In his new place he planned to set himself up seriously and in a big way.

They traveled in railway freight cars. In one were people on wooden bunks, and in the other were seeds, books, and some scientific equipment. They were a cheerful company, singing and joking: "There are rumors that the Nevsky Avenue is to be renamed the Avenue of Homologous Lines." But as they came closer to Petrograd the smiles faded from their faces. As they approached the railway station the people from Saratov saw a huge graveyard of locomotives and the ruins of dead factories. It was March, the same time that the Russian writer Maxim Gorky, who lived in Petrograd, was writing to his British friend H. G. Wells: "There is practically no food and it can be said without exaggeration that there will soon be famine in Petrograd. . . . I just can't imagine how our scholars are going to keep alive over the next few weeks."[9]

The situation was indeed catastrophic. Vavilov found Professor Regel's bureau in a sad state. One of the people who traveled with Vavilov wrote subsequently: "A picture of almost complete destruction, as if there had been an enemy invasion, greeted the new head as he entered the bureau's premises: the temperature in the rooms was freezing, the central heating pipes had burst, the bulk of the seeds had been eaten by starving people, there was dust and dirt everywhere, and only here and there were there signs of life: a few lonely and dejected-looking technicians lacking any leadership."

That account is confirmed by a letter that Vavilov himself wrote in the spring of 1921: "There are a million problems. We are fighting to get some heat into the premises, to get some furniture, to get apartments for the staff and to get some food. . . . I have to confess that it's a bit difficult to get a new laboratory and a new experimental farm working and to fix up 60 members of the staff."

Vavilov was not one to complain. Goodness knows how he himself lived, what he ate, and where he slept in those days. The wife of a Petrograd professor recalled that one evening Vavilov dropped in on them; with obvious embarrassment, he produced a small bag of millet and a minute piece of bacon and asked her to cook them. He was delighted with the millet *kasha* that resulted. When the meal was over, in response to pressing inquiries by his hosts, Vavilov admitted that he had not eaten a hot meal for more than a week.

Life in Petrograd could well have destroyed anyone's illusions. But Vavilov not only easily came to terms with the difficulties of daily life, at the slightest sign of improvement he would start rejoicing and making new plans. "The north is after all very fascinating," he wrote to friends in Saratov. "Very little has been done, but a great deal can be done. From the outside our laboratory is very beautiful. And in Tsarskoye it's absolutely lovely!" Tsarskoye, renamed Detskoye Selo after the Revolution (and now called Pushkin), had been the residence of the royal family near Petrograd. With great difficulty Vavilov had obtained buildings and land there for a genetics station. "There are many possibilities here," he wrote in his next letter. "There are books and museums and we have obtained dozens of hothouses. We are repairing the laboratories, making furniture and setting up the machines. . . . We are going to get on with our work and we shall try to carry on along the same path."[10]

But it was practically impossible in the first years after the Revolution for him to carry on with his own scientific work. In May 1922 Vavilov addressed a heart-rending appeal to the People's Commissariat for Agriculture: "We are receiving no funds at all for paying the employees or for our regular expenditures. . . . We have had to sell some of our equipment and seeds. . . . Despite the readiness of all the employees to be patient and to make do with practically nothing, the situation is becoming quite impossible. Rations arrive a month behind time and, as you know very well, they are not substantial enough for people to exist on. Employees have not received any pay for two months."[11]

In the autumn of that year Vavilov invited the Saratov professor Zalensky to move to Petrograd, promising him "every convenience" and reassuring him: "We are now maintaining a temperature not lower than ten degrees centigrade."[12] In May 1923 Vavilov reported in a letter: "These are now difficult times in Petrograd, and the employees are half-starved." Vavilov's bureau was supposed to transplant to Russian soil the most productive plants from other countries; yet there was not enough money even for the postage stamps.

Nonetheless it was in 1923 that Vavilov's expectations began to be realized, though in a most unpredictable way. In 1922, Lenin, forced by illness to abandon his duties of state for a time, had read a book of popular science entitled *The New Earth,* by an American author, William Sumner Harwood.[13] The book described the amazing achievements of agricultural science in the United States, the wonderful new varieties of cultivated plants, and the success of practical farming based on scientific knowledge. If this book, translated into Russian in 1909 by Professor K. A. Timiryazev, had come into Lenin's hands in the years 1910–13, he would not have paid any attention to it. But in 1922 he stood at the head of a state stricken by famine. The situation had to be changed at once, in one quick stroke. A magic wand was needed to make the devastated fields of the Volga region produce rich crops. Harwood unwittingly presented Lenin with such a wand.

As soon as he read the book, Lenin issued orders for the collection of information about the country's scientific resources and demanded the building in Soviet Russia of a major scientific center like the American research center in Washington. He even spoke of the need to set up an agricultural academy, but because of the shortage of funds it was decided for the time being to make do with just an institute. It took a long time to reach agreement on where the institute was to be situated, who was to head it, and where the money to support it was to come from. Finally, in the summer of 1925, when Lenin was no longer alive, the idea became a reality in the form of the All-Union Institute of Applied Botany and New Cultivated Crops. Nikolai Vavilov was appointed the first director and was described in the local press as "a scholar of world renown." As overlord of the whole project the government appointed Nikolai Gorbunov, who had been Lenin's personal secretary.

By this time Vavilov had indeed become a scholar with an international reputation. He had already spent some months in the United States and had gotten to know some of America's leading geneticists and plant breeders. The Academy of Science of the USSR made him a corresponding member in 1923. After that came a major expedition, producing an enormous quantity of scientific material, which Vavilov made to Afghanistan in 1924. In 1926 he set out on a tour of the Mediterranean: Algeria, Tunis, Morocco, Spain, Portugal, southern France, Italy, Greece, Crete, Syria, Palestine, Jordan, Ethiopia, and Eritrea. Hundreds of packets of seed from this expedition arrived at the handsome building on St. Isaac's Square where Vavilov's institute was housed. A unique collection of the world's most precious vegetation was being formed. The Mediterranean expedition was followed in 1929 by a visit to China, Japan, Korea, and the island of Formosa (Taiwan). The next year saw the beginning of a tour of the Americas. Every trip produced new finds, new friends, and new marks of international recognition. Scientists in the West became especially interested in Vavilov following the publication in Leningrad in 1926 in Russian and English of his *The Geographic Origins of Cultivated Plants*. From then on Vavilov became one of the most respected leaders of world biology.

Vavilov had had practically no spare time at all in Saratov, where he had worked on his law of homologous lines and had written a long monograph entitled *Field Crops of the Southeast*. Then had come the years of cold and famine in Petrograd and the task of organizing the Bureau of Applied Botany. In 1924 there had been the Afghanistan expedition and numerous articles about that country. Next came a period during which, as Vavilov wrote to one of his friends: "I am dashing between Petrograd and Moscow. They have made me set up an All-Union Institute of Applied Botany."[14] The institute demanded a tremendous amount of effort from him. Where did he find the time to develop his theory of the origin of cultivated plants?

According to most of his colleagues, Vavilov first raised the questions of the origins of the plants cultivated by peasants and of the countries in which humanity's principal foodstuffs first grew soon after he returned from his visit to Bateson in England. He continued to grapple with the problem during the following twelve years while at the same time creating university chairs, his bureau, and institutes, and amazing his contemporaries with his new writings. "Until 1926 he simply did not have two months in which to write down the views that had long ago taken shape in his mind," one of his colleagues said. At all events, Vavilov again set about solving a problem that the greatest minds in biology and geography had faced before him.

"The birthplace, the original homeland of the plants most useful to man is as impenetrable a secret as the question of the origins of domestic animals. . . . We do not know in what region first appeared in their wild form wheat, barley, oats and rye," the German explorer and natural scientist Alexander von Humboldt wrote in 1807. The Englishman Robert Brown and the Swiss botanist Alphonse de Candolle were the first people to propose some more or less serious ideas on the subject. De Candolle came to the conclusion that the native land of every cultivated plant was where its wild forebears and relations were found. It seemed a fairly credible theory, but when de Candolle tried, on the basis of books, collections of plants, and the reports of explorers, to discover the birthplace of 247 of the most widely distributed cultivated plants, he was sadly disappointed. The place of origin remained unknown in 72 cases. No ancestors could be found in the natural state for a third of the plants known to humanity, which meant that their birthplace remained unexplained.

Vavilov based his thinking about the origins of cultivated crops on de Candolle's original guesswork, but his own theory led him to reject his predecessor's views. De Candolle had been interested in the origin of oats, rye, and wheat *in general*. Vavilov pointed out, however, that in the previous century no fewer than eight species had been discovered and isolated within the genus *Triticum* (wheat). The species were so different in their structure and physiology that they could scarcely all have come from a single geographical region. The same was true of oats, barley, flax, and watermelon. It would be more correct to speak of different kinds of oats, flaxes, barleys, and watermelons and to try to trace the country of origin separately for each species or group of closely related species. It would be many times more difficult, but that much closer to the truth.

As for the ancestors of the cultivated varieties, it was not so simple a matter to find them as the Swiss botanist had thought. In fact, there was no point in seeking them. To find the place of origin of most cultivated plants, Vavilov asserted, it would be necessary to find those places in the world where the various forms of these plants were to be found in the greatest numbers. The homeland was the geographical center, where its variant forms had been created, where the greatest numbers of its sorts, varieties, and forms were found.

There was another obvious conclusion: where a large number of forms grew, even of the same species, it would be possible to identify many economically valuable characteristics of the grain. The geographical centers, where forms were created, had to be real treasure houses for plant breeders. Wheat immune to disease and resistant to drought, varieties of barley capable of producing rich harvests, flaxes with large oil-bearing seeds and strong, long fibers—they must all exist somewhere. According to the law of homologous lines, drought resistance and high yield were to be found in separate forms of wheat. Was it not reasonable to suggest that an expedition to the centers of form-creation would fill in the empty spaces in Vavilov's "tables of vegetable elements" with the most valuable varieties of grains and industrial plants, vegetables, fruits, and berries? It was simply necessary to set the expeditions off on the right road.

But where exactly were those promised lands? The centers of origin of cultivated plants were not to be found along the main highways of the world's agriculture. They had to be sought, according to Vavilov, in those few regions where primitive agriculture was still practiced, especially in the mountains, where from the earliest times people have tilled the soil. This conclusion was in direct contradiction to de Candolle's views, and not his alone. Historians had long accepted as an incontrovertible truth that agriculture had originated on the banks of the great rivers. They cited the valleys of the Hwang Ho and the Yangtze, the Indus and the Ganges, the Nile, the Tigris and the Euphrates, where what were believed to be the most ancient farming settlements had been discovered.

Vavilov stubbornly defended his own view: "After a detailed study of the centers where the forms of cultivated plants were created, a botanist acquires the right to dispute the conclusions drawn by historians and archaeologists." In his opinion the river valleys were not the cradles of civilization. Humans had moved down into the lowlands only in a later stage, their adolescence, so to speak. But what about the bunches of grapes carved into the stones of the Egyptian pyramids? And Chinese agricultural rituals going back five thousand years? Vavilov would reply that agriculture originated much earlier, long before people had become literate. It happened in the mountains, in places where the variety of natural conditions—from the desert to the oasis, from the stony screes to the rich soil of alpine meadows—gave rise to a great variety, an abundance of vegetation. It was there that the streams flowing down from the glaciers made it possible for primitive people to arrange for their first small cultivated plots to be irrigated by nature.

It was Nikolai Vavilov's opinion that these regions stretched in a broad belt from the mountain ranges of southeastern Asia (China) along the Himalayas and to their spurs; they continued in the mountainous plateaus of northeastern Africa and then crossed the

Caucasus, the Balkans, the Apennines, and the Pyrenees, while on the other side of the Atlantic they followed the line of the Andes from Chile to Mexico. In area they amounted to only about 20 percent of the world's land surface. But it was there that one had to go in search of variety of vegetation and the original source of the food we live on. This was the route that Vavilov followed on his expeditions, and he was not mistaken. He discovered the original home of maize and the potato in the Americas, of oats in the mountains of northern Spain, and of some species of wheat in Asia. It is hardly to be wondered at if, after all these discoveries, the author of *Geographic Origins of Cultivated Plants* won the universal respect of his colleagues on all continents.

Changes took place in Nikolai Vavilov's personal life as well. The agonizing uncertainty of his relations with his wife had continued for several years. Katya Sakharova did not move to Petrograd but, along with her son, settled in Moscow with relations. An outsider might have attributed the separation to the lack of food and a suitable apartment in Petrograd. But the famine was over and Vavilov was given an apartment, and yet Sakharova was in no hurry to leave the capital. Their married life had fallen apart even before their intellectual links had broken. In his letters from America in 1921 Vavilov continued to discuss with his wife political and scientific events and to describe the books he had read. In the years 1920 to 1923 Sakharova translated and Vavilov edited several specialized works, including a brilliant book by the English natural scientist R. Gregory entitled *The Discoveries, Goals, and the Meaning of Science.* But their personal relationship was marked by mutual irritation and misunderstanding. The family continued to exist only for the benefit of the outside world and perhaps also of their young son. Sensitive by nature, Vavilov tried to avoid a complete break. He took care that his wife and son had everything they needed, showered Oleg with presents, and had him stay at Detskoye Selo in the summer. Katya was also invited, but she did not want to leave Moscow.

Meanwhile, for Nikolai Vavilov a new young love took the place of the love that was dead. The face of this attractive young woman can be seen in snapshots taken even while they were still in

Saratov. Yelena Ivanovna Borulina—Lyonochka, as everyone called her on account of her very delicate, feminine appearance—was Professor Vavilov's first graduate student. Vavilov declared his love in the autumn of 1920, but the sweet-natured and indecisive Lyonochka was embarrassed at the prospect of becoming her professor's mistress while his wife was still alive. Vavilov soon left on business for Petrograd, where he received a letter full of doubts from a young woman who feared that his words of love reflected only a fleeting passion. Vavilov replied immediately in his usual decisive and crystal-clear manner, though he found it very difficult to write love letters; he had not made a great deal of progress in that field in the past ten years.

On November 27, 1920, he wrote:

> My dear friend, you are plagued with doubts as to whether the emotion, the burst of passion will simply pass. Dear friend, I don't know how to convince you, or what objective evidence I can offer you to prove that this is not the case. I myself would like to step aside and subject myself to unsparing analysis.
>
> It seems to me that, despite my tendency to bursts of passion and emotion, I am nevertheless a very constant and dependable person. I take love too seriously. I really have a profound faith in science, in which I find both purpose and life. And I am quite ready to give my life for the smallest thing in science. . . . And that is why, Lena, simply because I am a faithful son of science, I cannot, within myself, allow myself to treat matters of the heart lightly.

Then, after a whole page of reflections about science, Vavilov returned with some reluctance to the question of his future relations with Lyonochka:

> I do not have any great demand for comfort. True, I am not used to doing everything for myself, but I can do it when it is absolutely necessary. We shan't have any arguments about that, I am sure. I really don't know what we shall disagree about. Our life together should be very beautiful, both emotionally and in our everyday work.

And you agree on that. For some reason it seems to me that our union will be strong and lasting. It is true that in the past there were frequent near-quarrels [a reference to his relations with Katya Sakharova] but I did nothing to worsen them and I honestly consider myself to be tolerant and easy to get on with. . . .

It was my birthday yesterday. I am 33. For some reason I keep recalling the opening lines of Dante: "Nel mezzo del camin di nostra vita"—"Half way along life's path . . . I strayed into a dark forest, a dense forest. . . ." Now I have got to get out of that forest. And I believe we will get out of it together. It is a difficult forest, but is there any forest which does not have a way out? Yours, N.

Vavilov's forest consisted of his relations with Katya, which he lacked the courage to break off. It was Lyonochka who helped him to do it. She moved to Petrograd with the first group of Vavilov's students. For a long time their romance remained a close secret, and it was only in 1926, when he made a complete break with Katya, that Yelena and Nikolai revealed their secret to their friends. Even so, there was no wedding, because Vavilov was preparing for a major expedition and soon dashed off on a trip around Europe, Asia, and Africa, which lasted more than a year. The couple met again thirteen months later, in May 1927, when Vavilov managed to arrange for Yelena to join him in Italy; there they had a fortnight's honeymoon seven years after his first declaration of love.

Their relationship was on the whole successful. Time and again and without protest Yelena Ivanovna packed her restless husband's bags for some expedition. She often had to spend the weekend alone while putting up with the invasion of countless guests during the week. But her husband's works and his habits were sacred for her. Even after she had obtained her doctorate in science, Yelena Borulina remained the same faithful, helpful, and undemanding companion she had been to her teacher and lover during the hungry years they spent in Petrograd.

2 Michurin, Lysenko, and the Birth of "Progressive Biology"

Nothing is more constructive than the errors of genius.
Academician P. I. Kapitsa

It is still less than thirty years since the time when every public statement about the achievements of Soviet agricultural and biological science invariably began and ended with praise for the work done by the horticulturist Ivan Vladimirovich Michurin and the agronomist Trofim Denisovich Lysenko. Every article on the subject would include the stock phrases "Michurinist biology," "the teachings of Academician Lysenko," "the Darwinism of Michurin," and so on. The terms "Michurinist" and "anti-Michurinist" came into use at the end of the 1930s, and although at first they meant little to the general public, they soon achieved significance outside the boundaries of science. Schoolteachers giving lessons in biology, lecturers bringing science to the masses, and journalists writing in the daily press soon made it clear to the uninitiated that the relationship between the term "Michurinist" and the term "anti-Michurinist" was the same as that between heaven and hell. One of the first people to be labeled an "anti-Michurinist" was Nikolai Vavilov.

Vavilov first met Michurin in September 1920, at the end of the All-Russian Congress on applied botany in the provincial center of Voronezh. The organizer of the congress, the Voronezh professor Sokrat Konstantinovich Chayanov (who was later to become one of the organizers of Soviet agricultural science), invited his guests to visit the nursery where Michurin grew his fruit trees in the nearby town of Kozlov. The invitation did not arouse any great enthusiasm: it was a very unsettled period, there was a shortage of food, and the delegates were anxious to get back to their own homes as quickly as possible. But Chayanov insisted, and a special railway carriage took the agronomists from Voronezh to the small town of Kozlov. The delegates did not regret having made the trip: Michurin's orchard and the experiments he was conducting interested them all. But the conditions in which the talented horticulturist was working caused even people accustomed to the Spartan conditions in the provinces to throw up their hands in surprise. Vavilov wrote later: "I recall the squalid state of the experimental farm at that time: the wretched little wooden cottage in which one of the most remarkable plant breeders of our times lived and worked."[1]

When Vavilov, then thirty-three, first visited Kozlov, Ivan Michurin was already sixty-five. The greater part of his life was already behind him, and it had been a hard, lonely, and poverty-stricken life at that. There were very few people in Russia who knew anything about his experiments, his research, or the new varieties of plants he had bred. Even Timiryazev, who had written an excellent essay on the American horticulturist Luther Burbank, had not heard of Burbank's counterpart in Russia. In the first years after the Revolution Michurin was in special need of help: the orchard was unfenced and he had no laborers to aid him. In fact, this most inventive plant breeder did not even have the means to feed his own family. "After we have finished work, each of us has to set about patching up our boots and clothes, and then we still have to earn something on the side to support the family, because the wages we receive don't cover a tenth of what we need to spend," wrote Michurin to Chayanov in September 1922. Michurin did not mention that in his efforts to earn a living he had to mend worn-out buckets and repair old typewriters.

It was in those difficult days that Vavilov came to Michurin's aid. Even on the first visit, he acquainted himself with Michurin's ideas and realized that he was dealing with a talented and inquisitive researcher. Documents and letters of the early 1920s reveal the relationship between the two men and make quite clear what Vavilov was aiming at: having "discovered" Michurin himself, he tried to spread the news about the provincial horticulturist as widely as possible. That was typical of Vavilov. He was more eager to popularize other people's research, if it appealed to him, than he was his own. A lively exchange of letters and plant specimens ensued between Vavilov's Institute in Petrograd and Michurin's nursery in Kozlov. Vavilov drew up a list of everything that

Michurin had published and invited him to write an article summarizing his achievements, which Vavilov then published in his journal. Finally, he sent to Kozlov a well-known expert on fruit growing, V. V. Pashkevich, to write an account of Michurin's work.

But Vavilov did not consider that enough. Michurin was living in poverty and he had to be helped quickly in practical terms. At the beginning of 1922 Vavilov made a speech at an all-Russian conference on experimental work, in which he called upon the Russian Commissariat for Agriculture to give support to Michurin's nursery as soon as possible. Vavilov sent a letter to the commissariat proposing that it should celebrate forty-five years of scientific work by the outstanding Russian plant breeder Michurin and then went to Moscow himself to make sure his memorandum was attended to. His efforts were rewarded: on October 9, 1922, the Collegium of the Commissariat for Agriculture passed this resolution:

> 1. I. V. Michurin to be issued with a special document which will, firstly, record his services to the state performed in the course of many years of work on the breeding of a series of valuable varieties of crop plants . . ., and, secondly, grant him the ownership for the rest of his life of the smallholding in which his nursery is situated.
> 2. I. V. Michurin to be alloted the sum of 500,000 rubles in 1922 banknotes for him to dispose of personally without having to render accounts. . . .
> 3. The publishing department of the People's Commissariat for Agriculture to be instructed to collect and publish all Michurin's works along with his biography and portrait under the general editorship of Prof. N. I. Vavilov.[2]

This resolution played an important part in Michurin's life. His home and garden were freed from all taxes, he was no longer in need, and a year later he was appointed director of a considerably extended nursery, which was named after him. In another year's time his first book was published; in its introduction Michurin wrote that the publication of the results of his forty years' work had been made possible only through the efforts of Professor Vavilov. Vavilov himself contributed an enthusiastic introduction. Having only recently returned from the United States, where he had visited Luther Burbank, Vavilov wrote his introduction around a comparison of the work of the two self-taught experts:

> The conditions in which the Russian does his original work are immeasurably more difficult, but there are many striking similarities in the two men's intellectual qualities. They have both been working for more than forty years on the same problem. They have both come to the conclusion that the best paths to success in creating new strains and in improving existing varieties of plants lie in bringing together the widest variety of plant types from all parts of the country, the extensive application of cross-breeding between the various strains, and the cross-breeding of wild varieties with cultivated ones. . . . And toward the end of their lives and after half a century of untiring effort, they both continue to be explorers, striving to advance our knowledge.[3]

And what was Michurin's attitude to his benefactor in Leningrad? The agronomist of Lebedeva, a close friend of Michurin, wrote:

> I first heard about Nikolai Vavilov from Michurin himself. That year Vavilov was organizing a celebration to mark 50 years of Michurin's work. I arrived at Michurin's farm after the occasion and he immediately started to scold me: "Why didn't you arrive in time for the celebration; Nikolai Vavilov was here. Do you realize what a clever man he is, a great scholar with a wonderful character. You know, he makes such a fuss about my work and does so much to make our work more widely known. He is our great supporter. How he loves everything new! Where will you have another chance to meet him now?"[4]

Early in 1925 Michurin told the young A. N. Bakharev, later to be his secretary and friend, "Vavilov is an outstanding scientist, a brilliant mind. . . . He travels all over the world collecting the plants we need. . . . And it's quite amazing—he knows about a dozen languages. . . . And I must say he is very sympathetic to the work we are doing."[5]

In June 1932 Bakharev witnessed a meeting between the two men:

> A group of men approached the wooden shack near which Michurin had stopped. Vavilov was not alone. He was accompanied by the vice-president of the academy, Aleksandr Stepanovich Bondarenko, and the director of the agricultural publishing house. Vavilov had brought his son along with him, a boy of about 12 with a red neckerchief and a cap and carrying a camera. . . .
>
> Michurin and Vavilov shook each other by the hand like old and good friends, smiling happily and exchanging warm greetings.
>
> Vavilov picked a cherry, squeezed out a drop of juice and, as he let the sun's rays shine through it, exclaimed: "Ruby! A genuine ruby!" and, sampling some of the cherries with obvious delight, he eyed Michurin in a friendly way and then said rather earnestly: "If we could satisfy the demands of the Soviet economy for the development of the necessary varieties of all agricultural plants, as you are doing it, Ivan Vladimirovich, we would in a single decade leave the plant breeders of Western Europe and the United States of America far behind. You must propagate that cherry as quickly and as plentifully as possible." . . .
>
> "Everything that I've seen in the new gardens, the nurseries, the experimental plots, the laboratories and the museum causes great pleasure in that it shows that Lenin's wise forecast concerning the tremendous significance of your work for the state is being borne out," Vavilov said. And, as he always did when he wanted to stress the value of some institution, he added that Kozlov "will become a Mecca for plant breeders the world over."[6]

Plenty of other evidence has been preserved about the friendship between the two plant breeders. At Vavilov's request American seed firms sent Michurin seeds and plant specimens. The library of the Botanical Institute of the Academy of Agriculture in Leningrad contains a copy of the second volume of *The Results of Half a Century's Work*, on the title page of which is written in Michurin's distinctive handwriting: "To the much respected President of the Academy of Agricultural Science of the USSR Academician Nikolai Ivanovich Vavilov, with fond memories, from the author—I. V. Michurin. 8 April, 1933."

Vavilov visited Michurinsk for the last time in September 1934.[8] The town, as well as the rest of the country, was celebrating sixty years of Michurin's work as a scientist. The instruments in the brass bands, the scarves of the Pioneers, and the brightly colored costumes of the guests from the Ukraine, the Caucasus, and Central Asia mingled with the gold and crimson of the fruit-laden orchards. On the evening of September 20 a meeting was held in the local theater in Michurin's honor, at which Vavilov spoke on behalf of the two academies: "The Academy of Science and we, the scientists, are all proud to have Ivan Vladimirovich among us. His achievement teaches us how to live and how to work."

It was not by chance that Vavilov had stated that Michurin was worthy to be among the members of the Soviet Academy of Science. A few months later, on June 1, 1935, a record of a general meeting of the academy reads: "The permanent secretary reported the receipt of a proposal from twelve full members of the academy that I. V. Michurin should be elected an honorary academician." The first to sign the proposal was Vavilov, who had also composed the text. On the same evening Michurin was elected an honorary member of the academy by forty votes; only four people voted against.

A week later, on June 7, 1935, Michurin died. The sad news was reported in every newspaper in the country, and the next day an article by Vavilov appeared in *Pravda*. It bore the brief title "A Remarkable Achievement." In it the Soviet Union's leading theoretical biologist not only declared that Michurin's achievement as a practical plant breeder was of the very greatest value but also gave due praise to Michurin's contribution to theory: "His work was inspired by a materialist philosophy and many of his ideas were completely original. In all his works Michurin laid stress on the value of independent creative activity."

Such is the true picture of the relationship between Vavilov and Michurin. One would think that it would be very difficult to conclude from these facts that Vavilov was an "anti-Michurinist." But there were people who nevertheless declared that, although

Vavilov was not a personal enemy of Michurin, he opposed and fought against the theoretical principles underlying Michurin's system of plant breeding.

Let us examine this accusation. Addressing the younger generation, Ivan Michurin, then eighty years of age and a recognized expert in the field of plant breeding, had encouraged the young researchers to argue with him and, if his critics had their own tested observations, not to hesitate to try and prove him wrong. That summed up Michurin very well; he himself was a hard worker who had with his own hands brought new scientific facts to light, and he was now quite ready to welcome and help the next generation.

Vavilov was, it is true, a stubborn character, and no respecter of persons when it came to scientific disputes. In R. Gregory's *Discoveries, Goals, and the Meaning of Science*, which Vavilov edited in a Russian translation and provided with a foreword, there is a statement with which he was undoubtedly in agreement: "Progress consists of corrections being made in earlier researches. That is why criticism is so important for the progress of science."[7] Vavilov's critical faculty never left him even when he was dealing with the most renowned researchers. While he was still a student in England he voiced his disagreement with Darwin and wrote very astute comments all over the cover and margins of his copy of the great biologist's book. Even his much-loved teacher William Bateson did not escape impartial criticism on the part of his most conscientious student. Referring to one of the last articles Bateson wrote, Vavilov declared quite bluntly: "As they say in Turkestan, Mr. Bateson is shutting up shop and has already lost that quality which is especially needed in scientific work—the capacity to move with the times."[8] His principle was apparently that the more important the discovery, the greater the need for strict scientific analysis and scientific verification. Michurin's discoveries were extremely important, and Vavilov subjected them on several occasions to demanding but benevolent analysis.

Vavilov set out his views in great detail in his article entitled "A Great Day for a Soviet Horticulturist."[9] He defined three successive stages through which Michurin had passed, from his first unsuccessful experiments to the complete victory of his method. In an effort to extend fruit growing farther north, Michurin first tried prolonged acclimatization of southern varieties. When that attempt did not produce results, Michurin tried selecting seedlings grown from seeds of the best southern varieties. Once again, he had no success. It was only then that he realized that it would be impossible to extend fruit growing farther north without cross-breeding south-ern with northern varieties and submitting the plants to further strict selection.

Michurin's most important contribution, in Vavilov's opinion, was that "unlike anyone else in our country he promoted the idea of remote hybridization, of very original attempts to produce new species of plants by cross-breeding them with other species and he demonstrated both in theory and in practice the correctness of that method."[10] It was along the lines that Michurin had indicated that modern plant breeding advanced and continues to advance. And it was by that method Michurin produced some 350 varieties of apple, pear, plum, apricot, peach, and grape.

The second idea for which Vavilov also held Michurin in great esteem was "the collection of material for cross-breeding from every possible source." Long before the finest nurseries in the world did so, plant breeders in the little town of Kozlov were beginning, in their efforts to improve the local varieties, to make use of wild, cold-resistant, and disease-resistant kinds of fruit trees from Siberia, Canada, the mountainous regions of China, Tibet, and the Far East. "Ivan Michurin was the first to appreciate the exceptional importance of obtaining wild and cultivated specimens of every possible kind from the three main fruit-growing areas in the temperate zones—from North America, southwestern Asia (including the Soviet Trans-Caucasus and northern Caucasus) and eastern Asia."[11] Who could understand that side of Michurin's work better than Vavilov, who was himself a great collector of the Earth's plant resources and the founder of a world-famous collection of crop plant seeds? The two plant breeders had in fact come to the conclusion, quite independently of each other, that Soviet agricul-ture (including the Russian people's own gardens) had to be revived by using the plant resources of the whole planet.

On more than one occasion Vavilov reminded members of his staff of this remarkable discovery of Michurin's. In 1934, the same year he sent a group of his colleagues off to the Far East, Vavilov said, as though reprimanding himself: "It really is becoming quite disgraceful. . . . We know all about Abyssinia, but as far as the

Soviet Far East is concerned, we have wasted our time talking, and in the end it was Michurin who collected the material from there for the hybridization of fruit plants."[12]

But however much he admired Michurin's work, Vavilov, a supporter of the chromosome theory of the inheritance of characteristics, could not possibly agree with all Michurin's methods and conclusions. In particular he was quite unable to accept Michurin's assertion that the so-called vegetative hybrids (descendants of two different plants that have grown together) were exactly like hybrids obtained as a result of cross-breeding. (Incidentally, Soviet biologists have since rejected this view of vegetative hybridization and declared it to be unscientific.)

It must be remembered that, although the most important discoveries in genetics—those that completely overturned the old conceptions about heredity—were made by the 1930s, Michurin, who was already over seventy-five, could not follow everything that was happening in world science. This was not his fault. The self-taught Russian plant breeder had already made a substantial contribution to biology.

There were, however, in Michurin's work many unscientific, intuitive devices and methods bordering on miracle mongering. An account given by the Saratov plant breeder Nikolai Ananevich Tyumyakov, who visited Kozlov in 1926, gives some idea of what those methods were:

> Gorshkov [one of Michurin's closest collaborators] asked Michurin, "Ivan Vladimirovich, when are we going to get on with thinning out the seedlings?" Michurin stood up and said, "We'll go and do it right away." He took his stick and went off. Though he was already quite old he walked quickly . . . then he stopped and busied himself with something. I asked, "What's he doing?" "Oh, he's putting his label on them," Gorshkov replied. I was curious and went nearer. Michurin had stopped at one young tree, touched one of the buds, fingered a leaf and said, "It'll be slightly bitter, but never mind." He then pulled out of his pocket a leaden strip already prepared with numbers stamped on it, bound it round a branch, and went on his way. . . .

I took Gorshkov by the sleeve and asked him in a whisper, "Is he getting a bit too old for it?" Gorshkov replied, "No. We used to think so. But actually he has such a lot of experience. He feels the plant and says it will be rather bitter. And just imagine, the old man is not mistaken." I said, "All right, but what will happen tomorrow?" "Well, he's put five labels on, which means that tomorrow I shall replant them and the rest we shall dig up and throw away. Whether they are bitter or not will be known only in a few years' time, and Michurin says he needs the land at once."[13]

The geneticist N. V. Timofeyev-Resovsky, at the All-Russian Agricultural Exhibition in 1923, tried at Vavilov's request to explain genetics to Michurin. The conversation lasted for quite a long time, but Timofeyev-Resovsky did not succeed in making the horticulturist understand the ideas of Gregor Mendel and Morgan.

But there were around Michurin a number of people who wanted to create the impression that he was a great theoretician. They decided to exploit the nationwide admiration for Michurin that developed in the 1930s to set up in Kozlov an institute for the study of genetics. This prompted Vavilov, then president of the All-Union Academy of Agriculture, to write to the distinguished fruit-growing authority V. L. Simirenko:

> The comrades in Kozlov are wrong to make such use of Michurin's name. For all his great merits there are in his written works many elements of an unscientific approach, as there are also in Burbank's work. These questions can be discussed only in a calm atmosphere with a sufficiently prepared audience and group of arbiters, which, as you know, is not always possible. . . . It is one thing to recognize Michurin's great services, the value of the new varieties he has produced, and the value of Ivan Vladimirovich himself as a person who has labored with great determination and talent for fifty years. But the science of selection and plant breeding is quite another matter. Ivan Vladimirovich had no need of an institute; his work was really his own individual affair, whereas from an institute we require a scientific approach. And the rather superficial

approach and apparently scanty intellectual equipment that a number of the comrades at Kozlov display will be assessed objectively in the country, if not today, then tomorrow.[14]

There was nothing particularly offensive to Michurin in that assessment. Like every other major seeker after knowledge, he never claimed that his views contained the ultimate truth. In his first book, which was published with Vavilov's assistance, Michurin wrote:

I certainly do not lay claim to be presenting any new discoveries or to be disproving any laws established by those with authority in science. I am only setting out my conclusions and arguments, arrived at in the course of my own personal, practical work over many long years on the cultivation of new varieties of fruit-bearing plants. What is more, I may well have been mistaken in some instances and have not understood correctly various phenomena in the life of plants and the relevance of the laws of Mendel and other scholars in recent times. But such mistakes are unavoidable in all kinds of work and cannot be of great significance, since they will probably be corrected later by other workers in the field.

Michurin could really not be offended at what Vavilov, his opponent in science, had said. Michurin's magnanimous words about those who would one day correct his mistakes were inspired by the great tradition of science. You are invited to argue but not to quarrel, to object but not to fight.

Trofim Denisovich Lysenko was eleven years younger than Vavilov. He was born in 1898 in the village of Karlovka, in the Poltava region. He studied at a horticultural school and the Agricultural Institute in Kiev and then worked on an experimental station at Belaya Tserkov. In 1925 he joined the cotton-growing institute at Gandzha (now Kirovobad) in Azerbaidzhan, where he was put in charge of leguminous plants, which he sowed practically every five days throughout the year. Vavilov's Institute of Plant

Breeding was also conducting experiments at Gandzha, so Vavilov knew about Lysenko's experiments and took a keen interest in them.

Even then, when he was still under thirty, Lysenko managed to give the impression that he was an exceptional personality. A fellow employee and later close friend, D. A. Dolgushin, wrote:

> He was tall and thin and always covered in mud. He always threw his cap on in one quick movement and it would sit askew on his head. He paid no attention to himself or his own appearance. Goodness knows when he slept—when we came out to work he was already in the fields, and when we returned he was still there. He would spend all his time fussing around with his plants. He knew them and understood them perfectly and seemed even to be able to talk to them, delving right inside them. His plants would "want" things, "demand" other things, would "like" this and "be upset by" something else.[15]

Vavilov was presumably attracted by the same qualities in Lysenko as Dolgushin was: he liked people who could think for themselves and were absorbed in their work. At that time Vavilov knew very little about the views of his new acquaintance. He did not know, for example, that Lysenko had not read what had been published on biology in the world outside (his ignorance of foreign languages prevented him from doing so) and was especially contemptuous of the research carried on by geneticists. "Much of what we studied at the institute, for instance about genetics, he [Lysenko] considers to be 'harmful nonsense' and asserts that success in our work depends upon how quickly we manage to forget it all and 'rid ourselves of that drug,' " wrote Donat Dolgushin. Friends even made jokes about his views: "Lysenko is sure that it is possible to produce a camel from a cotton seed and a baobab tree from a hen's egg."[16] (Every joke contains its grain of truth, but who of the young wits could have thought that twenty-five years later their friend would write in all seriousness that he had obtained from a grain of wheat three plants of different genera—wheat, barley, and rye!)

Usually intolerant of anyone's lack of education in biology, Vavilov paid no attention at their first meeting to Lysenko's strange views. He was more interested in Lysenko's hypothesis, which Dolgushin described as follows:

> He [Lysenko] has established—and this is now beyond any doubt!—that all winter plants, which are generally believed to require rest in the winter so that they can flower the next year and produce seeds, do not, in fact, require any "rest" at all. They need, not rest, but *cold*, a relatively slight lowering of temperature (not below zero!).
>
> Once having been subjected to this cold they may develop further without any interruption and produce seeds. But that application of lower temperature may play a part even when the plant is not yet a plant but a seed that has scarcely begun to germinate. And so if, for example, seeds of winter wheat are made slightly damp and, after being kept for a certain time in the cold, are sown in the spring, they will develop normally and give a crop that same summer, like real spring crops!
>
> Just imagine, my dear friends, what that means. It means a reduction in the vegetative period in plants, the transfer of many crops farther north, and goodness knows what else! It is undoubtedly a discovery of major scientific importance. . . . That's the sort of man our Lysenko is![17]

Dolgushin's delight at this new agronomic method, which soon became known as "vernalization," is not difficult to understand. To a person who had just graduated from an agricultural college vernalization might indeed seem to be a new and significant discovery. But it is more difficult to explain Vavilov's attitude. It is true that at first acquaintance Vavilov was much more restrained in his assessment of vernalization than were Lysenko's friends. That plants had varying requirements of low temperature was an interesting point. Vavilov even found an application for it: it would be convenient to classify the many plants collected in Leningrad according to this criterion. "Taking this aspect into consideration in particular," Vavilov said, "we shall be better able to regionalize (i.e., distribute according to climatic zones) our varieties and crops." But Vavilov said nothing about growing southern plants in the north, although he considered Lysenko's experiments striking and original. That was his way: to support and encourage anyone who showed promise.

In 1929 Lysenko, still a young agronomist, received an invitation to speak at the all-union congress of geneticists and plant breeders in Leningrad. For a man from the provinces who had practically no written works to his name, this was a considerable honor. Although the meeting was described as an all-union congress, the attendance of numerous guests from abroad (including such distinguished biologists as R. Goldschmidt and E. Bauer from Germany and Federley from Finland) turned it actually into an international gathering of geneticists.

Lysenko's paper (prepared jointly with Dolgushin) did not, however, evoke any great excitement. In the course of the discussion, distinguished plant physiologists pointed out that Lysenko's vernalization was by no means novel: the Soviet scholar N. A. Maksimov had written about "cold germination," and the American Klippart had suggested it (unsuccessfully) as an agrotechnical method in the middle of the nineteenth century. Lysenko and his friend were highly displeased with their reception by the country's most distinguished plant breeders and geneticists.[18] Twenty years later Dolgushin wrote: "That was his first encounter with the enemy [!], from which it became clear to him that he would have to resort to other means in that battle."[19]

Vavilov, who presided over the congress, said in conversation with Professor Maksimov that Lysenko must certainly be supported, that he had an original mind, and that he had arrived at many of his conclusions independently of his scientific predecessors.

Two years later Lysenko had managed to move from Azerbaidzhan to the Institute of Plant Breeding and Genetics in Odessa and had transferred there the experiments he had begun in Gandzha. At Odessa he made just as strong an impression on his colleagues. Early in 1931, the director of the institute, Stepanenko, wrote in a personal letter to Vladimir Matveyevich at the Academy of Agriculture: "Comrade Lysenko's latest achievements offer us such possibilities for practical application as could not have been imagined only a few months ago." Stepanenko reported that Lysenko had made maize ripen two or three weeks earlier "by

subjecting seeds that had only just begun to germinate to darkness."
This method appeared to offer the possibility of transferring maize
to the far north. "With cotton equally remarkable results have been
obtained. . . . In a month or six weeks you can expect to hear from
me that the maize is going to cast off its panicles at the same time as
the early spring crops begin to flower and that the cotton will come
into bud some two weeks earlier than usual," he wrote. The
purpose of the letter was to obtain additional credits for Lysenko's
experiments. It certainly brought results, possibly because the
writer made a point of stressing that "Lysenko is very careful and
undemanding. He works literally day and night."

The letter from Odessa to Moscow was sent in May. But the
previous February Vavilov, who had been following closely the
experiments being conducted by Lysenko, invited him to give a
paper to the Presidium of the Academy of Agriculture. Lysenko
described the essence of his experiments in a businesslike manner
and made a good impression on the top people in the academy.
Though he was still ignorant of the scientific terminology and the
works of other biologists, his own ideas seemed to members of the
Presidium to have promise. Vavilov alone was in a position to note
that there had been no significant changes in Lysenko's ideas over
the previous five years: he was still talking about the fabulous effects
of vernalization.

It is true that Lysenko himself, the nature of his experiments, and
the conviction with which he defended his views, made a good
impression on Academician Vavilov and members of the Presidium
of the Academy, among whom were such prominent scholars as the
academicians G. K. Meister, A. S. Serebrovsky, and M. M. Zavadovsky. But by 1931 new factors, which had not operated in 1928,
were coming into play apart from Lysenko's personal merits.
Lysenko delivered his report in Moscow at the same time as the
authorities were impressing on all the scientific institutions dealing
with agriculture the need for practical achievements. Leaders who
had enforced collectivization at all costs and who were now planning to train biologists in the state farms and to extend the country's
cultivated area by forty or fifty million acres a year, now began
demanding that scientists "join in socialist competition" and produce immediate practical results. It was useless to try to explain to
them that the most important practical discoveries resulted from

pure theoretical research. At a time when "tempo" was everything, no one wanted to hear such views. "Logic" of a different kind was in fashion.

"Can such a situation arise in science where theory has made some kind of advance, a step forward, but practice derives no benefit from it? From childhood I have never understood how it could happen, and I could never tolerate people trying to demonstrate to me that such fruitless theoretical achievements with no practical value are worth anything at all." Those are Lysenko's words, not the words of an unpretentious agronomist delivering his first paper to the Academy of Agriculture, but of Lysenko, president of the academy, seventeen years later. Such were the views that triumphed at the beginning of the 1930s. The academy came under increasing pressure for scientific discoveries to produce immediate results in the form of bigger harvests.

In these circumstances the academy recognized vernalization as a discovery of practical importance. At another time, of course, the scientists would have demanded first that Lysenko's claims be verified on the experimental farms of other scientific institutions. But in 1931 there was simply no time for that sort of thing. And so, contenting themselves with Lysenko's own report, the academicians resolved that vernalization was to be regarded as a method of great practical significance. In that way, contrary to the main principle of biological science, the new discovery received backing and publicity long before anyone had succeeded in repeating Lysenko's experiments. If that was a mistake, no one drew attention to it. On the contrary, academicians were delighted to think that the science of agronomy was providing the country with visible, tangible benefits. In short, in 1931 Lysenko and his vernalization seemed to be a boon for everybody—for the civil servants as much as for the scientists.

Vavilov gave instructions for dozens of packets of seeds of different plants to be obtained from every part of the world and sent to Odessa for vernalization testing. In the summer of 1931 the Presidium of the Academy returned again to the question of Lysenko's experiments. A resolution was adopted unanimously: "For the purpose of developing and extending Comrade Lysenko's work on reducing the length of the vegetative period of cereals, cotton, maize, soya, vegetables, etc., it is considered necessary to allot the sum of 30,000 rubles from the academy's budget."[20] A year later forty machine tractor stations were given the task of carrying out "experiments in the vernalization of wheat according to Comrade Lysenko's method."

Because of his interest in this new development, Vavilov himself went to Odessa in the spring of 1932. Along with Lysenko he went around the institute's fields and visited the collective farms. He had no reason to doubt anything his companion told him. He had already given instructions for his institute to carry out its own experiments and to check Lysenko's claims, but it had not yet entered his head to suspect Lysenko of being dishonest or of falsifying his results. In a letter from Odessa to Leningrad Vavilov spoke enthusiastically about all he had seen: "Lysenko's work is remarkable. It means that a great deal will have to be put on a different footing. Worldwide collections will have to be subjected to the process of vernalization."[21] Vavilov was now captivated by the thought of shortening the period between sowing and fruit bearing in southern plants and, with the aid of vernalization, growing the best imported varieties farther north. Which agronomist would not be attracted by such a prospect? Vavilov did not see anything miraculous in it. Nobody possessed a monopoly over scientific truth. Harvey had said quite rightly, "Discoveries can be made by chance and anybody can teach anyone else: the young can teach the elderly and a simple fellow can teach a brainy one." There was nothing wrong about Vavilov learning from an observant agronomist. It is true that in the same letter from Odessa, Vavilov wrote, "I went around the state and collective farms with Lysenko; there are a lot of mistakes with the vernalization." But he saw only the mistakes committed in the fields. Nobody yet guessed that the whole idea of vernalization might be a mistake.

In the spring of 1932, as he prepared for the Fifth International Congress of Genetics in the United States, Vavilov had to draw up a list of the Soviet delegation. Along with the names of the doctors and professors of genetics he put the name of the agronomist Lysenko. In addition, he sent a personal letter to Lysenko inviting him to go to America, where there would be "much to interest a geneticist." In fact Lysenko did not go to America. But in his conference speech devoted to the successes of Soviet biology, Vavilov found it necessary to inform the world's scholars:

The remarkable discovery made by T. D. Lysenko from Odessa opens up tremendous new possibilities for plant breeders and geneticists working on individual variants. . . . The essence of these methods, which are specific to various plants and various group variants, consists in the effect on the seeds of different combinations of darkness, temperature and humidity. This discovery offers us the possibility of using tropical and subtropical plants in our climate for cultivation and for work on genetics. . . . This creates the possibility of extending the areas over which agricultural crops can be grown to an unheard-of extent.[22]

Because of the confidence he had in Lysenko as a colleague, Vavilov proposed that, from the end of 1931, all the experimental stations where the so-called geographical sowings were being done should test the effectiveness of vernalization. He was particularly insistent on its being tested in northern conditions. "What Lysenko has done and is doing is of quite exceptional interest, and the polar department must carry out these tests," he wrote to the agronomist I. G. Eikhfeld in Khibini.[23]

In plant breeding the process of testing is not a simple or a speedy business. Every experiment requires at least a couple of years and sometimes even more. It was bound to take many years to assess precisely the effect of vernalization on various crops in different parts of the country. But while the true value of Lysenko's ideas was being tested in the fields and nurseries, Lysenko himself was rapidly emerging as a leading "scientist." In 1932 Vavilov raised with the president of the Ukrainian Academy of Science, A. A. Bogomolets, the question of electing Lysenko a member of that academy.[24] A year later Vavilov submitted Lysenko's name to the government commission for aid to scientists as a candidate for a prize for his discovery of vernalization: "Both theoretically and practically Lysenko's discovery is even now, in its present stage, of exceptional interest, and we would regard Comrade Lysenko as one of the first candidates for receiving the prize."[25]

In 1934 it was again Vavilov who drew the attention of the Biology Section of the Soviet Academy of Science to Lysenko's research. Although the precise nature of vernalization required further study and would probably reveal a great deal that was new,

Vavilov said, nevertheless he considered the new method to be "a major discovery." Equally valuable in his view was Lysenko's teaching about the stages in the development of the plant organism. "For ten years Comrade Lysenko has been working steadily in the same direction," Vavilov wrote. "Although relatively few works have yet been published by him, his latest works represent such a major contribution to world science as to justify us in putting him forward as a candidate for corresponding membership of the Soviet Academy of Science."[26]

When he made his report to the government, in May 1934 about the achievements of the Academy of Agriculture, Vavilov, as president, again stressed the value of Lysenko's scientific discoveries. This repeated praise of Lysenko's merits meant that top officials very soon took note of his name. Visitors started turning up in Odessa from Kiev, the Ukrainian capital, and then from Moscow. Everybody liked the peasant-scholar, and he fitted in exactly with the demands of the time both because of his background and because of what he had to say.

Yakovlev, the commissar for agriculture, even granted a special privilege: Lysenko could approach him personally on any matter. Lysenko did not fail to take advantage of this offer. In 1932 and 1933, according to the archives, he wrote frequently to Yakovlev, on one occasion complaining about the shortage of staff in the laboratories, on another requesting that his friend Dolgushin should be moved to Odessa. As a rule his requests were granted. The commissar was obviously interested in Lysenko's work. He personally commissioned Lysenko to write an article about vernalization for the Soviet pavilion at an exhibition in Königsberg, and in 1932 he gave instructions for vernalization to be extended to some 250,000 acres on state farms and to be applied extensively on the collective farms.

It is quite clear from the documents that in the early 1930s Academician Vavilov opened the way for Lysenko to make a career in the government service and in science.

In an interview she gave to a Soviet journalist not long before her death, Lidia Breslavets said, "Nikolai Ivanovich himself raised Lysenko to the top. I was at a meeting in 1934 at which Vavilov said: We will now ask a young man to speak who is showing great promise—the scientist Lysenko. Lysenko was already behaving in such a way that we couldn't resist saying to Vavilov that it was strange that he should push him forward like that."[27]

Perhaps an explanation lies in what Professor Breslavets wrote on another occasion about Vavilov: "Unfortunately, the qualities of goodness and almost childlike naiveté, which it was so wonderful to find in so great a man, sometimes prevented him from understanding clearly enough the true character of other people. I would not wish to give the impression that Nikolai Ivanovich could not distinguish between one person and another. He saw the shortcomings in certain of his colleagues, but he reckoned that devotion to science would re-educate them."[28]

Vavilov undoubtedly hoped to see his own unlimited devotion to science repeated in others. But, alas, whether it is called trustfulness or gullibility, the hope became disastrous for Vavilov. In the early 1930s many people began to discover in science both a livelihood and a springboard to power. But Vavilov lived in the world of science and creative work and gave no thought to political ambition. He began to assist Lysenko in the firm conviction that he was dealing with an original and brilliant researcher whose discoveries would help the advance of agriculture. And he continued in that belief, apparently until the end of 1934 or perhaps the beginning of 1935. There were, however, other factors operating in the relationship between Vavilov and Lysenko.

In the 1920s and early 1930s the "intellectual" or educated person was characterized as a second-class citizen. The central figure in the newspapers, books, and films was the worker, the proletarian, or, at a stretch, the peasant–collective farmer. Educated people, the intelligentsia, were on the other hand subjected to constant repression and ridicule, if not yet mass extermination. They were reproached for their lack of backbone—they were known as "puny intellectuals"—for their real or imagined sympathy for the decadent West, or simply for their ties and white collars, their spectacles and hats. While proletarian origins would open the doors to the highest jobs, to educational institutions, and to science, an office worker, a doctor, or an engineer, or the child of such a professional, was treated, if not as an enemy, at any rate as a person to be eyed with suspicion. There was, for example, in the plant-breeding institute a special course to turn youths who were not particularly literate, but whose class origins were quite "clean," rapidly into scientists and the future managers of various institutions and enterprises. The educational and scientific demands placed on these young people were minimal, though the rights they acquired were more than sufficient. In particular they had the right to change the scientist in charge of them if they did not like him. Subjected to this "class" pressure and deafened by all the talk of "class science" in those years, many professors, whether with a sigh or a frown or a chuckle, carried out the orders of society—advancing the next generation "from the lowest level."

I believe that, consciously or not, Vavilov eventually became reconciled to this situation. In his own institute he chose to ignore the undisciplined and lazy adolescents in the special course. When Lysenko, with his perfect ancestry and upbringing and his many new ideas, appeared on the scene, Vavilov probably even rejoiced—Lysenko appeared to be energetic, hardworking, and gifted. There was nothing wrong in backing such a person, and at last it was possible to combine the demands of the state machine with those of one's own conscience. I would not say that Vavilov actually spelled out his attitude toward the young Lysenko so precisely to himself or anyone else. But no one who takes it upon himself to write the history of relationships within the world of Soviet science in the 1920s and 1930s can ignore the important fact of the difference in status that Soviet society gave Professor Nikolai Vavilov, a scholar and an intellectual, and his protégé Trofim Lysenko, the son of a peasant.

The protégé quickly realized all the advantages that might result from his impeccable background. Encouragement from his superiors and panegyrics in the newspapers soon started to spoil the character of the man who had only recently been a retiring agronomist. He became arrogant and rude, and his opinion of himself grew; these tendencies increased further following the arrest of the director of the Odessa institute, the talented plant breeder and geneticist Andrei Sapegin, and the appointment of Lysenko in his place. At the same time another event of the greatest importance in Lysenko's life took place—he met Isai Prezent.

Isai Izrailevich Prezent had never studied biology. In the late 1920s he completed a three-year course in social science at Leningrad University and then decided to specialize in the philosophy of biology. For several years he tried in vain to attach himself to some leading scientist in order, as a philosopher, to provide a theoretical framework for someone else's scientific ideas. This sort of "interpretation" work was fairly widespread in the 1930s, but Prezent had no success in his efforts to attach himself to a sufficiently important "boss". He offered himself to Vavilov, among others, but Nikolai Ivanovich did not like the "philologists" and Prezent did not last long in the plant-breeding institute. For Lysenko, however, a person like Prezent was a real gift. The agronomist from Odessa was moving up the social scale, and he now needed to consolidate his position on the higher level. For that purpose he needed some general ideas and theoretical views. He needed to look like a scholar. But Lysenko, who was ignorant of elementary biology, did not have such material at his disposal, and there can be no doubt that had he not met Prezent (apparently at the beginning of 1932), Lysenko would have faded out among his plants, just as so many "innovators" of the 1930s later vanished into obscurity.

The meeting with Prezent changed everything. The cunning, but by no means untalented, philosopher quickly realized the advantages of becoming the mouthpiece of the agronomist who was riding the crest of a wave. Prezent also realized that Lysenko, if he continued to confine himself entirely to practical work and flatly to reject genetics and any kind of biological theory, would not manage to stay long on the surface. Lysenko needed something to float on his own positive program. Prezent set about providing him with one.

A dilettante in scientific matters and unacquainted with the latest discoveries in biology, Prezent understood best the views of the nineteenth-century French naturalist Jean Baptiste Lamarck, which by the 1930s had already outlived their time. Lamarck's theory that by changing the external conditions in which a plant or animal was living, one could change correspondingly its inherited characteristics, seemed to Prezent to be the most suitable for Lysenko's philosophical platform. Lamarckism, sometimes called "progressive biology," was not only easy for even an ignoramus to understand, it was easy to link with the requirements of the age. People's Commissar Yakovlev demanded that scientists "revolutionize the life of animals and plants." Lamarck indicated how it could be done.

Prezent was also careful not to forget Darwin, because Marxist classics approved of the man who developed the theory of the origin of species. But since the teachings of Darwin and Lamarck did not go together very well, Prezent introduced the concept of "creative Darwinism" and began to adapt the great teacher of evolution to the conditions of "socialist reconstruction" and collectivization. Later, after Michurin died, Prezent added to his philosophical baggage some of the work of that generally respected horticulturist. He did it with his customary decisiveness. He approved of everything in Michurin's works that came closest to Lamarck's views and ignored the rest. Prezent even began to assert that Michurin had corrected and improved on Darwin, and the term "Michurinist Darwinism" was coined. It made no sense, but it looked good politically.

At the same time, in the first half of the 1930s, the more serious biologists began to comment on Lysenko's strange career in science. Some were put on their guard by the experiments that were being conducted simultaneously, without any proper control, over thousands of acres. Others were disturbed by Prezent's and Lysenko's crudely written articles and their unscientific contents, all disputing the tested facts of genetics and the world's leading experimental scientists.

In the summer of 1935 Professor Mikhail Zavadovsky of Moscow University, a member of the Presidium of the Academy of Agriculture, first drew his colleagues' attention to the strange alliance of Lysenko and Prezent. He told them that Prezent, teaching a course on Darwinism at Leningrad University, was saying that there were no genetics and no geneticists in the Soviet Union apart from Michurin and Lysenko, that Lysenko was the direct successor of Darwin. "I have formed the idea that Lysenko knows very little of what science is about," Academician Zavadovsky commented. "He does not have sufficient erudition. Prezent assists him in that respect, but *he* also knows nothing about physiology, though he has become interested in it recently. The result is a combination, a synthesis, which has produced, on the one hand, an interesting thought, but which on the other hand abounds in very questionable ideas. Insofar as the press seizes on certain statements by Lysenko-Prezent they become, in my view, rather menacing. . . . The fuss that is being made is not only turning the heads of the young people and graduate students; Lysenko himself is getting dizzy from his success, and this is putting him off his balance."

Zavadovsky also tried to draw attention to the moral side of the Prezent-Lysenko axis: Prezent had once been expelled from the university for seducing female students, and he was known to be both dishonest and immoral. His connection with Lysenko also looked very much like a business deal. As he reached the peak of his success, Lysenko, with all his energy and love of power, was dragging the clever opportunist along with him and at the same time benefiting from his shrewd advice. Having thus exposed all the unpleasant aspects of the "scientific" alliance, however, Academician Zavadovsky—either out of the kindness of his heart or because he foresaw the direction Lysenko's career was taking—limited himself to suggesting that the presidium of the Academy of Agriculture should help Lysenko to understand his mistakes and should explain to him how little substance there was in the claim that he was the Soviet Darwin.

At the same meeting of the presidium a plant breeder and geneticist from Saratov, G. K. Meister, declared that Prezent and Lysenko, without having read a single line of Morgan or Mendel, were disparaging the achievements of contemporary genetics:

> Our plant breeding is based on a study of genetics, and genetics has a mass of achievements to its credit especially in recent years. Not to take those achievements into account means to understand nothing at all. To criticize, as Prezent and Lysenko do, is quite improper, and especially so for us in the Soviet Union, where the Central Committee of the party and the government have decided to hold the international congress on genetics, while our academicians are being subjected to crude heckling criticism. . . . They say there are only two plant breeders, Michurin and Lysenko. . . . It is true that the Soviet Union did have an outstanding plant breeder in Michurin, who had tremendous achievements to his credit, but you cannot place Lysenko on the same level as Michurin when in the course of the last decade he has not produced a single new variety.[29]

Others spoke in the same tone, accusing Lysenko of ignorance and unethical behavior. In fact, his only defender at the meeting was Vavilov. While recognizing that some of Lysenko's arguments lacked substance—concerning the so-called in-breeding method, for example—Vavilov approved the general direction of his scientific work. "Lysenko is a careful and talented researcher and his experimental work is irreproachable," he said.

By 1935, much favored by the people at the top and equipped with a theoretical program, Lysenko was already in a position to ignore the displeasure of the established scientists, all the more so because he had just been made an academician by the Academy of Agriculture. What was that about reading the world literature on biology? In 1935 he could already permit himself to tell the booklovers: "Our first task is to absorb the rich scientific legacy left us by Michurin, that greatest of geneticists. . . . Yet here we are asking people first of all how much foreign stuff they have read."[30] On another occasion he expressed himself even more frankly: "It is better to know less, but to know just what is necessary for our practical work both at the present time and for the immediate future."[31]

Did Lysenko realize that the theoretical baggage that Prezent had palmed off on him was science fiction, a simple fraud? There is no easy answer to that question. But Lysenko's moral standards soon became much clearer.

In February 1935 the second congress of collective-farm "shock-workers" took place in Moscow in the presence of Stalin and members of the government, and Lysenko was invited to speak. His speech was devoted mainly to his vernalization method, of which there were both supporters and opponents among the scientists. Lysenko preferred, however, to give the scientific dispute a quite different gloss. Just ten weeks after the assassination of Kirov, he told the delegates:

> It is not only down on your collective farms that you can come across rich farmers out to wreck our system. You are well aware of them on your farms. But they are no less dangerous and no less active in the scientific world. I have had to put up with a good deal in all kinds of disputes with certain so-called scientists concerning vernalization,

in my efforts to develop this method, and I have had to withstand quite a few hard blows in my practical work. Comrades, it cannot be said that class struggle has not been going on, and is not still going on, on the vernalization front.

On the collective farms there were kulaks [well-to-do farmers] and semikulaks who would often whisper to the peasants: "Don't moisten the grain. It will ruin the seeds." There were cases like that, there were whisperings and similarly dangerous cock-and-bull stories put around by the kulaks, so that, instead of helping the collective farmers, they were doing their wrecking business; the class enemy always remains an enemy, whether he's a scientist or not.[32]

At this point the speech, which was nothing less than the work of an informer reflecting on the political reliability of his scientific opponents, was suddenly interrupted. "Bravo, Comrade Lysenko, bravo!" exclaimed Comrade Stalin. And he started to applaud. At this the whole of the chamber in the Kremlin Palace burst into a storm of applause. That "Bravo" marked the beginning of a new era in the life of the man who originated vernalization. Three months later the agronomist, Lysenko, became an academician, and in another three years he had become president of the All-Union Academy of Agricultural Science.

3 A Strange Debate

Lysenko's ideas are mistaken, very mistaken. . . .
And I consider that it was extremely unfortunate for
Soviet agriculture and Soviet biology that this man was
given such power to interfere with work which was, in
my opinion and in the opinion of the majority of
geneticists, very valuable.
John Haldane, Daily Worker, *December 1964*

When we look back, we are inclined to link Vavilov's misfortunes primarily with the excessive adulation of Lysenko. But in fact the first blows were struck at Vavilov long before Lysenko was finally and firmly established at the summit of Soviet biology and agronomy. There were other forces working against him from the beginning of the 1930s, as is apparent from the Vavilov's relationship with the Soviet authorities between 1925 and 1935.

For the first fifteen years after the October Revolution, Vavilov was a favorite of the new regime. The son of a millionaire, he wanted to prove to the new rulers of his country not only that he was politically loyal, but that he could also be of real use to them. Vavilov's ability and capacity for hard work were still appreciated in the 1920s, and his industry and talent were rewarded at the very highest rates. In 1926 he received the Lenin Prize and later he was made a member of the All-Union Executive Committee of the USSR, a deputy, president of the Academy of Agriculture, and a member of the People's Commissariat for Agriculture. The numerous trips he was allowed to make to foreign countries between 1924 and 1932 were also an indication of the trust placed in him. A country that from its very beginnings has boasted of the efficiency with which its frontiers are guarded grants only a chosen few the right to travel abroad. On the other hand, he did not remain in debt to his country: he set up the Academy of Agricultural Science, he was in charge of the Institute of Plant Breeding and the assembling of a unique collection of seeds, and he gained praise for the work of Soviet geneticists at international congresses.

But that was not enough to guarantee his high position in society. A citizen of the Soviet Union, even the most insignificant in rank, is obliged not only to serve the regime but also to carry out actively and unconditionally any and every order coming from his superiors. That is his main *political* duty. Although this obligation is not laid down in any legal document, everybody knows perfectly well what would be the consequences of the slightest violation of the unwritten law. For such an important figure as Vavilov, the responsibility for any neglect of his *political* duty was all the greater. It was not sufficient that he should demonstrate his complete subservience to the authorities; it was his duty, in speeches, articles, and conversation, to extol the party, its Central Committee, and its general secretary. All around him were singing their praises and trembling lest they lose their jobs. But Vavilov had no political ambitions, was open, warm-hearted, and democratic, and was quite unsuited for the bureaucratic rat race. Did he not find all the duties and privileges something of a burden?

Apparently not. In fact, it could not be said that Vavilov had no ambitions at all. But his ambition was centered not on a particular job, but on science itself. As the principal figure in Soviet agronomy and biology, he was very anxious that *his* laboratories should have the very best equipment the world could provide, and that *his* scientific libraries have the latest specialized material. He needed to finance further expeditions, better salaries for the scientists, foreign exchange for the purchase of seeds and subscriptions to international publications. All that required money, and only a person of influence and high rank could extract money from the centralized, bureaucratic state. Consequently Vavilov valued his position and prestige. He needed them as a means of improving the material and intellectual potential of his institutes.

Vavilov's attitude toward politics and politicians, wherever he came up against them—in Europe, America, or Russia itself—was rather one of faint disparagement, which did not, however, mean that he would have nothing at all to do with them. To help his own scientific cause he was ready to flirt with the Devil. On returning from his expedition to Afghanistan in 1925, he told Professor

Talanov an amusing story about how skillfully he had tricked the British and had photographed a fortress on the Indian-Afghan frontier in Kafiristan. The British would not allow foreigners to get closer than a gun could fire to the fortress, but Vavilov had scrambled up an obscure path that no European had even been along before. He had taken a whole album of pictures. Talanov, a refined intellectual, was shocked by the story—the act was espionage!—but Vavilov, the great traveler, the first European to have crossed the inaccessible territory of Kafiristan, only laughed. What did he care about politics? In Kafiristan he was trying to discover the birthplace of wheat. The pictures of the fortress were just a by-product. He did not suffer at all morally from the experience, but his stomach was sadly upset by the local food.

In a quite different part of the world Academician Vavilov was able to do the politicians yet another important service. In Argentina the Soviet embassy was carrying on a secret war with the German embassy. It was a period of considerable tension: in Berlin the Nazis were out to seize power, and in Buenos Aires the German embassy was trying to draw into its net the German colonists living there. Vavilov, the botanist and agronomist, managed to wreck the German diplomats' plans. Having arrived in the city for a few days, he gained the confidence of an influential landowner who was the leader of the local colony. As a result the German decided one day to refuse to attend a diplomatic reception in the German embassy and appeared instead at the Soviet diplomatic mission to spend an hour or so chatting with Vavilov. This incident apparently had important consequences for the Soviet Union, provoking a very lively exchange of messages between Argentina and Moscow. The Soviet diplomats thanked Vavilov and begged him not to break off his friendly relations with the "useful" German in Buenos Aires.

There was another important side to Vavilov's character. For all his cosmopolitan attitude in matters of science and his excellent relations with Western scholars, Vavilov never forgot that he was *Russian*. It was not a matter of politics or of cold calculation, but something handed down to him from Russian peasant and merchant forebears, an inherited perception of his native land as something irreplaceable and unique, which was not to be bought, sold, or exchanged. Vavilov never talked about his Russian patriotism. In any case that kind of talk—about ancient Russia, one's native land, and patriotism—was still banned in the 1930s. Not without reason, the authorities linked such concepts with the psychological outlook of tsarist times. But it was precisely in those "forbidden" terms that Vavilov, grandson of a peasant and himself a university teacher under the tsars, understood his profound links with his native land. Without being in any way a chauvinist, he loved everything Russian—the food, the language, and the countryside. Though he was not a religious man, he would always visit Orthodox cathedrals when he was abroad, and, though he was in effect a member of the Soviet government, when he was in Paris, Uruguay, or Brazil, he would exchange embraces with Russians whom the Bolshevik Revolution had scattered around the world. For him the exiles were in the first place compatriots, Russians.

A strict rationalist in everything that concerned science, Vavilov allowed his feelings to have their fling in this most important aspect of his life. He was prepared to make any sacrifices for the sake of Russia, irrespective of who happened to be governing it today, on behalf of that vague, almost symbolic Russia of history, whose great merit was the simple fact that it was his native land. It may well be that, when he took pictures of the forbidden fortress in the Pamirs or charmed a "useful" German in Argentina, Vavilov was simply acting as a true son of Russia. But his links with his country belonged to the realm of emotion rather than reason.

Those feelings prompted him to present his country with substantial and on occasion even very precious gifts. In the early 1930s he managed, with a good deal of effort and risk, to obtain in America a most important strategic raw material—the rubber-bearing plant guayule. It was then too that he obtained for the USSR from Peru the carefully protected seed of the quinine tree. His gifts to his country were worth millions of rubles. In any other country such an enterprising person would have become a millionaire. But he had no need of millions, because it was his research and his work that gave him his greatest satisfaction. In Vavilov's ebullient character an overt passion for science was mixed with a concealed *Russian* patriotism, and this complex internal chemistry turned the botanist into a trade representative, the traveler into a spy, and the scholarly lecturer into an undisguised political propagandist.

There was a good-natured but slightly Machiavellian smile on Vavilov's face when, in the spring of 1930, in a compartment of the Moscow-Leningrad train he told the geneticist A. Kuptsov the latest Kremlin story. "Maksimich [Academician I. M. Tulaikov] really put his foot in it yesterday," Vavilov said. "He and I were with Stalin, and he decided to demonstrate his knowledge of political affairs. He had been studying Bukharin's *Historical Materialism* and was quoting from it at every turn. But Stalin eyed him with a very disapproving air. You see, Bukharin is no longer in favor."[1] As he recounted this story with his childlike ingenuousness, Vavilov had no idea that in five years' time that disapproving look in Stalin's eyes would prove fatal for Tulaikov, a talented agriculturist, and that in ten years' time it would carry Vavilov himself to an early grave.

The times were changing. Even in 1931 and 1932, Vavilov could not understand why the Academy of Agriculture was turning so quickly into a bureaucracy or why the management of agricultural science was being taken over by people who were not serious scholars but semiliterate, boastful characters. The next three or four years apparently taught him a good deal. The tragic consequences of collectivization began to make themselves apparent, and there was a wave of arrests among the biologists, agronomists, and veterinary specialists, who were to be made to answer for the breakdown in agriculture. Eighteen leading members of the staff of the Institute of Plant Breeding were arrested, and the situation became more menacing every day. The innocent offenses that Vavilov, in the eyes of the authorities, had committed during the trips abroad in the 1920s were held against him in the early 1930s. On his way back from America in February 1933, as usual in Paris he met his old friends from the Institut Pasteur, Professors Metalnikov and Bezredkaya, who came to the station to see him off. A report was rushed immediately to Moscow: "Vavilov met with White émigrés." What is more he gave an interview to the wrong kind of newspaper and told a reporter that before the Revolution he had been "a lecturer under the tsars." That was not the way to behave, and Vavilov himself began to realize that it was wrong. After he had taken leave of his old friend Metalnikov at the station, he thought to himself: there will be trouble.[2]

The trouble soon started. Late one night in the spring of 1933,

Lidia Breslavets came running to Vavilov's Moscow apartment in a state of great alarm. She had just discovered that Vavilov was to be summoned to the Central Committee the next day and that he was going to get a good dressing-down. The people at the top were not happy about Vavilov's trips abroad, reckoning that they produced nothing of any use and cost a lot of money. Lidia had obtained the information from a friend who was also a member of the Central Committee, Georgi Lomov, a Bolshevik from Saratov who had fought in the underground before the Revolution. But Vavilov, who had just obtained at the risk of his own life in South America some seeds of the quinine tree, which the Soviet Union needed, and several thousand samples of other valuable plants, heard the news with a doubting smile. "That's nothing to worry about. The people in the Central Committee are not stupid; they'll understand," he said. We do not know what the party officials told Vavilov next day. But we do know that Vavilov, the great traveler, was never again allowed to travel abroad.

Vavilov was by nature an incorrigible optimist. Shortly after the unpleasant conversation in the Central Committee, *Pravda* made a bitter attack on the Institute of Plant Breeding and its director. The main accusation was that the institute was not doing work of any practical value and was not providing the country with any new varieties of plants. The argument that the microscope was not a suitable instrument for driving nails appeared in the party's main newspaper even before Lysenko began his triumphant campaign against theoretical science. Vavilov was about to rush to the defense of the institute he had created when even more serious events suddenly intervened.

From the summer of 1934 the Institute of Plant Breeding had been busy preparing to celebrate the tenth anniversary of its foundation and the fortieth anniversary of the institution out of which it had grown. At the same time a celebration of Vavilov's twenty-five years of work as a scientist was planned. As usual Vavilov was full of enthusiasm for the occasion. He may well have thought that the celebrations would increase the diminished authority of his cause in the eyes of the powers that be. He appealed to his colleagues to put their very best efforts into the work.

Many guests, including a large number of foreigners, were

expected in Leningrad. The Institute of Plant Breeding was receiving a stream of greetings from the leading biologists of the world, as well as congratulations from the prime minister of Turkey, and the secretaries and ministers of agriculture of the United States, Bulgaria, Finland, and Poland. Then suddenly, only four days before the ceremony was due to take place, it was canceled without any explanation. Vavilov was dumbfounded. He wrote a letter to Yakovlev, the former commissar for agriculture and later head of the agricultural department of the Central Committee. It was rumored that Yakovlev, who had fallen out with Vavilov at some point, had ordered the cancellation. There was a new figure in the ministry—Chernov. Vavilov appealed to him, in a letter that was a mixture of astonishment and indignation. "The sudden cancellation of the jubilee when the whole institute was already decorated for the occasion has had a very depressing effect on the whole staff, who feel as though they had received a vote of no confidence. . . . This has naturally prompted the senior members of the staff to wonder whether they are fit to carry on."[3] But Vavilov never succeeded in obtaining a reply to his letter. Chernov eventually followed Yakovlev into prison and the grave.

Following the cancellation of the anniversary celebrations, Vavilov came to realize quite clearly that it was not sufficient simply to be a good scholar. It was also not sufficient to pay the *political* price that he had been paying for the good of his scientific work: the authorities needed something else, something he did not understand and was not able to give. Vavilov did not yet know that the police had opened a file on him and that the first denunciations had already been entered in it. But with his sensitive ear and keen sight he had sensed that an irreversible change had taken place in the political climate. Vavilov concealed the fear he felt and suppressed it ever deeper, but it kept breaking through despite himself.

"There were only two occasions when I saw my friend [Vavilov] seriously upset," Herman Muller, the American geneticist and Nobel Prize winner, recalled. "The first time was when he told me what had just happened to him in the Kremlin. Hurrying to a meeting of the Executive Committee he went quickly around a corner in one of the corridors of the Kremlin, and bumped into Stalin, who was coming the other way. Fortunately they both realized that it was a chance encounter, yet even several hours later, after he had returned to the Institute of Genetics, Vavilov had still not recovered from the experience."[4]

As an American, Muller could not be expected to understand the full significance of what his Russian friend had experienced. According to the standards of the time (it was probably the spring of 1935), a meeting in a Kremlin corridor would not be regarded as such an innocent affair. Having bumped into Vavilov, Stalin, who was very much shorter, first recoiled and glanced with fear in his eyes at Vavilov's enormous briefcase. Even then, apparently, he was beset by the fears that later developed into a real psychosis. The briefcase with its loads of books might contain a bomb. But Stalin regained control of himself in a flash, and the fright that had swept across his face was replaced by a grim, suspicious expression. The dictator did not like anybody to see him afraid. That was the account that Vavilov gave to people much closer to him than Muller. He talked about the incident with his usual warm and faintly humorous smile as if it were some amusing and insignificant occurrence. But he is unlikely to have regarded that sudden encounter as a matter of little importance.

A totalitarian regime strives to make every one of its citizens, even those who are least involved, an accessory to its crimes, tries to spatter each and every one with the blood of its victims, and by involvement to make everyone dependent on everybody else. This is the purpose behind the mass political meetings at which people are forced to proclaim their loyalty to the regime and behind the letters of "protest" against real and imagined enemies. Sometimes the authorities need letters of "support," and the process of gathering signatures also becomes a test of people's moral stability. The higher a Soviet citizen rises on the social scale, the more difficult it becomes to avoid making public statements that discredit him. Writers, theater people, and scholars are especially sought after by officials, who consider it most important to obtain pledges of loyalty from them, the cream of society.

The year of 1937 was not only one of great bloodletting; it was also a year of oaths of loyalty to the regime. Among the various appeals published in the Soviet press on January 28 was a letter headed "We demand merciless punishment of the vile traitors to our great motherland." The signatories presented their joint demand:

kill, crush, and grind underfoot. Like all similar letters this document contained no facts at all, only abuse, threats, and slander. It might well have been forgotten were it not for the fact that the signers constituted a very select public: they included the chemist A. Bach, the plant breeder B. Keller, the geologist Gubkin, the parasitologist E. Pavlovsky, the locomotive designer N. Obraztsov, the physiologist A. Speransky, the mathematician M. Lavrentyev (now in charge of the Siberian section of the Soviet Academy of Science), and the epidemiologist P. Zdorodvsky. The third name on the list of signatories to the letter was that of Nikolai Ivanovich Vavilov. I produce this fact not to deliver judgment on Vavilov, but to set it alongside another incident that took place in the same year. I heard about it from Professor Nikolai Vladimirovich Timofeyev-Resovsky, the geneticist and radiobiologist.

In the 1920s the geneticist N. K. Koltsov sent his much-loved colleague, Timofeyev-Resovsky, to study in Germany. In those years Vavilov visited Berlin quite frequently and a cordial relationship developed between the two geneticists. After the Nazis came to power Timofeyev-Resovsky thought of returning home, but some time in 1937 he received a warning from the Soviet Union that he would end up in prison or suffer a worse fate. It was Vavilov who managed to send him the warning in a note delivered by the American geneticist Muller.[5]

Vavilov did these two things in one and the same year. Such were the tactics and strategy that the difficult times forced upon an honest man who was not at all interested in his personal well-being or in advancing further up the ladder of professional success.

I asked Professor Timofeyev-Resovsky in 1971 whether what he had told me meant that Vavilov had matured politically as late as 1937. After all, only a person who had at last come to understand the Soviet situation could advise a friend not to return. That warning required not only some courage but wisdom as well. "No," Timofeyev-Resovsky said, "Nikolai Ivanovich realized what was happening a good deal earlier—in 1934."

Playing with the Devil obviously demanded a good deal of diplomatic skill and plain intelligence. Perhaps it was that very game which saved Vavilov from arrest in 1937 and 1938. But time was working against him. However clever he was at the beginning, he could never have guessed that the authorities were grooming

Lysenko to put in his place, that the agronomist from Gandzha would one day trample down all the crops that had been cultivated by biologists in the Soviet Union and in the world outside, and that Lysenko would then destroy the biologists themselves.

Lysenko suddenly declared that the process of vernalization, which Vavilov considered a matter for experimentation and verification, was a reliable means that could be applied immediately to raise yields of wheat throughout the country. Soaking the seeds in water before they were sown, according to him, ought to increase yields by not less than a centner (a hundred kilograms) per hectare. Lysenko then multiplied this hypothetical centner by the one hundred million hectares sown to grain in the Soviet Union and proceeded by press and radio to promise the country additional trainloads of grain at practically no expense. Vernalization was declared to be the principal method to be employed to give the country an abundance of grain. If he was asked for proof, Lysenko would say that the best proof was for the method to be tried in the fields on millions of hectares. He would even argue that such an innovation had become possible only in the Soviet Union, where hundreds of thousands of collective farmers were engaged in experimental work.

Vavilov was dumbfounded. Many other instances of people coming forward with similarly "radical" advice for agriculture had come to nothing. In any case, every educated agronomist knew that one single method, even the most original, or a single agrotechnical process, however cleverly thought out, could not decide the fate of the harvest as a whole. Back in 1928, speaking in a debate about ways of raising the agricultural yields, Vavilov had told the "radicals" in agriculture: "We cannot fix on any one measure to serve as a panacea for all our ills, whether it is autumn ploughing or some other technical process."[6]

But in the 1930s nobody paid any attention to such reasonable warnings. The time had come for Lysenko, the principal advocate of "radical" solutions in agriculture, to try to escape altogether from scientific control.

What the Presidium of the Academy of Agricultural Science had let pass as an exception in 1931 Lysenko now tried to introduce as a permanent rule applying to himself. In doing so he played on the political situation. Much was being written in the papers about the movement of collective-farm experimenters and about the need for every village to have its own cottage laboratory. It was clear that, given the backward state of farming in the 1930s, such cottage laboratories staffed by amateurs could actually serve as centers for the education of the grain farmers. But Lysenko was now describing them as "people's academies," capable of introducing into farming practice not less but considerably *more* than the "city" scientists. He demanded that in the future, control of every new variety and every new farming technique should be in the hands not of research scientists in institute laboratories and on experimental farms, but of the collective farmers themselves on their farms and in their cottage laboratories. This proposal naturally offered tremendous scope for every kind of "scientific" double-dealing, the first case of which was the announcement that vernalization was the way to raise harvest yields.

Distinguished biologists with whom I have spoken took the view that there was something almost mystical about Lysenko's career, for regardless of his failures, Lysenko kept his position. Despite all the promises made by Lysenko's "progressive biologists" and "true Darwinists," harvest yields in the 1930s did not increase, and the campaigns organized by Lysenko ended in failure. For many years nobody mentioned the unfortunate business of vernalization. It was forgotten just as completely as the plan to sow grain in the stubble fields of Siberia, intravarietal pollination, promises to produce new varieties of wheat in only two and a half years, the planting of clumps of oak trees in the steppe lands, the plan for obtaining record yields of millet, and many other fruits of Lysenko's fantasy. Who prevented others from exposing, if not the lack of theoretical substance, at least the practical bankruptcy of his proposals?

There was really nothing mystical about Lysenko's tenacity. It was primarily Lysenko himself who prevented anyone from exposing him. The flow of his ideas was inexhaustible. New proposals followed one after the other at intervals of only a few months. Following the epic affair with vernalization he announced that it was absolutely essential to carry out the cross-pollination of wheat within one variety, which was supposed to give the collective farms greatly increased harvests. The newspaper *Socialist Agriculture* started up a mass campaign. Ten thousand collective farmers on a couple of thousand farms were engaged in the cross-pollination. But Lysenko considered that was too little. The next year, according to his reckoning, fifty to seventy thousand farms should be involved in the campaign. A little later cross-pollination was dropped, but Lysenko, with the same degree of enthusiasm, was by then asserting in the press and on the radio the need for a nation-wide campaign to achieve yields of millet of a hundred poods to the hectare. Millet was a crop with great prospects, the number one crop. Special brigades were organized on the collective farms, and the Academy of Agriculture developed a special new farming technique for millet. There was talk of nothing but millet, until the question of the summer sowing of potatoes in the south replaced all talk of millet and the fuss about cross-pollination of wheat.

On the surface the actions of this all-powerful agronomist always corresponded with the real needs of the time. Russia really was short of millet and other grains, and it was difficult to transport to the south every year a huge quantity of seed potatoes to replace the local ones that could no longer be propagated. It was precisely these central, fundamental problems of agriculture that Lysenko undertook to solve. He promised to increase the total grain harvest; he swore that he would obtain a hundred poods of millet from every hectare; and he guaranteed that potatoes planted by his method would not fail to sprout. He did not simply assert these things: he provided exact calculations. True, they referred to *future* harvests or the *next* crop. In that period, when big figures abounded, his calculations appeared credible. So much was said and written about them that it began to appear to uninformed people (and most people were uninformed, because the true figures of the harvests in those years were kept secret) that the problems of grain, millet, and potato production had been solved long ago in the best possible way by Academician Lysenko.

As for the actual results of his work, it was difficult to know what they were at a time when commissars for agriculture, heads of the agricultural department of the Central Committee, and presidents of the agricultural academy were being replaced one after the other. There were "enemies of the people" everywhere, and especially in agriculture. They were sought out and exposed and then held responsible for all the blunders, miscalculations, errors, and plain stupidities. They were also held responsible for the results of Lysenko's experiments.

The man at the head of "progressive biology" continued to be a favorite of Stalin's. Stalin was impressed by the scale and the daring nature of his experiments—eight hundred thousand pairs of tweezers for the collective farmers engaged in cross-pollination! But Lysenko had other qualities as well that Stalin liked to see in his subjects. He was a man of the people, the son of a peasant, and he conducted his arguments strictly on the basis of quotations from Marx, Engels, Timiryazev, and Michurin. He held materialist views, which meant that they were correct. All other views were idealistic and therefore wrong. And Lysenko would not make a single speech without singing the praises of the Soviet regime, Soviet science, Soviet "Michurinist Darwinism," and, of course, deep bows in the direction of the father of the people, the coryphaeus of the sciences—Comrade Stalin himself.

Stalin was also impressed, apparently, by another important circumstance: Lysenko's ideas were simple and understandable. For a person lacking in education an *understandable* statement always seems credible. And not only were Lysenko's assertions popular, they fitted perfectly into the philosophical system that Stalin himself preached. Lysenko said that it was sufficient to change the conditions in which an organism existed for the organism itself to change in a certain way, and also for it to hand down to its descendants the changes thus introduced. Meanwhile Comrade Stalin himself, through his court philosophers, declared that if the economic relations between people were changed, the whole human race would immediately be transformed, and its manner of life, tastes, morals, and social and personal relations would change too. Self-interest would disappear and there would be no more criminals, prostitutes, or drunks. The beautiful world of the future would be peopled by hosts of human angels and model human beings, true representatives of the working people. The identity of views between Lysenko, the agronomist, and Stalin, the "great gardener," eventually produced some very bitter fruits on Russian soil. And, as we now know, it was no accident. The American botanist Professor Conway Zirkl, of the University of Pennsylvania, wrote: "Genetics rejects the inheritance of acquired characteristics, but this type of inheritance seems to promise so much that it is always very popular with those who want to transform humanity quickly."

Stalin kept on presenting Lysenko with marks of favor. Lysenko was awarded a state decoration and elected a deputy in the Supreme Soviet. From 1935 not a single national conference on agriculture took place without the "scholar from the people" there to give some fundamental advice on every aspect of agriculture from plant breeding to fertilizers. Lysenko became a person beyond criticism.

No trace remained of Lysenko's former modesty. The servility displayed by research scientists, whose numbers grew along with Lysenko's influence, and the tremendous power allotted to him made him utterly intolerant of any other person's scientific thought. In fact science itself now became for him a source of the power he yearned for. In a couple of years he would gather into his hands all the reins of power and then he would show those "intellectuals" what they were worth. Lysenko believed sincerely in his own genius, and Prezent spared no effort to inflate that belief by providing a scientific wrapping for everything that came from his chief's mouth.

After Stalin's public applause in 1935, Lysenko's position in the world of science seemed inviolable. Then suddenly, some people began to question Lysenko's "discoveries." At the fourth session of the Academy of Agricultural Science in December 1936 the plant breeders and academicians Konstantinov, Lisitsyn, and A. N. Shekhurdin declared publicly that they considered Lysenko's agronomic methods completely valueless. They were difficult people to argue with because they were themselves the creators of new varieties of plants and drew their arguments from their own long experience. They declared flatly that the cross-pollination of grains within a variety "does not produce any real increase in harvest yields at all,"[7] and that large-scale cross-pollination would lead eventually to the complete loss of the country's best varieties. (This forecast of Academician Lisitsyn's was, unfortunately, later to be proved correct.)

Academician Lisitsyn also pointed to the extremely questionable effect of vernalization:

> We do not have now a precise idea of what vernalization does. Academician Lysenko says that it gives tens of millions of additional poods of grain. In this connection I recall a story from Roman history. A seafarer about to set out on a voyage decided to perform a sacrifice to the gods to ensure his safe return. He spent a long time searching for a temple in which to make the sacrifice. But everywhere he went he came across tablets bearing the names of those who had made a sacrifice and had been saved. "But where are the names of those who performed a sacrifice and were not saved," the sailor asked the priests. I would like to compare the powers of various gods.
>
> I would also like to put a question to Academician Lysenko: "You speak of harvests of tens of millions of poods, but what about the losses produced by vernalization?"

The next person to take the platform, Academician Konstantinov, supported Lisitsyn's questions with hard figures. Citing data from fifty-three plant-breeding stations in the Soviet Union that had carried out the vernalization of wheat from 1932 to 1936, he reported that in half the cases vernalization had slightly increased the yield, while in the other half it had actually reduced it. To take such an agronomic process seriously, he said, was to indulge in self-deception.[8]

"There are two sorts of ignorance: one is illiterate and precedes science; the other, full of arrogance, comes after it." Montaigne's thought apparently did not occur to the delegates who represented true science at the fourth session of the academy. There was no shortage of arrogant ignorance. Unchecked and unfinished "experiments" were quoted repeatedly as though they were the greatest achievements of science. To give their views a certain substance Lysenko's supporters kept earnestly repeating that their opponents did not know or understand Darwin. Earlier, however, the principal "Darwinist," at a conference and in the presence of members of the government, had admitted frankly, "I must honestly confess, comrades, here in the presence of Yosif Vissarionovich Stalin, that to my shame I have not studied Darwin properly. I finished in a Soviet school and I did not study Darwin, Yosif Vissarionovich. The only thing that people usually remember out of Darwin is that man is descended from the monkey."⁹

That was all that most of Lysenko's supporters "knew" about Darwin (though it is of course *not* what Darwin said), and their illiterate attitude received some sharp attacks from leading biologists who considered themselves Darwinists. A particularly outspoken speech was delivered by an American Communist, Herman Muller. His laboratory in the Institute of Genetics at the Soviet Academy had developed methods for actively intervening in the process of mutation-formation and of sudden changes in inherited characteristics. A possibility was emerging of speeding up the mutability of plants and animals and of exploiting this both for research and for practical purposes. Because he did not speak Russian well enough, Muller's speech was read for him by Academician N. K. Koltsov. But Muller asked to speak the concluding words himself. His words are remembered by everyone still living who took part in the session.

To the accompaniment of thunderous applause from the whole hall Muller said, "If our outstanding practitioners are going to support theories and opinions that are obviously absurd to everyone who knows even a little about genetics—such views as those recently put forward by President Lysenko and those who think as he does—then the choice before us will resemble the choice between witchcraft and medicine, between astrology and astronomy or between alchemy and chemistry."¹⁰

Academician Vavilov also spoke at the same session. But his speech, clever, sincere, and as usual packed with interesting facts, did not satisfy either his friends or his enemies: they both realized that he was simply defending himself. When Vavilov's speech had been discussed before the session in the institute, senior members of the staff had pressed their director to take a strong line in the dispute with Lysenko. But Vavilov did not follow their advice. He was shocked and amazed by the shameless way in which Lysenko's supporters lied and by their manifest ignorance of elementary biology. They should have been accused of plain dishonesty, and someone should have exposed the unethical and antisocial conduct of people who were cheating in their experimental work and destroying their opponents by means of political denunciations. But to conduct a debate in such a manner was profoundly distasteful to Vavilov. He considered that in a gathering of scientists the arguments must concern only scientific matters and in no circumstances carry over into personalities.

Vavilov was simply not able to cross that barrier. "He was quite incapable of carrying on what we call a battle. He was a scholar and nothing more," said a former member of the institute staff, Aleksandra Alekseyevna Zaitseva, thirty years later.[11] But when he came to talk about his beloved genetics, Vavilov made it quite clear to the Lysenko people that he was not going to retreat: "We consider the laws of Morgan and Mendel to be the basis of our understanding of heredity. We are not at the moment aware of any other theories of equal value, and we therefore have no grounds for departing from contemporary genetics."[12]

In the event all this criticism had not the slightest effect— Lysenko was at the height of his fame and "popular" recognition. The consequences in fact were not the ones desired. After 1937 the ranks of the genuine searchers after truth began to thin out. Academician N. K. Koltsov, who had been subjected to continual harassment, died. Herman Muller quit the Soviet Union to take part in the battle for Madrid in the Spanish Civil War. The president of the Academy of Agriculture, A. I. Muralov; the vice-president, A. S. Bondarenko; and Academician G. K. Meister were arrested and shot. In 1936 they all had dared to question the infallibility of Lysenko's ideas. Other leading geneticists, such as Levit and Agol, also disappeared.

It was said that the arrests had nothing to do with the scientific controversies that had preceded them, but the consistency with which the police arrested Vavilov's supporters, including members of the staff of his institute, while not arresting a single known supporter of Lysenko suggests the opposite. This pattern did not escape Vavilov. By 1937 or 1938 he could already see clearly the full extent of his mistake. He had deceived himself not only as a person, but also, what was more important for him, as a scientist. None of his friends heard him indulge in noisy lamentation, but they noticed that for some time their director would refer to Lysenko by name only in official correspondence and only when it was absolutely unavoidable. It was only in a letter to his friend Muller, sent from Leningrad to Madrid in the heat of the battle against fascism, that Vavilov admitted: "Professor Meister and I were recently in Odessa to check up on the work being done by Lysenko on plant development. I have to say that we came across too little convincing proof. In the past I expected more of him."[13] That was Vavilov's way. "Nikolai Ivanovich was very trusting and tolerant toward people," Professor E. N. Sinskaya wrote. "But there were limits. If he came across something a person had done that he could find no way of accepting or excusing, that person ceased to exist for him. Nikolai Ivanovich would simply cease to mention his name ever again, but he would not give vent to malice or annoyance."[14]

Vavilov's inability to use the same means that Lysenko used was, in my opinion, the main reason for his defeat and Lysenko's victory. Vavilov, a scholar and an intellectual, could not claim the ability at one stroke to double and treble the millet harvest throughout Russia. He knew well how very different were the climatic and soil conditions in the various zones of that vast agricultural state, and how long and complicated was the path to victory for scientific farming. He was incapable of announcing that he could produce a new variety of wheat in two and a half years, because it was impossible to do so with the resources that plant breeders had at their disposal in the early 1930s. For Vavilov it was just as wrong to lie to his country as it was to lie to his son or friend. He was as incapable of engaging in intrigues or denouncing other people as he was of printing counterfeit money or dealing in drugs.

The contest was between two different organisms, two irreconcilable characters, but the question of which of the two would triumph in the social and scientific arena depended also to a large extent on extraneous factors. A society that really depended for its advance on scientific progress would need people like Vavilov; but when the natural course of social development was destroyed and politics and propaganda took precedence, the demand for people like Lysenko was greater.

The fourth session of the Academy of Agriculture at last drew a clear line between the two camps in the biological sciences. Crude Lamarckism started taking over institutes, laboratories, and experimental stations one after the other. The Institute of Plant Breeding in Leningrad and the Institute of Genetics in Moscow remained the last outposts of genuine research. There they did not simply say that some farming process or other was wrong; they subjected anything doubtful to the strictest tests in the fields and laboratories.

Lysenko declared that forced self-pollination, the so-called in-breeding method, destroyed cross-pollinated plants and could cause plant breeders only trouble. The whole of the world's scientific literature on the subject was of a different opinion. Vavilov did not want to accept one view or the other. His institute set up long-term experiments involving the self-pollination of rye, clover, timothy grass, vines, and maize. Dozens of specialists worked on the experiments. Three years later, despite the variety of plants under examination, they all produced the same result: the in-breeding method was not dangerous to the plants and brought only benefit to the plant breeder. Only with the aid of this method was it possible to develop a hybrid maize that gave a third more grain and foliage.

Lysenko declared that he could easily convert spring cereals into winter cereals and vice versa, and cited this conversion as an example of how people could change plants in any way to serve their ends. Two members of the staff of Vavilov's institute, M. I. Khadzhinov and A. I. Lutkov, were given the task of repeating Lysenko's experiments. The two Leningrad geneticists studied every detail of the material produced by the people at Lysenko's institute in Odessa, who claimed to be able to change the character of cereals simply by subjecting the plants to high temperatures at some stage in their development. They regarded the transformation of winter crops into spring crops and vice versa as an incontrovertible fact. But there was no strict control over the experiments, and no one could be sure that, with the best of intentions, some winter varieties had not been mixed up with the spring varieties in the course of sowing.

Khadzhinov and Lutkov wanted to establish an absolutely sure experimental method that could not later be challenged or leave any doubts in people's minds. As soon as the winter wheat known as "Kooperatorka" had begun to germinate, they subjected it to a very delicate operation: they divided each plant into two halves, each of which could exist independently. One half was to serve as a control plant, growing in the field in the usual conditions, while the other half was subjected to heat treatment in precise accordance with Lysenko's instructions. The experiment was repeated dozens of times in different variations, and it was carried out on barley as well as wheat. The conclusion was that no transformation of the cereals from their winter to their spring form or the reverse took place. A whole pile of temperature records and logbooks of the experiments confirmed this brief conclusion, which had cost the two scientists thirty-six months of intensive work. Lysenko was again exposed.[15]

But Lysenko's capacity to come up with new ideas appeared to be inexhaustible. One fine day he announced that it need not necessarily take years or decades to develop new varieties of wheat, as had hitherto been the case. Two and a half years would be quite sufficient, he claimed. Plant breeders received this latest discovery of Lysenko's with skepticism. When he offered two new "varieties" produced by the fast method, the Saratov plant breeder Academician G. K. Meister pointed out, with good reason, that a single crossing does not produce a new variety. Variants capable of producing a good crop in the nursery frequently turned out later to be useless. Anything that could be considered for labeling as a new variety had to be subjected to a long period of testing in field conditions. A plant breeder should not be put off by the length of time required, because only that method could demonstrate that the qualities required in the plant had actually become constant.

In 1938 Academician Meister was executed; the idea of high-speed plant selection continued to flourish. True, it was only the idea that flourished, because not a single new variety was produced in the course of two years. But that was not the end of Lysenko's exploitation of the question of producing new varieties. Once he had become president of the agricultural academy, he began to demand that every scientific plant-breeding institution produce some new varieties. On the surface this appeared to be perfectly reasonable. It was up to the scientific plant-breeders to demonstrate the correctness of their theoretical views and to create good varieties of cereal, vegetable, and industrial crops and so bring wealth to the population by their discoveries.

The demand for new varieties was soon directed at Vavilov's Institute of Plant Breeding as well. Members of his staff were criticized in the press and at conferences for not wishing to be involved in practical work and for getting bogged down in theoretical research work that was no use to anyone. This campaign was obviously quite dishonest. Its organizer knew very well that plant science did not consist simply of selection and that plant breeders could create something new only if they had the right material and parental forms for cross-breeding and selection. But where were such forms to be found? For hybridization, plant breeders sometimes needed plants from the most distant lands. They also needed to know the chemical composition of the parent plants, their physiological qualities, whether they would tolerate cold and lack of moisture, and whether they would react with rapid growth and development if they were given large quantities of fertilizer. Plant breeders also had to ascertain in advance the genetic qualities of the plants they were working with: how and to what extent the plants passed on inherited characteristics to their descendants, and whether the descendants were economically valuable or harmful. Then there was the question of the plant's immunity to disease: it was hardly possible to start the process of selection without ascertaining beforehand to which diseases the new variety was most exposed and from which ones it might be protected.

This was exactly what the staff of the Institute of Plant Breeding was doing. Vavilov was certainly not an opponent of plant selection. At a meeting of one of the learned councils in the summer of 1935, he explained his attitude to the staff in very precise terms: "We are now coming to the stage of producing a decisive transformation of plants and of varieties and we are about to perform very far-reaching research into the very essence of plant selection, which will however require tremendous assistance from biochemistry, genetics, physiology, technology and other related disciplines."[16]

This statement was made at the very beginning of the "boom in varieties" initiated by Lysenko, although Vavilov had already foreseen the danger that was emerging on the horizon of science:

It is not possible for us to devote all our attention to plant breeding or to turn the whole staff of a leading scientific establishment into plant breeders. We have something like 60 physiologists, and many geneticists and biochemists. Naturally we must work closely with the plant breeders and not conceal physiological characteristics from them. But one must surely not take Comrade

Lysenko to mean that a man must turn himself into an encyclopedia and do everything himself. That is carrying it to absurdity.[17]

At the end of his speech Vavilov again stressed the inflexibility of his position: his Institute of Plant Breeding was going to remain a center of genuine scientific research into agronomy and genetics.

Vavilov did not make that statement simply because Lysenko had made such a fuss about the production of new varieties. He saw further than that. He wanted to raise the process of plant selection, which had for centuries remained simply a personal skill of the more gifted plant breeders, to the level of a science. He was impatient to replace the chance successes of individual seekers after the "golden ear" by developing new varieties strictly according to scientific laws. To teach plant breeders the fundamentals of the scientific approach Vavilov had, as far back as 1933, started on the preparation of a three-volume collective work entitled *The Theoretical Foundations of Plant Selection*. In a chapter entitled "Plant Selection as a Science," Vavilov set forth his thesis: "The socialist system in our country, with its purposefulness, the unlimited scope it offers for our work and its huge company of researchers, has a greater need than ever of plant selection as a scientific discipline."[18]

He never abandoned this view to the end of his days. In one of his letters to Harland written in 1938 Vavilov said, "Plant-breeding stations are springing up like mushrooms in our country. You understand the need we have for scientific plant selection. There is a deep rift between the art of plant selection and genetics and a great deal has to be done to put a bridge across it."[19] He hoped that the people on the staff of his institute would be the bridge builders.

The Institute of Plant Breeding appears to have coped well in the 1930s with the task set it by its director. In 1934 the Imperial Scientific Bureau of Plant-Breeding in Britain devoted a whole book to the achievements of Soviet plant breeding and to the plan for research work in the second Five-Year Plan, which had been drawn up mainly by the staff of Vavilov's institute. In the same year a well-known British plant breeder and geneticist Biffen, reviewing the achievements in plant selection throughout the world, had to admit that the Soviet Union occupied the first place in research into plant breeding.

Such assessments of Soviet biological science were by no means rare at that time and were reported in the newspapers, so that Lysenko could not fail to know what a high position Soviet plant breeding occupied in the eyes of the world's scientists. But the success enjoyed by Vavilov's school was not likely to cause Lysenko any pleasure. In his battle with those who did not share his views, Lysenko sought to have quite different judges and quite different supporters. At the second congress of collective-farm "shock-workers," speaking as though he did not know the true facts and utterly ignoring the testimony of the world's leading scientists, Lysenko announced that the plant-breeding situation in the USSR was catastrophic. He went on to propose that he should save the situation.

> So long as the collective farmers do not take a hand in the business of plant breeding things will never be right there. . . . Many scientists have been saying that the collective farmers are not drawn into work on genetics and plant breeding because it is a very complicated matter and that to deal with it you need to have studied at an institute. But that's not true. Problems of plant selection and genetics dealt with on the basis of the theory of plant development [the theory of vernalization] that has been evolved by Soviet science on the collective farms, are now handled differently. . . . Initiative on the part of the collective farmers in this matter is essential, and without it we shall have only specialist plant breeders, just a few individual skilled men.[20]

It is difficult to decide what is the most striking in these words—the fanatical sense of his own importance (implying that, thanks to vernalization, the science of genetics had become accessible to every ignoramus) or his undisguised mockery of the scientists. Only a man quite convinced of his own impunity could permit himself to make such a speech. But however great his influence as a favorite of Stalin's, Lysenko still realized in 1935 that Vavilov and his best colleagues would never recognize his claims to primacy in scientific matters or reconcile themselves to his diktat. They would continue to carry out experiments to verify his claims and they would go on publishing articles refuting them. Vavilov's institute would have to be dispersed, and Vavilov himself, the most dangerous of Lysenko's enemies, would have to be silenced.

But to crush Vavilov was not a simple matter. His authority as a scientist was too great and his importance as an organizer of scientific work was enormous. The value of Vavilov's ideas and achievements must be questioned, and his character discredited. His enemies decided that the best way to destroy Vavilov would be to engage in a scientific debate on biological problems. Although the argument would appear to be about profoundly scientific matters—concerning the ways in which inherited characteristics were transferred—Lysenko's supporters essentially attacked Vavilov as an idealist, an advocate of old and obsolete conceptions, and a person not worthy of trust. There is no point in repeating here the scientific arguments used in those verbal encounters. Today the chromosome theory of heredity, which Vavilov defended, and his approach to plant selection have been accepted beyond question, whereas the views of his principal opponents—Lysenko and Prezent—have not stood the test of time.

In 1887, the same year that a son called Nikolai was born in the family of the Moscow merchant Ivan Vavilov, a book was published in London called *The Life and Letters of Charles Darwin*. It was written by Francis Darwin, the son of the great natural scientist, who painted an honest and realistic portrait of his father, revealing the diverse aspects of the elder Darwin's character. "Worthy of note was the polite tone in which he addressed the reader," the young Darwin remarked. "The reader feels like a friend being addressed by a polite person, and not like a student being lectured to by a professor. The whole tone of a book like *The Origin of Species* is that of a man convinced of the correctness of his views but by no means certain of convincing others. He was the very opposite of a fanatic who wanted to force other people to believe him."[21]

But the manner of the fanatic became a constant feature of the campaign that Lysenko's supporters started against Vavilov. His enemies began to speak of him and those who stood by him, at public meetings and in the press, only in what were, from their point of view, terms of abuse, calling them "Mendelists," "Morganists," "anti-Darwinists," and "anti-Michurinists." Other epithets were employed as well, but these four principal ones were as effective as a lash.

It is not easy today to understand how calling somebody a "Morganist" or a "Mendalist" could be regarded as an insult. The geneticist Thomas Morgan won the Nobel Prize in 1933, and the whole scientific world celebrated the centenary of Gregor Mendel's experiments in 1966. But the situation in Russia in the years 1937 to 1940 was very different. The journals dealing with biology and agriculture were mostly in the hands of supporters of "progressive Michurinist biology." Their publications, in particular the journal *Vernalization*, edited by Lysenko and Prezent, were repeating over and over again that there was no single science of biology: there was the rotten, spurious biology of the West, which was not concerned with human well-being, and there was the only true "Michurinist" science of biology. Anyone who drank from the unclean spring of the former was regarded as a transmitter of falsehoods that were of no practical use and did nothing to increase the harvest yields on the country's farms.

This question was worked over so often in the pages of the press and in speeches made by Lysenko's supporters that it was sufficient to call Vavilov a "Morganist-Mendelist" or an "anti-Michurinist" for people to understand without any additional proof that he was (1) a defender of the teachings of a monk—a member of a religious order!—Gregor Mendel, who after his death was praised by German nationalists; (2) a person sharing the same view as the American geneticist Thomas Morgan, who was both a representative of Western imperialism and the winner of a prize from the fund set up by Alfred Nobel, the inventor of dynamite; and (3) an opponent of the widely respected Soviet biologist and plant breeder Ivan Michurin, who had developed 350 important varieties of plant. If a speaker were to add in passing that a person was also an "anti-Darwinist," it became clear he was a dangerous opponent of the views of Charles Darwin, whom the world recognized as the man who first stated the theory of evolution.

Lysenko's people kept hurling these four epithets in Vavilov's face. Among those who did so were people who knew that several of Darwin's books had been published in Russia on Vavilov's initiative and edited by him, and who knew that Michurin and Vavilov had been great friends both as scientists and as people. But facts played no part in that extraordinary debate. What mattered was *who* spoke and what was said. Lysenko declared that the All-

Union Institute of Plant Breeding was a center of "Mendelism," adding: "I do not consider formal Mendelist-Morganist genetics to be a science."[22] Anyone following the debate from the sidelines could understand that Academician Vavilov, the staff of his Institute of Plant Breeding and all their supporters were no more than imposters pretending to be scientists, adherents of a nonexistent and spurious science.

Lysenko's people kept fanning the fire of the debate. It caught light at conferences at the Academy of Agriculture, burst into flame at meetings in the Commissariat for Agriculture, and gave out clouds of smoke, making constructive work impossible, at every kind of meeting. "It was mainly Lysenko's people who spoke. They would say nothing new but just keep repeating the epithets and labels which people had already had more than enough of," recalled E. N. Sinskaya, who was present at those meetings. "That constant repetition of all those crude attacks day after day produced a sort of feeling of physical sickness."[23]

The younger scientists quickly caught on to Lysenko's style. Graduate students at Vavilov's Institute of Plant Breeding, whom Lysenko's supporters had turned against the older generation of teachers, became zealous in their rejection of the science of genetics at every meeting, though again without producing any hard facts.

On May 8, 1937, a trade union meeting was held in Vavilov's Institute of Plant Breeding, and once again Vavilov was under attack. Kuprianov, an agronomist, stated:

> You are afraid of criticism, mortally afraid. It strikes home. Vavilov's theory [. . . is] a harmful theory which ought to be branded with a red-hot iron, because the working class has coped with its tasks without the bourgeoisie and has begun to rule on its own and has achieved definite results . . . .
>
> The whole country knows about the Institute of Plant Breeding and the debate taking place between Vavilov and Lysenko. Vavilov will have to change his ways, because Stalin said that they must work not the way Vavilov does but as Lysenko does.[24]

A student named Donsky argued:

Lysenko said straight out: it is either me or Vavilov—clear and precise, and it makes sense. He says: whether I am right or wrong, one of us has got to go. There is no way of reconciling Lysenko's and Vavilov's ideas. It is time we realized that we are at a stage when it is essential that the achievements of experimental science should be used in the service of our socialist country. Hence the bitter struggle and hostile attitude to Vavilov's teaching.[25]

The archives of Vavilov's institute contain innumerable records of similar speeches made in those years. In the years 1937 to 1939 Vavilov was forced to spend hours and days listening to similar exhortations and trying to reply to them. It is painful to think that he was obliged, as Sinskaya described him, "with his hair wet from perspiration, in a tone at once of restraint and of bewilderment, but with indignation in his voice, to try and explain sincerely his objections and to persuade his opponents that everything they were saying was the result of ignorance, and that he knew his Darwin and respected him, and then to have to descend from the platform amidst whistling and booing."[26]

The organizers of the campaign never forgot their main objectives: to demonstrate first, that Vavilov had contributed nothing to agricultural practice and even obstructed any such contribution, and, second, that he was connected politically with ideological enemies of the Soviet Union. These two themes, which were rather muted in 1937, were openly discussed closer to 1940. In 1939, for example, Lysenko wrote: "The genetics of Mendel and Morgan have contributed and can contribute literally nothing at all with any practical application to life. . . . One can point to numerous instances when their false teachings have hindered those scientists who want sincerely to do useful work." And stated: "Formal genetics—Mendelism-Morganism—not only retards the advance of theory, it actually hinders such an important matter for farming practice as the improvement of plant varieties and animal strains."[27]

Not quite so far from the truth, but no less impudent, was future Academician P. Yakovlev:

In order to assemble 300,000 specimens for his collection of world plant resources, the Institute of Plant Breeding had to organize dozens of excursions to every part of the Old and New Worlds and spend millions on them. And what benefit did plant breeding derive from that? Not a thing. Once they have frozen away in their plant stores hundreds of thousands of plants, many of them of the greatest value for farming and plant-breeding work, the staff of the institute jealously protect their collection like greedy knights sitting on their chests of gold. . . . True, Michurin occasionally received from the institute a few seeds or some plants, but they usually failed to germinate. . . . To get rid of Michurin and his insistent demands the institute probably sent him the first seeds they could lay their hands on from their old stock which had long since lost any chance of germinating.[28]

The political part of the attack on the institute and Vavilov was directed by Prezent, Lysenko's trusted spokesman. "I simply get on with my work and Prezent works out the philosophy for me," Lysenko said after his assistant had announced that from the philosophical point of view the whole of genetics should be dismissed as a delusion.[29] Prezent continued himself and through others to philosophize on Lysenko's behalf. In 1939, for example, Prezent wrote:

Academician Vavilov builds his theory of homologous lines . . . entirely on the basis of the metaphysics of Morganism, thus further extending its pseudoscientific teaching. Vavilov rightly considers his teacher to have been that most reactionary of geneticists, the Englishman Bateson. It was Bateson who, in Australia in 1914, in a speech shameful to science, defended views opposed to evolution and drew openly fascist conclusions from his anti-evolutionary ideas. . . .

We can see just how new the philosophy of contemporary Morganism is. These novelties of science were expressed in general philosophical form by Dühring, a violent anti-Darwinist and racist, and were destroyed theoretically by Engels in his famous *Anti-Dühring*. Ought we not to reflect on this parallel between the statements of Dühring and the Morganists?[30]

So that was it: Nikolai Ivanovich Vavilov was a student of a fascist and a racist and was spreading ideas identical with those of Dühring, the enemy of Marxism. But Prezent's underlings went further. Writing in the magazine *Soviet Subtropics*, a certain G. Shlykov said, "N. I. Vavilov is trying to hide behind the fact that his theory has won approval in world, i.e., bourgeois, scientific writings. But who does not know that those authors do not recognize the significance for science of Marxism-Leninism and reject materialist dialectics?"[31] There follows a whole page of argument to the effect that Vavilov's law of homologous lines is not only a product of bourgeois science but also the scientific foundation of fascist, racist "Draconian laws."

That was all written at a time when much milder accusations might cause a person so attacked to disappear forever in the depths of Stalin's extermination machine. The authors of such "scientific" articles undoubtedly knew perfectly well where their work was leading.

In their replies and counterarguments Vavilov and his supporters were not in the least apologetic, but I have not found in any of Vavilov's articles a single political attack. He discussed only scientific issues, nothing else. The poisoned weapons of slander and denunciation were not for him. Moreover, among all the accusations and slanders hurled at him, he continued to seek for some element of reason. "We must take advantage of the criticism to review our scientific stock-in-trade and rid it of errors," he said on more than one occasion. Ready to have confidence even in his opponents, he remained convinced that "people who spend their time criticizing others will see, in the course of their work, their own mistakes and will in the end follow the path of experimentation and the collection of verified facts."[32] For this reason Vavilov constructed even his most polemical speeches in the form of educational lectures, quoting a mass of experimental data, his own and other people's, with references to the authoritative views of the world's major laboratories. Lysenko's speeches, with their dogmatic conclusions not based on any serious or honest experimental work, astonished Vavilov. "Is it some kind of religion?" he exclaimed once following a lecture particularly lacking in scientific proofs and full of empty promises.

4   The Destruction of "Babylon"

If scientific research is carried on for the purpose of material gain, that gives it an element of egoism . . . if the aim of the research work is to gain power, then it can even become a danger to society and lead to a sort of learned barbarism.

R. A. Gregory, Discoveries,
Goals, and the Meaning of Science

It is difficult now to recall who first put the word into circulation or when it happened. But sometime in the middle of the 1930s the obviously unfriendly label "Babylon" was firmly attached to the Institute of Plant Breeding. Not very strong on ancient history but quite skillful when it came to political intrigue, Vavilov's enemies kept repeating "Babylon must be destroyed," apparently having in mind Cato's *"Delenda est Carthago."* However that may be, the label attached to Vavilov's institute symbolized the doom that threatened the last stronghold of "classical" biology.

They attacked "Babylon" in a variety of ways. In the spring of 1940 at the agricultural exhibition in Moscow Professor I. V. Yakushkin, one of Lysenko's circle, commented to Vavilov maliciously, "What's this I hear, Nikolai Ivanovich: you've already sent eighteen people to the scaffold."

"What do you mean?"

"Well, everybody knows that no one is arrested without the approval of the director."

Vavilov flared up and was about to answer the slander with some violent language, but restrained himself. Through his clenched teeth, without lifting his eyes from the ground, he said, "Apparently they didn't always know where to find me."

But Yakushkin had got his numbers right: from the time of the death in 1934 of Sergei Kirov, who had been a defender of the

Institute of Plant Breeding, to the spring of 1940 no fewer than eighteen scientists on the institute's staff had been arrested.

Every arrest shook Vavilov. People he had known for many years were disappearing. He could, of course, simply have argued that he was helpless and kept silent. That was the way many people, even honest ones, acted at the time. But that was not Vavilov's way. In the institute's archives are preserved many letters that Vavilov sent to various departments in an effort to help his colleagues. In one he begged the authorities to send back to Leningrad people who had been arrested and exiled, vouched for their loyalty, and affirmed that they were unique authorities on some crop or other (as was most often the case) and that without them work of importance to the state would stop. He made approaches to the head of the NKVD in Leningrad concerning the fate of T. A. Maksimova, S. I. Korolev, G. P. Kuzmin, A. A. Orlov, and G. A. Levitsky. After the arrest of G. E. Spangenberg, Vavilov gave the man's wife a marvelous letter setting out the work that her husband had done as an outstanding phytopathologist. He did not, however, succeed in saving anybody.

The institute's publishing house was closed when Lysenko's people seized all of the country's agricultural publishers. It thus became impossible for Vavilov's supporters to have their works published. Then the institute lost its experimental farms one after the other. Situated in zones with different climatic and soil conditions, they were essential for the testing and propagation of the institute's plant collections. The Ukrainian and Byelorussian farms were taken over, so that it became impossible to test and propagate many industrial and vegetable crops. The institute lost the long-established farm in the Kamennaya Steppe near Voronezh, with the result that scientists were no longer able to study the resistance of wheat to drought conditions. Farms in the northern temperate zone used for testing rye, oats, and barley were seized along with the Severo-Dvinsk station. It became impossible to carry out research into a huge collection of subtropical crops following the removal of the experimental base near Sukhumi. Along with the experimental farms the institute lost the employees, every one of whom was an irreplaceable world expert on one or even several crops. The institute lost its most important quality, which Vavilov valued so highly: its encyclopedic resources.

Even those who remained with the institute no longer enjoyed the conditions necessary for steady, planned work. Sinskaya described conditions:

> Stupid compulsory campaigns followed one after the other. First of all for several years we had to visit collective farms to set up "experiments" on vernalization, where for the most part there was no scientific method applied and no proper comparison with an established norm. Then Dolgushin invented some special scissors for cutting the ears of corn and the whole country was forced to take up intravarietal cross-breeding. . . . Instead of going on expeditions or carrying out urgently needed observations in their own nurseries, scientists were ordered to go out and collect ears of corn.[1]

The dispatch of scientists on these excursions became a real disaster. In a letter to the commissar for agriculture Vavilov informed him that in the spring of 1939 alone his commissariat had issued orders "to send to various republics and regions to help with the sowing campaign 77 scientists with higher degrees. The institute spent 117,000 rubles more than its budget on those trips, and this has had an exceptionally bad effect on the institute's main work."[2]

It was not only the useless excursions into the countryside that were wrecking the institute's budget. From 1937 the Commissariat for Agriculture made serious cuts in the funds allotted to its most important scientific institution. The battering ram of finance began to play a quite important part in the siege of Vavilov.

"I consider it my duty to bring it to the knowledge of the Presidium of the Academy [of Agriculture] that the financial position of the Institute of Plant Breeding is catastrophic," Vavilov told the Presidium in February 1939.[3] It was indeed catastrophic: in the main laboratories expenditure on research was reduced by 50 percent. A month later the commissar, I. A. Benediktov, declared publicly that he would not give any assistance to "Morganists": "The People's Commissar for Agriculture supports Academician Lysenko in his practical work and his theoretical views and instructs plant-breeding stations in the USSR to apply his methods in the work of seed growing and plant selection."[4]

The pressure was steadily increasing. At the beginning of May

1939 the Presidium of the Academy of Agriculture considered a report on Vavilov's institute and, on a proposal by Lysenko, declared it to be unsatisfactory. The work carried out by a staff of a thousand people over a whole year was declared to be useless and the management of the institute to be faulty: "Babylon must be destroyed."

To demonstrate how useless the institute was, it was refused permission to exhibit at the All-Union Agricultural Exhibition. The Leningrad scientist V. S. Lekhnovich recorded a typical episode, which took place in Lysenko's office in the year 1939:

> Lysenko was sitting, his eyes closed, at the end of a long, narrow table. Vavilov sat opposite him. The secretaries and I were at the side. Vavilov had in his hand a list of names and gave the reasons, briefly and in a businesslike way, why the institute recommended that the work of members of the staff should be exhibited. Throughout the meeting Lysenko did not once say a word or open his eyes. He would simply indicate his acceptance of a partic- ular person by slowly nodding his head. If a particular candidate did not appeal to him Lysenko made no move at all. Then, when Vavilov had finished, a painful silence reigned over the table. Our list of names had been sub- stantially reduced. Nobody was accepted who had ever in any circumstances criticized Lysenko's views. Among the very few who were accepted were T. Y. Zarubailo, who had discovered the phenomenon of "vernalization on the root." Among those not accepted were A. Levitsky, the world's leading authority on plant cells, whose work on the morphology of wheat chromosomes was continued after his arrest and death by the Japanese; G. P. Karpe- chenko, who was the first person in the world to produce a fertile intergeneric cabbage-radish hybrid; M. A. Ro- zanova, a leading authority on berry-bearing plants, and many others.[5]

What was to be done? Appeal to Stalin, or to Molotov? Complain to the Central Committee about the lawless behavior of the president of the Academy of Agriculture? By the end of the 1930s that was already impossible. After 1935 Vavilov ceased to be elected a member of the Executive Committee. In the same year Vavilov, the founder of the Academy of Agriculture, was forced to resign the position of president and remain only as a vice-president. The higher Lysenko's stock rose, the less value was attached in the Kremlin to Vavilov. At one conference Stalin chatted affably with Lysenko and encouraged one of his followers: "Keep on experimenting—we will back you up"; he left the room ostentatiously when Vavilov began to speak. Stalin demonstrated his dislike for Vavilov even more openly in the mid-1930s at another meeting. The late Sokrat Konstantinovich Chayanov recounted this brief and extremely unpleasant conversation as told him by Vavilov himself. Stalin declared firmly that scientific expeditions abroad by botanists were no use to anybody, and that many botanists did not bother about the harvest but spent their time on useless work in the laboratories and institutes. "Go and learn from the shock-workers in the fields!" Stalin advised Vavilov.[6]

Molotov immediately adopted Stalin's tone of contempt for Vavilov once the scientist was in disgrace. Molotov, as chairman of the Council of People's Commissars, interrupted Vavilov on several occasions when he was speaking about the Academy of Science. Once, when Vavilov was delivering a report about the rearing of wild animals in artificial conditions—a development that was then very novel but that has long since been generally accepted—Molotov exclaimed in the middle of the report, "What a silly idea, to try and domesticate foxes! When are you, Academician Vavilov, going to stop fooling about with such useless things?" The newspapers quickly noticed this episode and articles began to appear about scientists who were cut off from real life and who had gone so far as to try and domesticate foxes. Although Vavilov himself had nothing to do with this matter, it was he whom the papers attacked.

Was there any justification for the talk about the ineffectiveness of Vavilov's work in science and practical life? We have already mentioned the new varieties developed by his institute and the collection of plants from all over the world that provided the plant breeders with their basic material. What else was there?

It is true that Vavilov, botanist, geneticist, and geographer of plant life, by virtue of his character as a scientist, was interested mainly in the future prospects and development of agriculture. But that interest did not mean that he was not concerned with the present day. The story of his efforts to produce a hybrid maize is instructive. The development of this essentially new variety was due entirely to the science of biology or, more precisely, genetics. One of the methods used in genetics—a lengthy artificial self-pollination (in-breeding), followed by the cross-breeding of the self-pollinated lines—helped to create a plant that produced 30 percent more crop than had previously been obtained from the very best varieties.

The first person to take up hybridization in Russia was Vavilov's close friend and colleague Professor Talanov, and Vavilov had always encouraged his research. But in 1935, when the theoretical work was already coming to a conclusion and the Americans were rapidly increasing the areas sown to hybrid maize, Lysenko announced at a meeting in Odessa that the "in-breeding method" was contrary to biological science and in effect closed the door to this new crop in the USSR.

Vavilov conducted a very vigorous correspondence about the fate of the maize hybrids, which is almost dramatic in character. News of the speed with which the area sown to hybrids was growing in the United States prompted Vavilov to suggest that the Russians should follow suit. Professor A. V. Gursky later wrote:

In 1937 a special conference on this subject was held under Molotov's chairmanship. Vavilov spoke, proposing that they should immediately get on with hybridization. Molotov turned to Lysenko and asked him: "Well, what do you think about that, Trofim Denisovich?" Lysenko's reply was short and definite: everything connected with formal genetics was quite useless. The American idea should not be followed. When he told me about this Vavilov exclaimed: "Just imagine! The government turned down the possibility of doubling the maize harvest!"[7]

Lysenko's dictatorial rule prevented Vavilov from carrying out essential research work even in the experimental nurseries belonging to the Institute of Plant Breeding. Lysenko ordered all experiments with forced self-pollination to be halted. But Vavilov had not given up hope of persuading Lysenko, with the aid of hard practical economic facts, that he was right. After receiving the latest issue of the British journal *Nature* in September 1938 he wrote to Odessa:

Dear Trofim Denisovich!

In view of the fact that you were interested in the possibility of using first-generation hybrids from self-pollinated lines of maize, I am sending you the latest very interesting data, which has just appeared in a report made by the United States secretary of agriculture.

This year about six million hectares, or about 15 percent of the whole area sown to maize in the United States, has been sown with crops of first-generation hybrid lines. It has been calculated on the basis of comparative experiments that this will yield up to 100 million bushels extra at the harvest. Moreover the secretary—[Henry] Wallace, who is himself a plant breeder and seed grower—attaches exceptional importance to this method and considers that all the other methods employed for improving maize in the last 40 years have produced no substantial results.[8]

It might be thought that such an important piece of information would excite anyone seriously concerned about the success of the nation's agriculture. But Lysenko pretended not to have received the letter and to have heard nothing about the success of the hybrid crop in America. In the course of a discussion he said with feigned concern, "For the last 10, 15 or 20 years all the plant-breeding stations have been using the in-breeding methods. With what results? Name a single new variety produced by this method. This is what the Mendelists, and above all Academician Vavilov, forget."[9]

Similar situations arose for Vavilov more than once in those years. But what was he to do if a respected opponent lied in public? Friends advised him to protest, but he shrugged off their advice: if he were to give his time to such nonsense, he would not have enough time for his main work. "To fight against the 'Rasputin approach' is the most difficult thing in our life. I am fifty-two. I have no more than eight years of productive work ahead of me. And there is so much I have to do!" he said.[10]

But all Vavilov's efforts to introduce hybrid maize into farming practice were in vain. His appeals came to nothing in the face of a deliberate, malicious refusal to listen. The journal *Vernalization,* edited by Lysenko and Prezent, which set the tone for the whole of agricultural science, published in February 1940 an astonishingly cynical series of articles ridiculing the in-breeding method. An editorial said:

> The balance of the work of all in-breeders in the world, including our own compatriots, is negative. They have created a rich variety of forms, from which it is impossible, however, to extract a single variety which could be compared even with the standard variety. . . . The latest attempt of the Morganists to demonstrate the validity of their theory was their reference to American maize. Yet it was not so much the Americans as our own Morganists who made the fuss about the success of maize over millions of hectares in America and of the in-breeding method which they preach.[11]

Six months later Vavilov was arrested. But it was nearly another twenty years before the subject of his research—hybrid maize—was finally established in the fields of Russia. In 1955–56 the Soviet Union, which through the fault of Lysenko and his followers had not developed the seeds for hybrid maize, was obliged to purchase seed stocks for foreign currency from the American farmer Garst. It was indeed an irony of fate that Garst's business was a branch of a firm founded by the plant breeder Henry Wallace, who had been the United States secretary of agriculture to whose farming experience Vavilov had tried in vain to direct attention back in 1938.

A glance at Soviet agricultural science and biology between 1935 and 1939 reveals yet another way of "destroying Babylon." Lysenko involved Vavilov and hundreds of other plant breeders, geneticists, agrochemists, and cytologists in activity that had nothing to do with science. In 1935 a campaign was started to make the employees of every scientific institution help with the harvest on nearby collective farms. Lysenko announced that he was going to turn practically the whole of the southern Ukraine into a region of record harvests. The employees of Vavilov's Institute of Plant Breeding adopted the collective farms in the Leningrad area. For scientists this was the beginning of a period of endless inspection excursions, consultation visits, exhibitions, and harvest celebrations, and of a political (certainly not scientific) campaign that was of interest only to the reporters from the *Evening Leningrad.*

Then Lysenko started to make a fuss about the cottage laboratories, making speeches and writing articles about this great national movement; he forecast for them a brilliant future and pointed out on every occasion that in remote corners of the country the peasants were doing real scientific work, which was far more important than what was being done by all those biochemists and geneticists. Vavilov was also required to make speeches, to send valuable seeds to the cottage laboratories, and to provide instructions in farming methods. All this produced unnecessary correspondence, used up personnel, effort, time, and material resources, and finally did practically nothing to help farming. The cottage laboratories disappeared as suddenly as they had appeared. Lysenko consequently became known as the "people's scholar," while Vavilov was reproached for being cut off from the people.

But the indefatigable Lysenko did not stop there. He proposed that Vavilov's Institute of Plant Breeding and Lysenko's Institute in Odessa should enter into a competition. The competition was accompanied by a newspaper campaign, by innumerable excursions of people from Leningrad to Odessa and people from Odessa to Leningrad, and by a stream of slander attacking Vavilov, his followers, and his "obsolete" teachings based on Western models. All these excursions, inspections, and supervisory visits and the hysteria whipped up by the newspapers played on the scientists' nerves, disorganized the scientific life of the Institute of Plant Breeding, and disrupted the work that agriculture really needed. The only people to derive any benefit were Lysenko's supporters. They were demonstrating to the authorities their activity, energy, and close links with the population, and at the same time the social and political passivity of their opponents. That was the way to prove that "Babylon must be destroyed."

Vavilov's family archives preserved a telegram that he received early in May 1940. It reads:

> The American national committee, consisting of 75 prominent scientists, which is organizing the Second In-

ternational Congress on Pure and Applied Sciences—
physics, chemistry and biology—at Columbia University,
New York, in September 1940, is very anxious to ensure
your participation and that of other scholars from your
country, which will add to the international character of
the congress. Expenses will be covered. Please reply to
Columbia University, New York. Chairman of National
Committee—Millikan. [12]

This telegram from New York is a remarkable document.
When the organizers of an international congress wanted to invite a
delegation from the USSR, they did not approach the Soviet
government or the president of the Soviet Academy of Science.
Instead they wrote to Leningrad to the director of the Institute of
Plant Breeding. It was in fact entirely natural for them to do so: at
that time Vavilov was the best-known Russian scientist outside the
Soviet Union. Hundreds of researchers in various countries were
his personal friends and correspondents. The people in New York
thought quite reasonably that such a person would enjoy considerable authority in his own country. Who better than Vavilov, the
famous Soviet natural scientist, to get together a delegation to the
international congress?

But in Moscow in 1940 they had different ideas. After receiving
the telegram Vavilov informed the Presidium of the Soviet Academy
of Science about it, and also asked Molotov, the prime minister, for
instructions. But no instructions came; Molotov remained silent.
No Soviet delegation attended the congress.

Vavilov received an enormous number of telegrams like the one
from New York. Organizers of international congresses were always sending him invitations. He had a rare talent for making
friends. People fighting in the International Brigade in Spain shared
their private thoughts with him, and so did the peasants on the
"Vavilov" collective farm in the Penza district. A porter in the
South American Andes, a ruler in Ethiopia, the suspicious inhabitants of the remote Afghan province of Kafiristan, as well as top
civil servants in Paris and London, all felt a certain affection for the
professor from the country of the Bolsheviks fifteen minutes after
first meeting him. But those who were particularly well disposed
toward him were the biologists, his scientific colleagues.

"I just don't understand how he manages to captivate us so," the Bulgarian scholar Doncho Kostov once exclaimed, with delight and amazement. As if in reply, a quarter of a century later a geographer, botanist, and corresponding member of the Soviet Academy of Science, Pavel Aleksandrovich Baranov, wrote an article about Vavilov entitled "A Scholar's Charm."

In the 1930s people working in Vavilov's Institute of Plant Breeding had little difficulty in obtaining the seeds they needed from any country in the world, however remote. Yefrem Yakushevsky, who was in charge of the sorghums, wrote:

> Our laboratory needed to get some sorghum from the Sudan. I mentioned this to Nikolai Ivanovich when I met him in the corridor. He immediately looked into his notebook and said: "I know a man in Khartoum. Here's his address. Write and say 'Mister Vavilov sends his greetings and asks you to send him a selection of sorghum varieties.' " . . . The letter was sent off right away and a couple of months later we were the proud possessors of dozens of valuable samples. In the same way, by using Nikolai Ivanovich's name, we obtained rare varieties of sorghum from Senegal, Mali, and Guinea. Incidentally, that same Guinean sorghum is the one which is now used very extensively on our farms.

Yakushevsky said that from 1932 to 1940 the Institute of Plant Breeding obtained, thanks to Vavilov's contacts, nearly a thousand samples of sorghum alone. The number of samples of wheat, vegetable seeds, and seeds of fruit trees arriving by post from all over the world ran into tens of thousands.

There was no element of self-promotion or of excessive admiration for foreign successes in Vavilov's continual exchanges with the West. For him there existed in the world only one single biological science, and any serious researcher, whether he lived in Michurinsk or in Washington, was primarily a comrade in a common pursuit. It was inevitable that there should be differences of opinion, but they were differences among colleagues equally interested in discovering the truth. Like Goethe he was convinced that "the history of science is a great fugue into which the voices of the people slowly join." There was of course no question of refusing to listen to people simply because they were using a different language. In a letter to the Leningrad geneticist G. D. Karpechenko, who worked for a time in the United States, Vavilov said: "Write and tell us about the wonderful things being done and take the best: we need everything that is good. We want to catch up at all costs."[13]

In his speeches and articles and at meetings of scholars Vavilov kept insisting that Soviet science should not lag behind but should catch up and overtake the West. He had every right to do this, since nobody knew better than he did the strong and the weak points in Soviet biology. "On the theoretical front we are still ahead in our knowlede of crops, of geography, cytology and genetics and in the extent of our understanding of genetic interrelationships," Vavilov said at a meeting in his institute in February 1937. "As far as knowledge of physiology goes, despite the imperfect state of that field, I dare say we are still ahead. But in chemistry, technology, plant selection and in certain branches even of genetics we are not ahead, and for that reason we have to do some serious study and borrow a lot from others."[14]

The institute's output was considerable. Vavilov's letters of that period are full of the titles of new monographs and collections of articles and manuals issuing from the institute. He wrote to Professor Karpechenko:

> Work is going full steam ahead. The monograph on wild oats has appeared. Maltsev had assured himself of immortality by it. It is a book of which we can be proud. We have published a volume on fruit growing, dealing with the wild fruits of the Caucasus, Central Asia and the Far East. You can recommend it to anyone. It is full of original material. . . . Borodin's book is out. It has a very important article by Kuleshov on maize and its worldwide distribution. Advise your comrades from America to have a look at it—it will do them no harm at all.[15]

The "comrades from America" were indeed able to learn a lot from that volume published in Leningrad, because it was in Russia and not in America, the home of maize, that Nikolai Kuleshov, Vavilov's pupil and colleague, first described and classified maize on a world scale. In 1936, when it seemed there was not a single work by Vavilov that had not been criticized by his opponents, a German publishing firm applied for permission to translate the three-volume *The Theoretical Foundations of Plant Selection,* the publication of which Vavilov and his pupils were most proud.

Vavilov and his colleagues were connected in a thousand different ways—scientific, commercial, and friendly—with the world's centers of learning and with the leading biologists and public figures of Europe, America, Africa, and Asia, from whom they received a steady flow of the latest scientific information. It was by Vavilov that the West measured the level of Soviet science. Every speech he made abroad was a sensation. The intellectuals from the capitalist countries who attended his lectures frequently overcame the barriers of intolerance and suspicion more quickly than did the diplomats and ministers.

But then these long-established threads of friendship and scientific exchange started to be broken off. On three occasions in 1936, the Czechoslovak Agricultural Academy, having just elected Vavilov a member, invited him to Brno to give a lecture. But when he applied to the people's commissar for agriculture for permission to travel abroad, he was refused.[16]

In 1937 an even more painful blow was struck. The Seventh International Congress of Geneticists was due to take place in the USSR. Back in 1932 Vavilov had handed the organizers of the previous congress an invitation from the Soviet government to hold the next meeting of geneticists in Moscow. On that occasion he had been elected president of the congress and he had been looking forward impatiently to the summit meeting of geneticists. It seemed to him that the arrival in the Soviet Union of the world's leading geneticists and their speeches would help to alleviate the state of pitiless intolerance in science created by Lysenko.

"We are undergoing a very serious examination," Vavilov wrote in *Izvestia.* "World congresses, especially those in such important branches of science as genetics, are indicators of a country's cultural level. . . . We have to demonstrate our ability to organize international congresses. We must display the high level achieved by Soviet science."[17]

However, when seventeen hundred of the world's geneticists had written to confirm their intention of attending the congress and the preparatory work was nearly complete, Molotov suddenly refused to allow it to take place. This refusal was followed by an order that the meeting be postponed by a year. All the enormous work put in by the organizers went for nothing. But something more important was also lost. Instead of bringing the world's scientists together in a progressive atmosphere, as Vavilov had hoped, the arbitrary decision to cancel the congress evoked a wave of indignation in scientific circles in the West, which was immediately exploited by scientists in the fascist countries—Germany and Italy—to impose their own anti-Soviet views on the international committee.

The congress finally took place in Edinburgh instead of Moscow, but even then Vavilov was not able to act as president. He was not allowed to leave Russia.

Many years later, when Vavilov was no longer alive, his friends in Moscow and Leningrad received reports of what had happened at that congress and read these bitter lines: "You have invited me to play the part which Vavilov would have so adorned," the British geneticist F. Crew, who presided over the Edinburgh congress, said. "You are placing his mantle on my unwilling shoulders. If I look rather awkward in it you must not forget that this mantle was made for a much bigger man."[18]

It was no accident that the Moscow congress of geneticists was canceled. If top geneticists from all over the world had gathered in Moscow, the tremendous achievements of Soviet science undoubtedly would have received confirmation. Academician Vavilov's position as the leader and organizer of Soviet biological thinking would have been further strengthened. But that was what Lysenko's patrons did not want. Scarcely had the ban on the international congress been imposed than Lysenko got together his own "congress"—the fourth session of the "Lenin" Academy of Agriculture—in December 1936. But he miscalculated: on this occasion the "progressive biologists" did not gain a scientific victory over classical biology. There was nothing left for them but to pin their hopes on administrative measures.

In the latter years of his life Vavilov became especially attached to the family of the Bulgarian scholar Kostov, an extremely good and sensitive man, but he was obliged in the end to part from even that friendly home. From 1936 the position of foreign scholars in Vavilov's Institute of Plant Breeding became increasingly difficult: Vavilov was criticized publicly for bringing allegedly disloyal foreigners to Russia. In fact, everybody Vavilov invited became very fond indeed of the new socialist country. Kostov even married in the Soviet Union and was proposing to settle there forever. Nevertheless, foreigners were forced to leave.

The first to decide he could not stand any more was Muller. His departure evoked fresh slanders. There was talk about the flight of a reactionary geneticist and his retreat in the face of the "unquestionable" achievements of Lysenko's advanced biology. There was even talk of the American's "bourgeois" tendencies. But this lie was short-lived. Following the usual stream of invective against Muller in the hall of the institute, one of the members of the staff read out a letter sent from Spain. Herman Hermanovich (as Muller called himself in the Russian manner), now a member of the International Brigade, in which he was working on blood tranfusion, asked that they put off all disputes about genetics until complete victory over fascism. "The most important thing now is to hold Madrid," he wrote.

The campaign against everything foreign, which had begun with the ban on expeditions abroad, was gradually extended to include all foreign writings, according to Professor Sinskaya. The words "world literature" came to be regarded as bad language. Lysenko's people encouraged the campaign, since they reckoned they had achieved the summit of biological thought and had no reason to waste their time getting to know other people's theories. There was no need to read any publications on biology other than their journal *Vernalization*. Zealous editors strove to eliminate from every publication or manuscript any reference to foreign writings and any hint of respect for scientific work outside Russia. Special efforts were made to eliminate all foreign words and words of foreign origin that had crept into the Russian language.

Professor Sinskaya records that in the late 1930s a great deal of valuable written material was taken out of circulation at Vavilov's institute and elsewhere and much of it was destroyed. Some was hidden away or released only to a limited circle of readers. There thus grew up a special generation of people for whom the history of science, especially biology, began with the present day and who often wasted a lot of energy "discovering America."[19]

By the beginning of 1940 Lysenko had already succeeded in depriving the teaching staffs at universities and medical, pedagogical, and agricultural institutes of the right to teach their students genuine biology, which was replaced by "Michurinist" biology. He then turned his attention to schoolchildren. "Questions of Mendelism and Morganism should be removed from the syllabus on Darwinism for the secondary schools," he wrote to the deputy commissar for education in the Russian republic. "This is in my view logical if only because the secondary schools ought to be teaching the children the foundations of science, and Mendelism and Morganism have, of course, very little to do with the foundations of science."[20]

Vavilov did what he could to fight against the impoverishment of biology. On his initiative in the middle of the 1930s the Institute of Plant Breeding undertook the publication of three capital encyclopedic works: *Plant Breeding in the USSR*, *The Theoretical Foundations of Plant Selection*, and *The Cultivated Flora of the USSR*. But it proved possible to complete only the second work, the one in which the Germans were so interested. That unhappy year 1937 marked the end of Vavilov's publishing activity. Only a part of the first volume of his *Plant Breeding in the USSR* was actually published, and only an insignificant part of *The Cultivated Flora of the USSR* appeared, although it was to have summed up all the enormous botanical and geographical work done by Vavilov's staff. "Manuscripts were passed from one reader to another and were finally submerged forever in the publishers' rubbish," one of the authors, Professor Kuptsov, recalled.

Vavilov also edited for Soviet publication collections of important articles by T. Morgan and J. Meller (1937). It was at his insistence that Charles Darwin's fundamental work *The Effects of Cross and Self-Fertilisation in the Vegetable Kingdom* (1876) was published for the first time in Russian. This translation of Darwin and the introduction to the work were the last successes by Vavilov, the great booklover and spreader of scientific writing, in his efforts to disperse the gloom hanging over Soviet biology. Although he continued to work hard on his manuscripts, nothing more of his was published. Professor Nikolai Rodionovich Ivanov, who talked to Vavilov shortly before his arrest, told me that in Vavilov's Moscow apartment at the time there were some twenty-five hundred pages of unpublished manuscripts. They included a thousand-page manuscript entitled "Combating Plant Diseases by Breeding

Resistant Varieties," which the institute submitted for a Stalin Prize, as well as some unfinished works: "Field Crops of the USSR," "World Resources of Varieties of Grain Crops and Their Use in Plant Selection," "Plant Breeding in the Caucasus," and a large volume entitled "Farming Regions of Five Continents," in which Vavilov described his journeys through fifty-two countries of the world. Most of these manuscripts disappeared without trace after his arrest and have not been recovered.

Nevertheless one document has by some miracle survived and makes it clear that Vavilov remained to the very end faithful to the ideals of world science. In the summer of 1940, at the height of the campaign of persecution and when arrests were still taking place at his institute, Vavilov handed the commissar for agriculture a brief report entitled "The Uses of Foreign Agricultural Experience, the Latest Foreign Inventions, and Improved Seeds and Plants." It was like a cry of despair: Vavilov could not tolerate the transformation of science into an affair of village amateurs. That report, written many years ago, can tell us a great deal even today:

> One of the special qualities of such outstanding Russian scholars as Mendeleyev, Timiryazev, Pavlov and Pryanishnikov was that they trained us to study attentively the achievements of world science. . . . Gorky also taught us the need to study carefully the experience of world culture. But in many branches of agriculture and agricultural science recently there have been signs of an unhealthy tendency to ignore foreign experience and even to treat it with contempt. The publication of reference works and of translations of the best foreign handbooks and original works has ceased, as has also the recording of new inventions and advances in plant breeding that have taken place in the last decade, especially in Canada, the USA, Germany and Sweden. There is a tendency to dismiss indiscriminately all scientific work done in the capitalist world. But people forget that science and technology in capitalist countries are advanced mainly by intellectuals and people who work in science. The fact that the views of certain influential Soviet comrades do not correspond with the main lines along which scientific work is being

carried on abroad has come to serve as an excuse for dismissing the whole of foreign science. This attitude is usually the result of an ignorance of foreign languages on the part of even leading agronomists in our country.

Restrictions recently imposed on the exchange of seeds have in effect halted the import of improved varieties from other countries, since that whole business can be based only on a two-way exchange of innovations. . . . Radical steps must be taken to correct this state of affairs.[21]

Vavilov went on to describe the steps he had in mind. He provided a list of books by plant-breeding experts that should be translated immediately into Russian; he suggested the appointment of agricultural consultants in certain Soviet embassies "both to take advantage of foreign experience and to collect the seed stocks we need"; and he appealed to the commissar for agriculture to organize "an operational office to handle the application of foreign experience, for example: the latest machines and equipment, new ways of combating plant diseases and pests, new plant varieties."[22]

There were of course people who sought to derive some personal benefit from the policy of isolating Russia from the outside world, just as there were some who were skillful at extracting some benefit from the policy of repression and the atmosphere of fear and suspicion. The man who in 1939 asserted that "the science of biology and in particular the teaching about heredity in capitalist countries are dominated by metaphysical distortions" and that "by no means all of our biologists have yet rid themselves of their admiration for everything foreign and their pursuit of foreign fashions in science"[23] knew very well that such statements would please Stalin. It also suited Stalin that Lysenko promised to provide him with very rich harvests, new varieties, and other good things in double-quick time without any outside participation and through the efforts of Russia's own home-grown science.

How did it happen that in such extremely unfavorable circumstances Vavilov decided to hand the commissar for agriculture that report? Was it naiveté on his part? Or obstinacy? Or was it a case of attempted suicide? I questioned some of Vavilov's closest collaborators in his Institute of Plant Breeding—Professors Sinskaya, Bukasov, and Ivanov. They heard me out patiently and sadly, as if they were dealing with someone incapable of understanding the simplest truth: "There was not the slightest element either of naiveté or of obstinacy in him. How shall we put it—Nikolai Ivanovich was a person of complete integrity. He was simply incapable of acting otherwise."

5 Nineteen Forty

I envy our grandchildren and great-grandchildren,
who will have the good fortune to see Russia in the year
1940 when she will be looked up to as leader of the
educated world, legislating for both science and the arts
and enjoying respect and reverence from an enlightened
humanity.

V. G. Belinsky, 1840

A few years ago I was shown in Tashkent two pages torn out of
a school exercise book, upon which a brilliant epidemiologist and
virologist, Professor Nikolai Khodukhin, had scribbled his last
testament. He had headed this work, written on his deathbed,
"What I would like to achieve in science." The man who had
brought sanitation to the Central Asian republics left his followers a
carefully drawn fourteen-point program for the further campaign
against diseases. Reading that document I reflected on the courage
of the scientist, or rather on the tradition of courage in scientific
work.

Francis Bacon caught cold when he was cooling down a
chicken for an experiment in physiology. His last words, recorded
in his logbook of experiments, were "Experiment successful." A
few hours before the destruction of Pompei, Pliny the Elder was
writing to friends, who were begging him to escape, to say that he
was more interested in the raging elements than he was in his own
safety. In 1912 Ippolit Deminsky, dying from pulmonary plague,
spent the last minutes of his life composing and dispatching a
telegram concerning scientific matters: he urged his colleagues to
dissect his body, since it was the first known instance of a man being
infected with the plague by a gopher.

The final acts of heroism performed by Khodukhin and Bacon,
Pliny the Elder and Deminsky, are separated by centuries, but for
us these men stand side by side, all of them heroes. "When a scholar

dies, the world dies," says an Eastern proverb, for with the scholar dies a whole world of uncommunicated ideas, uncompleted discoveries, and unrevealed truths.

I have two pages removed from Vavilov's archives headed "Work Plan for 1940–41," which he had drawn up for himself at the beginning of 1940 or the end of 1939. It is by no means a complete plan of what Vavilov intended to do in the next two years. There is nothing in it about his duties as vice-president of the Academy of Agriculture or as director of the Institute of Plant Breeding, or about his expeditions and visits to experimental stations: there is only a list of the books and articles he intended to write. Even so it is a very striking personal document. In the next 720 days of his life Vavilov was planning to write a whole library— twelve books. Three of them were going to be written in English, while two were to have a lengthy English summary. Apart from that Vavilov was committed to writing five long articles for learned journals, one of them in German.

In the history of science, Vavilov's work plan can be placed alongside Deminsky's telegram and Francis Bacon's last words. It is frightful to think of the libraries of books that have been destroyed by fire and of unique books—compact distillations of human reason—that no longer exist. But the fate of those twelve unwritten volumes is no less tragic.

Persecution did not deprive Vavilov of his capacity for work. He was squeezing ever more work into his already overloaded days. To write twelve books in two years meant hours of work every single day. People who remember Vavilov in those final months say that was the way he worked. When he was on his expeditions around the country, he would set aside for sleep only the few hours when he was actually traveling, snatching an hour or two in a car or even in a small plane on a local flight in which he had to curl up on the parcels and suitcases. "Life is short—we must hurry." These words were now permanently suspended over him like a whip: "Hurry . . . hurry."

But, apart from his enormous industry, this concern for haste also reflected a sense of alarm that was quite unlike Vavilov. It was not fright, not fear for himself, but the natural alarm of a researcher who was not going to have the time to complete his work or to pass on to others the riches of his mind, his experience, and his erudition. There were plenty of grounds for alarm. The time had long since passed when, in the words of Professor K. I. Pangalo, "what was so typical of the Institute of Plant Breeding was a special festive atmosphere, a generally lively mood of elation."[1] By the end of 1939 and the beginning of 1940 the picture painted in the memoirs of Professor Sinskaya is far more typical:

> Life in the institute had been uneasy for a long time, but there were still periods of relaxation. But as the Lysenko psychosis grew and consolidated itself those relatively calm intervals disappeared altogether. . . . The attacks on the Institute of Plant Breeding and on Nikolai Ivanovich himself developed into a permanent campaign of persecution. The situation of the institute was seriously shaken. All sorts of audits, commissions and inspections became more and more frequent.[2]

Meanwhile the institute was embarking on yet another major work: the process of so-called cyclical crossings was being carried out on a large scale. Vavilov was spending whole days at the experimental station at Pushkino, bent down for hours over the rows of wheat and flax plants. He wanted to establish exactly which combinations of parent plants gave the best results for plant selection. He was taken up with a new idea. The cyclical crossings promised to give important results for the development of new varieties of agricultural plants. But at that point an inspection commission drew up a report stating that Vavilov's institute was suffering from a decadent bourgeois influence. As proof of this the commission cited an incontrovertible fact: all the nameplates on the doors of the laboratories in the institute were written in two languages: even the lavatories and the office of the party committee had nameplates in English! The director was hauled up for a reprimand, explanatory notes were written, and the commission's conclusions were discussed at a general meeting of the institute.

The institute was engaged in a complicated and extremely laborious attempt to draw up an original systematic classification of all crop plants, another work that had the most direct connection with efforts to develop new varieties. But the procuratura of the October district of Leningrad chose that moment to draw the attention of the director of the institute to the fact that, "according to information in the hands of the procuratura's office," Vavilov was not replying with sufficient regularity to comments posted in the institute's wall newspaper.[3]

These were all trivialities, but it was no accident that this stream of trivial unpleasantnesses descended on Vavilov at that time. Cracks began to appear on the surface of the once impassive facade of the institute. Among the graduate students of the institute there were ever more frequent instances of what Vavilov described half jokingly as "mutations." The young people who had only recently been seriously engaged in their research work suddenly declared themselves to be opponents of Vavilov's ideas and demanded to be given a new director. Various factors prompted the young people to change so suddenly: some of them wanted to abandon genuine scientific work, believing quite sincerely in the infallibility of "progressive biology"; others simply concluded that it would be easier to read two or three books and so absorb the one and only "true" theory than to spend their whole lives groping their way through the jungle of the unknown to reach the truth. There were also the usual careerists, whose dream of rising rapidly up the official ladder suddenly acquired an entirely real form: Lysenko was always ready to take in defectors.

In 1937 Vavilov used to say of the relatively few "mutants" in ironic terms: "They'll come to their senses." And he would advise students to read Darwin more often. But now he had to reflect on the moral reasons for the flight from science. Vavilov's friends detected increasing pain and bitterness in his words when he talked about the institute's future scholars. "They've turned the young people's heads," he said. "One man cannot put himself in place of science. If that happens we shall fall behind world biology by at least fifty years." Speaking about the young "defectors," Vavilov concluded sadly: "Nothing much is likely to come of *those* people. And it's a pity, because there were capable ones among them." His forecast came true: from among those who, having adopted another person's views, rejected Vavilov's way of independent thinking and thoroughly testing every new theory, no scientists of any importance emerged. A lack of moral standards in science is not without its effect. Half jokingly and half in earnest, Vavilov said of them: "If there's no honesty in their genes, there's nothing you can do about it."

The continual battle and the years of nervous strain took their toll. "He became somehow less colorful in that last year. The old sparkle went out of his eyes and he lost his usual slightly ironic cheerfulness," wrote Professor V. E. Pisarev. The untiring traveler who had at one time made his way easily across untrodden passes and journeyed thousands of miles on foot and on horseback, now, though he was only fifty-two, had difficulty in climbing the stairs to the third floor. "It's my heart, my dear fellow," he admitted to the institute's doorman, who was first to notice the change in the director's health.

Vavilov concealed his state of health from everybody, even from his wife. Yelena Ivanovna, with whom he had lived happily for fifteen years, tried in vain to extract from him what was the matter. But Nikolai Ivanovich either refused to answer or turned the conversation to something else. Ever more frequently, both at home and at the institute, he was seized by bursts of pointless rage. The people around him at home and at the institute tried to limit these outbursts. And when they had passed he himself would be embarrassed and simply mutter, "The brakes are getting worn down."

Bouts of nervous frustration, heart trouble, and intellectual fatigue became steadily worse in the stifling atmosphere of the storm that seemed to be hanging over the institute and to be enveloping the whole of biological science. I asked several members of the institute staff whether they thought Vavilov realized the inevitability of the approaching storm and the hopelessness of his own situation. Opinions differed. "Everybody considered him to be doomed," replied Professor Sinskaya. "He was less inclined than others to give in to such moods, but then they even overwhelmed him." Anna Anatolevna Kostova confirmed that view: "In the summer of 1939, Vavilov's old friend Doncho Kostov sent him a diploma recording his election as a doctor of science of Sofia University. In the same envelope Kostov sent the citation about Vavilov that he had read out in the crowded hall of the university. 'Thanks for your obituary notice,' Vavilov wrote with gruesome humor in reply. A presentiment of early death never left him."[4]

Professor A. V. Gursky, a member of the institute staff, did not agree with this view. "In the summer of 1940," he recalled, "I dropped in on him in his Moscow apartment. We started talking about the future of the institute. Nikolai Ivanovich voiced the conviction that his cause was far from being lost. He said firmly, 'If all our enemies were to be drowned in the Fontanka, they are so insignificant there wouldn't be any bubbles.' He did not believe there was a real possibility of his being arrested—'They won't dare,' he said."

Who was right? One of the older members of the institute staff, Dr. Aleksandra Ivanovna Mordvinkina, explained the conflicting views: "In public he still kept up appearances, but at home on his own he became depressed and seemed quite an old man." This is apparently the truth. The blows of fate had destroyed the mind and body of a powerful man. He could not fail to see the end that was approaching so rapidly. But in public, at his school and his institute, Vavilov remained the personification of energy and courage. That was his duty, his last duty—to make a heroic effort to control himself for his staff's peace of mind and to preserve in the laboratories the last vestiges of a truly scientific atmosphere.

In the middle of March 1939 scientists from the whole Leningrad region held their conference in the Institute of Plant Breeding. The debates lasted for two days, and the conference hall was overflowing. Opponents and supporters of Academician Vavilov followed one another on the platform, and all the weaknesses and all the failings of the institute were exposed. It became quite obvious that the two sides—science and pseudoscience—could not be reconciled. Vavilov's speech was yet another attempt to protect the thousand-strong scientific staff from destruction. P. Pomerantsev described his style:

> Vavilov did not go in for fine speeches—that was simply not in his character, but his carefully and precisely delivered remarks always left an indelible impression. In his pleasant, sonorous voice, without any sentimental overtones, he would enunciate every word and every sentence with maximum clarity, as though he feared that otherwise his listeners would lose the main thread of his argument. His speeches reflected the way he thought, weighing with absolute precision every element of it, so that not only each sentence and word but each letter had its place.[5]

I have read that speech of his in a recorded and corrected text. Even in that form it gives the impression of a work of art because of its intellectual content and striking form. At the same time he was dealing with what might seem to be profoundly specialized matters. He spoke of the enormous territories in the north and east of the country that had not yet been brought into cultivation, of the deserts and mountain valleys where the farmers were expecting help from the scientific plant breeders, of the duty of biologists to be constantly improving the quality of the varieties they had already bred, and of the valuable crops that were not yet growing in the fields. It was essentially a speech about the great work still to be carried out by the institute and its staff and about the responsibility of the scientist to the people. It was intended to restore to his pupils and colleagues the intellectual balance they had lost and to give them a more businesslike attitude toward their work. Vavilov appealed to them to get down to work again together, but it was not in any sense an appeal to abandon their own views and ideas. The record conveys his unyielding, passionate mood: "We shall mount the fire and we shall burn, but we shall not give up our convictions."[6]

There can be no doubt but that in his last year of freedom Vavilov knew that his days were numbered. No matter how he tried to conceal this from the people around him, the bitter truth, relieved by a joke, would from time to time show through in his conversation. On one occasion, as he was getting into the car, which, with all his duties as director, he simply could not do without, he said to a colleague: "I've got used to all sorts of comforts, but fate is so inconstant." On another occasion, as he was signing a reference for one of his students, he said almost casually, "I am giving you a reference now, but soon, maybe, I shall not be able to do even that." Nevertheless he was too fond of scientific work and attached too much value to every minute of his work and life to allow himself to be idle. He continued to draw up plans for years ahead and strove to finish what he could still do.

In his correspondence with friends abroad Vavilov did not conceal, as far as that was possible, the battle that was going on in Soviet biology. Nor did he conceal his own scientific position: "As for the situation with genetics, it is stable," he informed Doncho Kostov in May 1940. "They have arrived logically at Lamarckism. Vegetative hybridization is considered not only to have been demonstrated but is acceptable as a method in selection. I stand firmly and steadfastly on my own views."[7]

Vavilov was indeed still director of both the Institute of Plant Breeding and the Institute of Genetics, but it was a long time since he had been in charge of the Academy of Agricultural Science or a member of the Central Executive Committee. It was already seven years since he had traveled abroad, although he was president of the Geographical Society. Vavilov was on the way out. Everybody could see that, and especially his enemies. Every trip Vavilov made to the Lenin Academy in Moscow became a moral ordeal for him. At meetings Lysenko simply treated him with contempt.

A typical instance occurred when Vavilov was reporting on the Institute of Plant Breeding's plans and discussing the development of immune varieties of wheat, the breeding at the institute of cancer-resistant varieties of potato, and the need to set about producing a hybrid maize. As usual, he did not think it necessary to conceal shortcomings, and when he came to talk about the work of the biochemical laboratory, he admitted regretfully that the biochemists had not yet discovered how to recognize varietal and specific differences from the proteins. "We are not yet able to distinguish the lentil from the pea by analyzing the protein," he said.

Lysenko (from his seat): I reckon that anyone who tries them on his tongue can tell a lentil from a pea.

Vavilov: We are unable to distinguish them *chemically.*

Lysenko: What's the point of being able to distinguish them chemically if you can try them on your tongue?

Another no less revealing exchange took place at a meeting of the Presidium of the Lenin Academy when Vavilov proposed that they should use for breeding a variety of oats known as "Byzantium," which he had found on the Mediterranean and which was not subject to rust. So as not to delay the matter, Vavilov pulled a packet of seeds out of his pocket there and then and handed it to the secretary. It emerged that the label on the packet was written in Latin.

> Vavilov (by way of explanation): Botany is an international science and the most convenient terminology is therefore Latin.
>
> Lysenko: So that ordinary people shouldn't understand.
>
> Prezent: Then there is no need for research.[8]

Vavilov kept himself under control. He did not reply to the gibes even when they acquired an obviously mocking tone. It was a matter of principle for him.

By no means all the people at his institute had the courage to carry on with their work from day to day, apparently unconcerned. One after the other members of the staff would turn to him and say: "Perhaps, in view of the forthcoming changes at the institute, we should wind up some of the experiments in genetics? Should we not halt experiments that will in any case soon be no use to anyone?" Their concern was by no means without reason. After Vavilov left the scene, the most outstanding members of the institute's staff were arrested, others were dismissed, and the subjects being researched were radically changed. The research workers, realizing the futility of their efforts, were right in a way. But Vavilov did not know how to capitulate. He wrote his colleagues letters begging them to carry on and do as much as they could for science. Typical of such letters is one sent to Professor Konstantin Ivanovich Pangalo, the leading expert on melons and gourds:

Dear Konstantin Ivanovich,

Carry on quietly with your work. Give serious attention to the matter of summing up your great work on melons in a fundamental monograph. We must hurry to produce immortal works! Nodin probably worked faster than you,[9] but you must catch up with him and overtake him! It is not for nothing that I am always behaving like an alarm clock. . . .

There are no terribly threatening circumstances, so carry on with your work quietly. . . .

When Faraday was asked how he had achieved such great results, he replied that he worked hard and regularly summed up the results of his work in a brief, intelligible form and then published them.

That's the complete recipe for success.

I have just returned from the Caucasus. In Maikop, Derbent and especially in Sukhumi the work is going ahead at full speed. The crops are in excellent condition. They are doing a real and necessary job with great skill. . . .

We shall go on pursuing our policy of setting up a

new institution for plant breeding irrespective of any obstacles.[10]

In his efforts to protect the people working with him, Vavilov did more than make speeches and write letters. Knowing that, in the event of his arrest or dismissal, the genetics laboratory that Lysenko hated so much would be the first to be swept away, he moved several of the more gifted geneticists (including the maize specialist M. I. Khadzhinov, who subsequently won a Lenin Prize) to other departments. Dr. R. L. Perlova recalled that at the beginning of the summer of 1940 she and several other members of Vavilov's institute who were on an expedition started to receive telegrams from their director suggesting they should take jobs in the places the exhibition was passing through. They could not understand what had happened. Was Vavilov trying to get rid of them? Some were offended, others suspicious. Only some months later, when Vavilov was no longer with them, did they understand. Foreseeing the fate that was hanging over his institute, Vavilov tried to protect the more honest and capable biologists.

Talk about an expedition to the western Ukraine and western Byelorussia had been going on in the institute since the spring of 1940. It was being organized by the Commissariat for Agriculture for the purpose of studying the state of agriculture in the areas that had just been annexed. The rumor went around that the group of plant breeders would be headed by Academician Vavilov, and nothing had given him more pleasure for a long time. New places, untrodden paths—in his thoughts he was already breathing the air of the Carpathian mountains and striding through the forests of the Bukovina. But this expedition was to be something more than just another excursion to unfamiliar regions. It would serve to release some of the emotional tension that had built up in the institute. Even the indefatigable Vavilov was longing for a change, if only for a time. But the people in the commissariat dragged their feet— somebody was stubbornly opposing Vavilov's appointment.

The document authorizing the trip was not signed until July 23, and Vavilov left immediately for Moscow. He had everything ready—the members of the expedition had been chosen and the route planned. He had prepared a case full of books from the academy library, covering every aspect of the agriculture, flora, soil, and climate of the western regions. In his office before setting out he had a few parting words for those who were going on the trip: "Ladies and gentlemen," he thundered. "Ladies and gentlemen, we have been entrusted with a most responsible task." His eyes and teeth sparkled, his movements were full of life and vigor. It was as though the dreary years of "biological" debate, of foul denunciations, wicked prosecution, and pointless commissions and inspections, had all been forgotten. Vavilov was as cheerful and businesslike as he had been eight years previously, when he had set out on his last expedition abroad.

They were due to leave Moscow for Kiev on the evening of July 25. In the course of the day Vavilov had a talk with Dr. A. I. Atabekova at the Institute of Genetics. She had just been taken off her work at the Timiryazev Academy for embarking on "seditious" research work: she had dared to study the action of x-rays on plants.

"Everything is going to change now," Vavilov told his young colleague with conviction. "What I'm telling you is something more than smelling salts. I am not in a position to name the person in the government I have been talking to,[11] but, believe me, it will now be possible for us to do as we wish. We will develop a huge cytology department. The Americans will be green with envy!"

Delighted with the opportunities that had suddenly opened up before him, Vavilov talked long and enthusiastically about the rate at which biological research was going to develop henceforth in the Soviet Union. But a couple of hours later there was a sudden change in his mood, following a meeting with Lysenko, president of the academy. They started by talking about a doctoral thesis on genetics that Lysenko would not accept, but their exchanges became steadily more heated and extended to more general topics, until they developed into a bitter argument.

According to Professor Breslavets, when Vavilov finally slammed the door and rushed out of Lysenko's office, one of the scientific staff whispered, "Now he's going to be arrested." "What for?" Breslavets asked. "Because he said a terrible thing to Lysenko. He said, 'Thanks to you our country has been overtaken by other countries.' You just wait—he'll be arrested."

The last people to see Vavilov in Moscow were members of his

institute—Nikolai Rodionovich Ivanov, Nikolai Vasilevich Kovalev, and the newly appointed deputy director of the institute, Ivan
Alekseyevich Minkevich. They called on Vavilov in his Moscow
apartment that evening and found him extremely nervous and
exhausted. All he would mutter about his clash with Lysenko was:
"I told him *everything*." Minkevich received final instructions for
the work of the next few weeks, and Vavilov discussed the manuscript lying on his desk, which he still had to work on, and future
publications. He urged his colleagues not to slacken the pace of
their work. He even managed to raise a smile as they left, but it was
a forced smile, and his eyes had a tired look, clouded by bitter
thoughts.[12]

Yet people who met Vavilov on July 26 at the Kiev railway
station found him once again in full control of himself and bursting
with energy. Not a word was said about the troubles in Moscow.
There was thought only for the expedition. The three days in Kiev
were filled with activity: a meeting with the president of the
Ukrainian Academy of Science, talks with the commissar for agriculture and the deputy prime minister, arrangements for a small car
to take them around the western regions. Vavilov found time to visit
a sugar-beet research institute and an archaeological exhibition, to
discuss with Ukrainian scholars the organization of a conference on
the history of agriculture, and even to make a speech at a Re-
publicwide gathering of Pioneers. As an experienced traveler, he left
nothing to chance—all the maps and reference materials were
collected. He had remembered that it was going to be cold in the
mountains of the Bukovina and that woolen clothing would be
necessary.

At last the little black Soviet-made Ford was spinning along the
main highway from Kiev to Lvov. Vavilov did not like casual
conversation when he was on the road. On the other hand, everything that was going on in the fields along the road was of the
greatest interest to him, and he was particularly taken by the vast
areas of high-quality wheat stretching far away into the horizon up
to the old state frontier. But even more interesting in the western
Ukraine were the peasants' fields, which reminded him of a ragged
blanket. In that region Vavilov would stop the car every two or
three miles, and before it had come to a halt he would be running

toward the nearest field to take samples of rye, barley, and oats and put them into his cloth bags.

From Lvov the expedition moved on to Chernovitsy, still gathering seed samples from ripening crops by the wayside. They got to know the local farms and had conferences with botanists and agronomists. They had their midday and evening meals in canteens and village cafés. As in Leningrad, Vavilov would invite everyone with whom he happened to be talking to join him at the table and would always pay for his guests and colleagues out of his own pocket. His consideration for others took another form. In the hotels and inns in which he, the driver, and his two colleagues, V. S. Lekhnovich and F. K. Bakhteyev, generally occupied the same room, Vavilov would stubbornly refuse to take the bed farthest from the door. "The leader's place is near the door," he would say. But Bakhteyev and Lekhnovich soon realized why he did it. Vavilov was in the habit of rising an hour or so earlier than the others to work on his books and notes before going out into the fields. His place by the door allowed him to work without disturbing the others.

According to his plan, on August 6, Vavilov was due to make a trip in three cars with a group of local scientists and agronomists from Chernovitsy to the mountainous region of Putilya. They had to cover something less than a hundred miles to reach the heights of the Carpathians. It was a sunny day and the members of the expedition and their hosts were in an excellent mood. But quite early on, while they were still in the foothills, the car in which Lekhnovich was traveling (Bakhteyev had stayed in Chernovitsy) had several punctures, fell behind, and soon turned back.

"On the way back," Lekhnovich told me, "we met another black Ford, just like ours. The people in it stopped us and the four men wanted to know where Academician Vavilov was. We explained to them the route the other two cars had taken. When we asked them why they needed Vavilov, they replied: 'He has taken with him from Moscow some documents concerning the export of grain that are urgently needed.' The black Ford went on its way in search of Vavilov and we went back to Chernovitsy."[13]

That evening, after supper in the canteen, Lekhnovich and Bakhteyev went back to the student hostel where Vavilov's group was spending the night. It was getting dark; an elderly servant was standing at the gate. Bakhteyev later recalled, "He said that the professor [i.e., Vavilov] had just returned in his car and had been about to go to the hostel when another car drove up and the people who got out of it had invited him to go off with them for urgent talks with Moscow. The professor had then put his rucksack down and asked the doorman to tell the other comrades that he would be back soon."[14]

It was a quiet moonlit night, and the hostel was also quiet. The driver had gone to bed, but the two scientists continued to wait for their leader, occasionally exchanging remarks about the day's events. There was no reason for concern. Vavilov was often called by telephone from Moscow on government business. It was even a good thing that Moscow should remember Vavilov.

Bakhteyev was sorting out the plants collected during the day. He carefully removed from Vavilov's rucksack a sample of grain and examined it. What a find! Even in Kiev Vavilov had been asking the archaeologists what the inhabitants of the Black Sea steppes had sown four or five thousand years ago. For a long time he had been trying to discover the route along which agricultural crops had traveled from their original centers to the farming areas where they are found today. According to his calculations wheat must have arrived in Europe not only by way of the Caucasus but also through the Balkan countries. If that were the case, then somewhere in the remote mountain valleys there ought still to be some survivors of the original wheat plants. At the Dublyany Academy and at a conference of teachers at Chernovitsy University on the evening of August 5, Vavilov had kept asking the local botanists and agronomists what ancient plants they came across in the Carpathians. But they were unable to tell him anything about such survivals. And then, on August 6, 1940, Vavilov himself had discovered in the mountains a sample of that much-traveled grain, of that ancient spelt emmer, the wheat that had provided food for Babylon and Egypt in the time of the first pharaohs.

Around midnight there was a knock on the door. Two young men entered, and asked for Lekhnovich, and handed him a note. On a small sheet of paper Vavilov had written in his bold handwriting:

Dear Vadim Stepanovich. In view of my sudden recall to Moscow, hand over all my things to the bearer of this note.

    6.8.40.   2315 hours.   N. Vavilov.[15]

The young men added that the professor was flying off urgently to Moscow and was already beside the plane at the airport.

Bakhteyev described what happened in the next fifteen minutes:

> We quickly gathered Nikolai Ivanovich's things together, although we had the idea at first of leaving something out, thinking he would soon be back. . . . But the messengers insisted, very politely, but at the same time quite firmly, that we should hand over literally everything, not leaving even a scrap of paper. We shrugged our shoulders, extremely surprised by such insistence. Having gathered his things together and packed them up, we ourselves prepared to go and see him off from the airport. The young men did not object to this. But once the things had been taken out and put in their car, it turned out that there was no room for us two in the back, since there was a third man at the wheel. We decided that I would go and see Nikolai Ivanovich off and discuss with him the future of the expedition, while Vadim Stepanovich would stay behind.
>
> I was about to get into the car alongside the man in the back seat when he suddenly dropped his polite ways and said sharply: "Is it worth your while going?" I replied that the comrade was presumably joking and that, if there was not room for both of us, one of us at least must have a word with Vavilov. As I said this I took hold of the rear door and was about to step in and sit down when the man I was talking to struck me a swinging blow and I fell. That was followed by a brusque order to the driver: "Let's go!" The door slammed with a bang and the car disappeared in the darkness. It was only then that, utterly stunned, we realized at last that Nikolai Ivanovich was in real trouble."[16]

6   State Prisoner

*I am sure the time will come when everyone in
Russia will be given his due, but it is impossible in the
meantime not to be concerned at the dishonest way our
contemporaries are hiding the truth from posterity.*
                                    P. A. Chaadayev, 1854

*I conducted the investigation into the case of N. I.
Vavilov with complete objectivity. It was a case
involving a great deal of work. . . . N. I. Vavilov did
not have any criticisms to make of me as the
investigating officer, either during the investigation or
when it was completed.*
                              Colonel A. G. Khvat,
                      former police investigator, 1954

"You have beern arrested as an active participant in a subver-
sive anti-Soviet organization and a spy for foreign intelligence
services. Do you admit your guilt?"

"No, I do not. I have never been a spy or a member of any
anti-Soviet organizations. I have always worked honestly for the
good of the Soviet state."

With these words on the morning of August 12, 1940, the first
interrogation of Academician Vavilov began in the prison of the
People's Commissariat for Internal Affairs (NKVD) in Moscow.
The dialogue between Aleksei Grigorievich Khvat, then senior
lieutenant of State Security, and Vavilov continued for eleven
months. Not only does the case file no. 1,500 contains the records
of the interrogations and the confrontations with witnesses, the
statements made by the prisoner, and the testimony of experts; it
also reveals to a certain extent the characters of the participants in
this drama.

At the age of thirty-three Aleksei Khvat stood on the threshold
of a major task. As deputy head of the investigation department of

the principal economic section of the NKVD, he had been given a job that was to a large extent going to determine his future career. He had to demonstrate by any means at his disposal that Nikolai Vavilov was not a distinguished scientist, not the pride of Soviet science, and not the organizer of Russian agronomy, but a sworn enemy of the Soviet regime and consequently a person to be destroyed.

Looking ahead a little, it must be said that Lieutenant Khvat justified fully the trust placed in him by his superiors. He got the whole Vavilov case down on paper without a single hitch. He later reached the rank of colonel and in 1948, at the height of his powers, he retired on a full pension. The former police investigator's peace of mind has been disturbed since then only once. In September 1954 he was summoned to the office of the chief military prosecutor and asked to explain how he conducted the case of Academician Vavilov. Khvat was presumably alarmed at receiving such a summons. His two bosses, Beria and Abakumov, had just been executed; there was a purge going on in the security organs; and many former investigators were losing their pensions and being expelled from the Party for their past sins. But Khvat got away with it. He had a clear head and a quick mind and, fourteen years after the event, he was able to put his hand on the very paper from among the hundreds of sheets in the ten-volume Vavilov case that alone could relieve him of any responsibility. It was a certificate to the effect that in September 1940 Investigator A. G. Khvat had approached his superior officers for advice and had received confirmation that "the facts stated by Vavilov concerning his wrecking activity in agriculture actually took place."[1] Once he had produced this document in his own defense, Khvat relaxed and wrote confidently in an explanatory note that he had conducted the Vavilov case "with complete objectivity" and that Vavilov had made no criticism of him. The reference to his superior officers got him off the hook: although the prosecutor had admitted that the Vavilov case was entirely false, Khvat was allowed to depart in peace. He continued to live in the center of Moscow in a fine official apartment, receiving his colonel's pension.

Police file no. 1,500 tells the whole story of the relationship that developed between Lieutenant Khvat and Academician Vavilov in May 1940. In the days immediately following his arrest, Vavilov was full of determination to prove his innocence. The replies he gave during the first interrogation session were firm, even spirited: "I declare categorically that I have never engaged in espionage or in any other kind of anti-Soviet activity. . . . I consider that the documents in the possession of the police are one-sided and throw an incorrect light on my work. They are obviously the result of differences of opinion that I had in my scientific and governmental work with a number of people. I regard it as nothing but a slanderous attack on me."[2]

He continued to assert the same at the second, third, and fourth sessions: "I have not engaged in anti-Soviet work and cannot provide any testimony on that question." But Khvat had had plenty of experience of how to "soften up" such stubborn subjects. From August 14 he started questioning Vavilov for ten, twelve, even thirteen hours at a time. He would call Vavilov out in the early hours of the night and finish his talk with him at daybreak. A day's rest and then off again.

Practically nothing is known about what went on during these all-night vigils, because the longer the interrogation sessions lasted, the shorter were the written records. The protocol dated August 21 contains only one question: what countries had Vavilov visited? The great traveler named a few dozen states and places he had been to. It must have taken no more than five minutes to put the question and receive the answer. But what did the two of them do for the remaining ten and a half hours? On the following day—they took no break!—another twelve hours were spent "elucidating the truth" and again the protocol took up only three or four pages.

It was on August 24, after twelve hours of questions, that the investigator heard his victim make a confession for the first time. "I admit that I was guilty of being from 1930 a participant in the anti-Soviet organization of right-wingers that existed in the People's Commissariat for Agriculture."[3] Vavilov then named "others involved in anti-Soviet work." He listed all the commissars and deputy commissars for agriculture who had been executed by that time—Yakovlev, Chernov, Muralov, Gaister, who had all been declared to be "enemies of the people"; the vice-presidents of the All-Union Academy of Agriculture—Gorbunov, Volf, Chernykh, Tulaikov, Meister; and members of the academy staff who had been arrested—Margolin and Khodorovsky.

Through the next night Vavilov continued to incriminate people who had occupied important posts but who were already dead. The records of the interrogation became steadily more detailed. Under investigation Vavilov did not spare himself or those whose bones were already rotting in mass graves. He confessed that when he was in charge of the Academy of Agriculture he had set up useless, highly specialized institutes with a view to harming agriculture. This action resulted in a dissipation of personnel and a deliberate waste of state funds. Vavilov confessed to having used his authority to increase the areas under cultivation in the USSR, resulting in a shortage of seeds with which to sow those areas. Consequently, in 1931 and 1932 the country's fields were full of weeds and the rotation of crops was disrupted. Moreover, in 1930 he had campaigned for an increase in the area sown to maize and had thus caused the country tremendous losses.

Lieutenant Khvat liked documents and knew how to use them. Although Vavilov's testimony was taken down in shorthand, and the records were afterward typed out and signed on each page by Vavilov himself, the interrogator still wanted him to set down his evil doings in his own handwriting. The result was a whole treatise, dated August 6, 1940, that Vavilov entitled "Wrecking Activities within the Institute of Plant Breeding, of which I was in charge from 1920 until my arrest." In that twelve-page composition Vavilov again confirmed that the increase in the cultivated areas, the setting up of specialized institutes, and the cultivation of the maize were acts intended to harm the country.

If in his search for the truth Lieutenant Khvat had taken the trouble to study the documents published in connection with the first and second five-year plans and the resolutions passed at the party congresses and congresses of Soviets in the late 1920s and early 1930s, he could easily have established that the man he was questioning was grossly deceiving him. Everything that Vavilov declared to have been done by him personally and with evil intention, had been written into state documents and approved at party meetings. That included the extension of the area sown to grain by fifty million hectares from 1931 to 1934.

Moreover, it was the policy of the government, aimed at bringing the whole administration of agriculture under one centralized command, that led to the breakdown of experimental work in the localities and the establishment of separate institutes for each branch of agriculture. The Academy of Agriculture had been ordered to set up a *single* scientific administration for all branches of agriculture and, in obedience to the command from above, the academy had started creating narrowly specialized institutes like the Institute for Coffee and Chicory, the Institute for Soy Beans, and the Institute of Rabbit Breeding. Plenty of scientists and others in those years had protested this centralization of scientific work. They had argued that because Russia was a vast country with a great wealth of soils and climates, experiments with agricultural crops and breeds of cattle should be conducted according to local conditions. But such people had been arrested as "enemies of the people" out to undermine the foundations of agriculture. The most distinguished organizers of experimental work in the provinces all landed in prison—Pisarev, Talanov, Chayanov, and Doyarenko—not to mention lesser folk, agronomists and plant breeders, who were arrested in the hundreds. But now, in 1940, the specialized institutes had been declared harmful, and Vavilov was expected to take upon himself the blame for the stupidities, deception, and sheer nonsense committed in the "period of the socialist reconstruction of agriculture."

Lieutenant Khvat would have had no difficulty at all in establishing the complete innocence of the man he was interrogating. But he was not in the least interested in the true interconnection between historical events and Vavilov's part in them. His aim was the very reverse. His duty was to prove, in the face of all the facts, that Vavilov, president of the Academy of Agriculture, was the person responsible for the ruin of Soviet agriculture and the breakdown of agricultural science. For this purpose anything was good enough—Vavilov's lies about himself, denunciations by his enemies, and documents forged by the police.

What broke Vavilov's will and made him lie about himself and people who had already perished, including some who had been dear and close to him? A good deal may be explained by the severity of the system of interrogation. Even our generation, which has not experienced personally the horrors of the prisons of Stalin's day, knows from books and accounts of witnesses the sort of methods used in those years to extract the wildest sort of confessions. It is not difficult to understand that a fifty-three-year-old scholar was unable to withstand the humiliations, threats, sleepless nights, and physical maltreatment, and that he simply gave in and agreed to sign everything the authorities demanded of him. To admit this is not to insult Vavilov's memory, but nonetheless I cannot accept such a hypothesis.

Nikolai Vavilov was known as a fearless traveler, a man whose courage was known the world over. In 1924 he was the first European to dare to journey across Kafiristan, an inaccessible mountainous region of Afghanistan, without roads, without maps, and without experienced guides. He had spent a night in the Sahara after his plane had crashed and he and the unarmed pilot found themselves next to a lion's den. In Ethiopia he had come up against bandits. In the Caucasus he had been caught in a landslide and with a heavy rucksack on his back had scrambled across the rocky scree, which might at any moment have resumed its descent into the gorge beneath. Vavilov's companions on his travels had had the opportunity to discover that in really dangerous circumstances he was resourceful and courageous, that he possessed an iron will and would never abandon a comrade in disaster.

Was it possible that such a person had given in after only twelve nights in the Lubyanka? It seems to me that something different happened. With his deeply analytic mind, Vavilov very soon must have realized that his arrest was not a matter of chance but a carefully planned move cleared with all the authorities. He would have been convinced of this above all by the numerous depositions made against him, which Lieutenant Khvat, like an experienced cardplayer, kept producing one after the other. These depositions included slanderous statements made by Commissar Yakovlev, long since executed; the "confessions" of Gorbunov, a government official who was murdered in prison; and the written testimony of Talanov, the plant breeder who had died after being arrested for the third time. Khvat produced thirty-eight such extracts from the files of people who had long since been condemned and executed.

Fifteen years later, having checked through the files in Vavilov's case no. 1,500, the military prosecutor, Kolesnikov, came to the conclusion that most of the documents were no more than crude forgeries. Neither Gorbunov nor Commissar Yakovlev had said anything about Vavilov; Talanov had not produced any concrete facts; Academician Meister, the plant breeder who lost his mind in his cell, declared Vavilov to be a wrecker on several occasions and just as often withdrew his charges; the vice-president of the Academy of Agriculture, Bondarenko, who was later executed, withdrew his testimony in court. In 1955 Khvat's dishonest tricks were fully exposed.

But even in 1940 Vavilov realized that Khvat was playing with marked cards. The number of denunciations that had been collected indicated his arrest on August 6 had been decided long in advance and cleared with all the appropriate departments. In that case there was no sense in trying to obtain justice or in demanding unbiased treatment. He would have to play the game Khvat was forcing on him and play it with the least possible losses. This knowledge was the origin of Vavilov's plan, which was to admit his guilt in "wrecking" Soviet agriculture and claim as accomplices people who were no longer alive and could not suffer from his testimony.

The only charge Vavilov rejected utterly was that of espionage. He admitted that he had been abroad and had called on foreign embassies and missions, but he denied that he had ever been recruited by, or had ever carried out any tasks for, foreign intelligence services. Here it seems Vavilov's analytic mind let him down. Apparently forgetting that he was in the hands of people for whom the codes of law meant nothing at all, Vavilov fought sutbbornly with his investigator against being characterized as a spy. The arguments he made reveal clearly that Vavilov was still cherishing a naive faith in the law—the law that punished a spy working for a foreign state more severely than it punished an internal enemy. Khvat probably had a condescending grin on his face as he read the passionately stated protests of the arrested academician. Although there was not a single document in the files to prove that Vavilov was a traitor to his country, nevertheless Khvat managed to include the charge that Vavilov was a spy in the indictment. Nobody at the trial recognized the absurdity of this charge. After all, Vavilov had not denied that in 1933 he had embraced the White Russian émigré Professor Metalinkov at a railway station in Paris.

Nevertheless Vavilov won the first round in this diabolical game. At the beginning of September 1940, after he had confessed to being a "wrecker," the night interrogations ceased. Lieutenant Khvat was busy preparing for the second round.

It is quite clear now that Vavilov's arrest had been planned long ahead. The distant thunder of the coming storm had been rumbling away over his head ever since 1931, at a time when he appeared to be at the peak of his success. But it was then that secret police dossier no. 268615 was opened in his name in the depths of the OGPU. While Vavilov was solving problems connected with the growing of quinine and rubber in the Soviet Union, grappling with the difficulties of developing agriculture in the polar and desert regions, developing drought-resistant wheat, making speeches at international congresses and national conferences, and pursuing research into the crop plants of the Transcaucasus, the Far East, and Canada, his secret dossier was growing in size and the files were getting fatter with each new line of inquiry. By the time Vavilov was arrested, there were seven volumes of police reports in his dossier.

Vavilov's secret dossier is fascinating to study. Official reports by members of the staff are mixed in with denunciations by people in the scientific world, and cuttings from newspapers are found along with letters from highly placed statesmen. Everything is in good order—each document is numbered, filed, and indexed. Vavilov's dossier reveals that the first stone was thrown at him by a professor at the Timiryazev Academy, Ivan Vyacheslavoch Yakushkin. A descendant of the famous Decembrist who, in Pushkin's words, "drew the dagger that killed the tsar," Professor Yakushkin directed his dagger at the most brilliant of his contemporaries. As an informer he liked especially to write slanderous statements about academicians and corresponding members of the Academy of Science, but he did not object to doing the same for mere doctors of science.

In the course of his career Yakushkin had experienced plenty of difficult moments and some sharp reverses. In 1920, unable to get along with the Soviet regime, Yakushkin, then a young professor, plant breeder, and pupil and follower of V. R. Vilyams, tried to get out of Russia by way of the Crimea along with the retreating forces of General Wrangel. Unfriendly sources asserted that only an accident prevented him from settling abroad: Yakushkin was simply thrown off the boat at the last minute as it set sail for Turkey, and he had to lie low in the Crimea. In the late 1920s the unsuccessful defector decided that his sins must have been forgotten and he moved to Voronezh, finding work on a beet-growing experimental farm in Ramoni. There he became a research worker, and a quite good one. But in 1930, during the first wave of mass arrests, he was held by the police. It was a time when the police were especially keen to get hold of agronomists, plant breeders, and scientists involved in agriculture, who were characterized as "wreckers" and blamed for the collapse of agriculture caused by collectivization; many of them perished without trace. But Yakushkin managed to survive and, what is more, to leave prison with good prospects. Many years later he wrote: "In 1931, immediately after my release from prison in Voronezh, I was recruited into the OGPU to work as a secret police informer, which I continued to be until November 1952 or 1953, when I was released from that work."

It cannot be said that this "work" proved to be a great burden to Yakushkin. On the contrary, he was soon made a professor at the Timiryazev Academy of Agriculture and acquired considerable skill in combining his personal interests with those of the state. Those who did not get on with Professor—later Academician—Yakushkin or who appeared to be his rivals were removed from his path in the blink of an eye. Some power acted so quickly and with such skill that the academy, which had been rich in scientific talent, was soon left with no one likely to eclipse the brilliant Yakushkin. "As a secret collaborator with the OGPU I was sending secret reports to the OGPU, particularly about Vavilov," Yakushkin informed the prosecutor Kolesnikov. He delivered his first ten-page report as far back as September 1931, and in it he had demonstrated point by point that Vavilov's Institute of Plant Breeding was a center of anti-Soviet activity and that its director was the organizer of "wrecking activities" in the fields of plant selection and seed growing.[4]

Professor Yakushkin was naturally not the only person working as an informer. Another man who did very well in that profession was the head of the institute's department of plant introduction, Aleksandr Karpovich Kol. He was ten years older than Vavilov, imagined himself a great scholar, and complained that his work was not appreciated. His contemporaries remember Kol, however, as a troublemaker who was extremely careless at his work. Whenever Vavilov dispatched parcels of seeds from his distant expeditions he would always, as far back as 1927, mark his accompanying instructions: "To everybody in the introduction department and especially A. K. Kol." Nevertheless seeds that got into Kol's hands were lost or their labels would disappear. Although he was usually very understanding about human weaknesses, Vavilov could not forgive slovenliness that could undermine the work of the whole institute. Kol was reprimanded on several occasions. But instead of correcting his mistakes, he started complaining that Vavilov was persecuting him because of their differences over scientific matters. He even engaged in a public scientific debate with Vavilov in 1931. Although the debate produced nothing but confusion, it helped Kol to revenge himself on Vavilov. Vavilov's dossier contains all the documents in the debate. Somebody was following very closely the squabble that the ambitious Kol had started with the director of the Institute of Plant Breeding.

In 1933 Kol was arrested. At his first interrogation he testified that a counterrevolutionary group led by Academician Vavilov was operating in the Institute of Plant Breeding. Kol was allowed to go free and started to work as a secret collaborator with the NKVD, providing his employers with compromising material about Vavilov and other leading scientists at the institute.

By the late 1930s quite a few such people at the institute were acting as police informers, some voluntarily and some more reluctantly. The cytogeneticist Yelena Karlovna Emme had rather unwisely submitted some of her scientific works to foreign journals, and she had also been seen talking to foreign scientists. In 1937 and 1938 that was quite sufficient to cause a person to disappear without trace. But Emme did not disappear: an NKVD officer forced her, frightened for her life, to write slanderous reports about Vavilov. These reports were all the more effective since Emme was friendly with Vavilov's wife and was often in the Vavilov home. It was only after the war, on her deathbed, that Emme confessed to her son Andrei that she had for years been giving false testimony about people who had treated her as a member of their family.

Professor Emme wrote her false reports because she feared arrest. But others found the atmosphere of repression, suspicion, and fear to their taste. The Vavilov dossier contains the writings of some who hoped that, by slandering Vavilov, they might advance themselves one or two steps up the career ladder. The regime that destroyed thousands of manuscripts and diaries and tons of personal letters and scientific works decreed that the reports of its voluntary informers should be "preserved forever."

On September 3, 1937, Fyodor Fyodorovich Sidorov, thirty-two years of age, a scientist working at the institute's experimental

farm at Pushkino, turned up on his own initiative at the office of the
representative of the State Security police in Pushkino. "I want to
make a statement concerning the wrecking activity of the men in
charge of the Institute of Plant Breeding—Vavilov, Aleksandrov
and Lepin—as a result of which work on the development of
varieties of agricultural crops resistant to disease and pests has been
wrecked," he said.[5] What illegal acts on the part of the men in
charge of the institute had driven the well-intentioned Sidorov, a
former graduate student there, to expose them? Vavilov's "wrecking
activities" consisted, apparently, of his closing Sidorov's laboratory, because he considered the younger man insufficiently educated. In its place Vavilov organized elsewhere a whole station for
the study of immunity in grains. A matter that at any other time
could have been solved by the local committee or by the institute's
Learned Council found its way into the safes of the secret police.
Sidorov's libelous report was entered in Vavilov's dossier as one of
the most incriminating documents, and Sidorov himself quickly
advanced to the position of deputy director of the institute. When,
after the war, what had been secret became public knowledge and
Sidorov was asked to leave the institute, the Leningrad district
committee of the Communist party found him an equally well-paid
job in another institute. It did not occur to anybody that an
informer should be expelled from the party.

Meanwhile Grigori Nikolayevich Shlykov, a biologist, did not
suffer even that inconvenience. He continued to head one of the
departments of the institute until a very advanced age, although the
entire staff knew practically by heart the text of a letter he had sent
to the secret police on March 7, 1938. It was shortly after the arrest
of the two commissars for agriculture, Chernov and Yakovlev, and
the head of the Agriculture Department of the party's Central
Committee, Bauman. Shlykov wrote:

> Before the bandits Chernov, Yakovlev and Bauman are
> destroyed we must discover what they were doing in the
> way of wrecking the organization of agriculture, experi-
> mental farms and the testing of new varieties. I am ever
> more convinced that there could have been a division of
> labor with Vavilov, the actual head of the country's scien-
> tific research in the field of plant breeding. . . . It is

difficult to believe that those restorers of capitalism could
pass over such a figure as Vavilov, who had such authority
in agronomy, particularly of the old sort. I cannot think
that such a person, well known for his right-wing views
and coming from a family of millionaires, was not involved in their organization.[6]

Shlykov's report consisted of nothing but speculation and
suspicions: "It is difficult to believe . . . ," "I cannot think. . . ."
Neither he nor the people to whom he was writing were interested
in facts. His unfounded guesses were turned so quickly and so
unquestioningly into part of the indictment that the little informer
felt himself to be indeed the sword of justice. Bursting with pride,
he was unable to restrain himself from boasting to his friends: "It
was I who got Vavilov sent to prison!" But it was not, of course,
just Shlykov. There were plenty of people around Vavilov like
Yakushkin, Kol, Emme, Sidorov, and Shlykov—frightened, ambitious, or simply vicious—but even they were not the people who
actually decided his fate. Who did?

Most of the documents in Vavilov's dossier relating to the years
of 1931 to 1933 seem to have been assembled more or less by
chance. The purpose for which the OGPU had begun to collect
them had apparently not yet been finally determined. Along with
the obviously slanderous statements by Kol and Yakushkin, the files
of those "liberal" years also contain, for example, an enthusiastic
article in *Izvestia* about Vavilov as the organizer of a campaign
against drought. The same file contains a newspaper clipping of a
report that in February 1931 the Soviet government appointed
Vavilov to be a member of the State Planning Commission, while in
March of the same year he was made a member of a commission to
draw up the second Five-Year Plan. His dossier also includes some
extremely favorable testimony made about him by Professor S. K.
Chayanov, who was arrested in 1931. Most of the documents in the
dossier relating to the early 1930s contain favorable opinions of
Vavilov. Even the slanderous statements were of a fairly "academic"
character—Vavilov was blamed for the excessively theoretical direction of his experiments, which had allegedly "caused harm to
socialist agriculture."

The character of the slanders changed sharply from the end of

1937, when Lysenko became president of the Academy of Agriculture and relations between the two academicians were beyond repair. From then on everyone giving information to the secret police dutifully stressed the fact that Vavilov was an opponent of Lysenko. Sensing the new direction being taken by the authorities, the interrogators started distorting the testimony of their prisoners in the same way. The change in the interrogations can be seen in the work carried out at the time by a certain Stromin, who was head of the Saratov district office of the NKVD. In July 1937 Stromin had been questioning the well-known scientist N. M. Tulaikov. God alone knows what Stromin did with his victim, but in his hands Professor Tulaikov put his name to utterly fantastic accusations against the country's most distinguished plant selectors and breeders, including Vavilov, with whom he had been for many years on the most friendly terms. Tulaikov "exposed" Vavilov's links with Bukharin, and even with the White Russian émigré and monarchist Milyukov. There can be no doubt that, if Stromin had required it, Tulaikov would have testified to Vavilov's connections with the Romanovs. In the summer of 1937, however, it suited the NKVD very well to have Vavilov as a Bukharinist and a monarchist. But the situation changed in the autumn. Stromin received new instructions, with the result that all the people he was interrogating started to declare, almost in unison, that Vavilov's counterrevolutionary attitude found its clearest expression in his refusal to accept Lysenko's discoveries.

"An important nucleus of leading members of the academy, led by Vavilov, Koltsov, Meister, Konstantinov, Lisitsyn and Serebrovsky, actively opposed Lysenko's revolutionary theory of vernalization and intravarietal cross-breeding," stated Rudolf Eduardovich David, an academician and director of the Institute for the Study of Drought, under interrogation on November 27, 1937, in Saratov. "It became quite apparent to me that, behind the statements being made by the group of academicians I have named, there was a single political line and that they were undoubtedly united in a single anti-Soviet organization. . . . In an effort to verify my suppositions I asked Academician Meister about it straight out. . . . In conversation with me Meister confirmed that the attacks against Lysenko and Vilyams were led by a group of academicians, members of a right-wing Trotskyist organization."[7] Thus Vavilov, the scholar who belonged to no party and had throughout his life refused to engage in any kind of political activity, was in the autumn of 1937 finally included among the active *political* enemies of the Soviet regime.

Although he had tortured quite a few scientists and agronomists with his own hands, Stromin, down in Saratov, could not have thought up this new version. The idea that Vavilov and the other plant breeders and geneticists were disputing Lysenko's "discoveries" because they had been ordered to do so by a right-wing Trotskyist center originated higher up and was passed on to the provinces. Similar testimony was demanded in Moscow from Gaister, deputy commissar for agriculture, and from Muralov, president of the Lenin Academy, in Saratov from Academician Meister, and in Leningrad from Naumov, head of the district land administration.

After 1937 the nature of Vavilov's "guilt" finally became clear both to the informers and to those who read their reports. From that date reports of his anti-Lysenko (and therefore anti-Soviet) actions started to arrive in his dossier by the dozen. One file bearing the number 300669, which was opened in 1938, was simply labeled "Genetics." It included three volumes of documents aimed at proving that Academician Vavilov had gathered scientists with anti-Soviet views around him not only in the Institute of Plant Breeding but also in the Institute of Genetics. These counterrevolutionaries were alleged to be defending the reactionary racial theories of "bourgeois" scientists, opposing Academician Lysenko and refusing to recognize his works.

Why then, after having such charges leveled against him, did Vavilov still remain at liberty? For a certain time he was protected by his international fame and his reputation as a great scholar. But, wherever explosive material is steadily piled up, a catastrophe is sooner or later inevitable. At the beginning of 1939, shortly after Stalin and Lysenko were "elected" members of the Soviet Academy of Science, Beria's deputy, Kobulov, doubtless on instructions from his boss, summed up the results of the many years spent secretly observing Vavilov in a special report entitled "The Campaign Waged by Reactionary Scholars against Academician T. D. Lysenko." Disaster now threatened Vavilov and his teacher Pryanishnikov, who, in Kobulov's words, "pose as defenders of Soviet genetics against Lysenko's 'attacks' " and were "trying hard to discredit Lysenko as a scholar." Kobulov also named as opponents of Lysenko V. L. Komarov, president of the Soviet Academy of Science, G. I. Krzhizhanovsky, vice-president of the academy, Academicians E. A. Fersman and L. A. Orbeli, Dr. N. K. Kotsov, and many others.

There was no mistaking where Kobulov got the inspiration for his report. One of the heads of the security police declared himself ready to crush the life out of anybody (even the president of the Academy of Science or Lenin's friend, the elderly Bolshevik Krzhizhanovsky) who dared to criticize the sacred dogmas of Trofim Denisovich Lysenko. It is difficult to imagine that Kobulov (who was, incidentally, quite illiterate) had come to the conclusion that Lysenko's Lamarckism was more reliable as a biological theory than Vavilov's Darwinism. It was not the president of the Lenin Academy or Michurinist biology that Beria's organization was taking under its wing, but the dearly loved favorite of Stalin. It must have been in the spring of 1939, at some top-level reception, that Lysenko had complained about the difficulties that Vavilov's supporters were causing, not to him, of course, but to Soviet agriculture. Lysenko was an excellent actor who knew how to arouse sympathy and fellow feeling when necessary. It is reasonable to suppose that he performed especially well in the Kremlin. He had succeeded in evoking a cry of displeasure from Stalin, and that was sufficient for Beria immediately to draw the "organizational conclusions." The fate of Nikolai Vavilov had been decided then, in the summer of 1939, and it was only circumstances of an international character that delayed his arrest for a few months.

In the summer of 1939 the Seventh International Congress of Geneticists was due to take place at last in Edinburgh, and there was much discussion in the world press about who was to preside over the congress—whether it was to be Vavilov or whether his place would be taken by the distinguished Scottish geneticist Dr. Crew. Vavilov received many letters about this issue from friends in Britain and America, most of them supporting him and hoping to see him in Edinburgh. With only two months to go before the congress opened, Vavilov applied for permission to leave Russia to attend it. He wrote first to Komarov, then to Molotov, the prime minister, and to Litvinov, the foreign minister, and did his best to persuade them that his trip was not a personal affair but something that would raise the country's international prestige. He argued that there was political advantage in having the congress under the aegis of the Soviet Union, a country that had had brilliant successes in the field of genetics, and he thought it would influence Western intellectuals in the Soviet Union's favor.

In promising the Soviet leaders that they would derive some *political* benefit from the congress, Vavilov was employing an innocent diplomatic trick. But the idea of the country's prestige apparently had a different sense for Stalin and those around him from what it had for Vavilov. Komarov called on several government offices, but Molotov kept stalling, refusing to commit himself in reply to Vavilov's application. He was of course a clever enough politician to know the sort of international scandal there would be when it became known in the West that Soviet geneticists had been refused permission to attend the congress. But he was much more concerned with the domestic situation—with how Stalin regarded the question.

The domestic situation became clear in July when Molotov received a letter from Beria devoted especially to Vavilov and the situation in biology. As commissar for state security, Beria informed Molotov that, according to information in his possession, following Academician Lysenko's appointment as president of the Academy of Agriculture, N. I. Vavilov and the bourgeois school of so-called formal geneticists that he headed had organized a systematic campaign aimed at discrediting Lysenko as a scholar. Beria did not conceal the purpose behind his letter: he expected Molotov, then in charge of science in the Central Committee, to agree to Vavilov's arrest. There was nothing in Beria's letter about Vavilov's Trotskyist views, his "wrecking activities," or his alleged association with Bukharin and Milyukov. In official correspondence between two statesmen there was no need for such window dressing. Both Beria and Molotov knew that Academician Vavilov had to be destroyed because he would not accept Lysenko's "discoveries," which annoyed Comrade Stalin. Such was the unvarnished truth. To dress it up in suitable forms and manufacture charges against Vavilov as a "wrecker" and a spy—those were details, pure practical matters that would be dealt with later by the *apparat* of the NKVD.

Among the papers I was able to examine I did not come across

Molotov's assent to Vavilov's arrest. There can be no doubt that he gave his blessing to Beria's proposal, as he had done many times in the past, but he delayed giving Beria an answer for several months: there was no point in making a fuss by arresting the president of the international congress just when it was meeting if this arrest could be made quietly a little later.

And so, no matter what clever traps Lieutenant Khvat laid for Vavilov, what new documents and testimonies were entered into case no. 1,500, or what incriminating things Vavilov said about himself, all the participants in the drama knew that Vavilov had been arrested because he would not recognize Lysenko's "discoveries," and that he was being tormented because he would not accept a state of affairs in which the Rasputin of agronomy wielded absolute power over Russian science. But this truth was kept concealed. In eleven months of questioning Lieutenant Khvat did not once pronounce the name of Lysenko in Vavilov's presence. Yet the unsavory truth seeped through every crack. It even crept into the decree for Vavilov's arrest, a document in which everything else is complete falsehood from beginning to end, but which says clearly:

> It has been established that, with the object of refuting the new theories in the field of vernalization and genetics put forward by the Soviet scholars Lysenko and Michurin, on instructions from Vavilov a number of departments in the Institute of Plant Breeding carried out special work to discredit the theories of Lysenko and Michurin. . . . By putting forward deliberately hostile theories, Vavilov campaigned against the theories and practical work of Lysenko, Michurin and Tsitsin which are of decisive importance for Soviet agriculture.[8]

After confessing to having been a "wrecker" and an "enemy of the people," Vavilov was left in peace. From September 1940 to March 1941 Lieutenant Khvat did not summon him for questioning. He remained alone in his cell and was able, at last, to rest. He was later to look back on that period of solitude with pleasure. His cell was dry and warm, well ventilated and well lit. From eleven o'clock at night till six in the morning he was allowed to sleep on a folding bed, and he did not go hungry. True, he was not allowed to

have books, but there was paper and pencil at hand—in case the
prisoner, seized by a desire to repent, wanted to provide further
testimony. Vavilov, always full of energy and plans, decided not to
waste a single day in the cell. He had long been impatient to write a
book summarizing his reflections on the evolution of world agriculture since earliest times. As the director of two institutes and vice-
president of the academy, he had not had time to work on such a
"narrowly theoretical" monograph. But as a prisoner he had time
on his hands, and he was not discouraged from embarking on the
composition of a major work without the aid of encyclopedias,
maps, and reference books. His own memory served as his library.
All we know about this work, however, is a reference to it in one of
Vavilov's letters to Beria: "During my stay in the NKVD's internal
prison while I was being interrogated, when I was able to have
paper and pencil, I wrote a long work—'A History of the Development of Agriculture'—dealing with the world's farming resources
and their use, dealing mainly with the USSR."[9]

While Vavilov was writing his last work, Lieutenant Khvat was
also not idle. From autumn 1940 to spring 1941 he managed to
arrest another five "accomplices" of Vavilov. In Leningrad the
police seized Leonid Ipatievich Govorov, one of Vavilov's oldest
friends and collaborators from his student days. Very like Chekhov
in appearance, Professor Govorov was a leading authority on
leguminous plants and knew all there was to know about the pea,
the runner bean, the French bean, the vetch, and the marsh pea. A
good family man, a serious scholar, and an extremely peaceable and
obliging person, Professor Govorov let his feelings have their head
only once, on the day when people at the Institute of Plant Breeding
first learned of Vavilov's arrest. Without saying a word to members
of his family or his colleagues, Govorov dashed off to Moscow to
seek an audience with Comrade Stalin. He considered it his duty as
a scholar and a citizen to open the Soviet leader's eyes to what a
remarkable person and scholar Russia was losing in the person of
Academician Vavilov. He was not allowed to see Stalin, so he tried
to get to Malenkov, also without success. It is said that, in his
efforts to be received in the Kremlin, Govorov neither ate nor slept
for several days. When he made his way back to Leningrad at last,
physically exhausted and spiritually destroyed, they arrested him as
an accomplice of Vavilov.

At about the same time a young professor of genetics, Georgi Dmitrieyevich Karpechenko, one of the most gifted geneticists of the twentieth century, was arrested in Leningrad. Educated in Europe and with a fine sense of humor, Karpechenko "confessed" at his very first questioning that his experiments on the doubling of a set of chromosomes were anti-Soviet in character. He assumed that such an absurd statement would attract the attention of the judges and enable him to demonstrate his innocence.

In addition to these two men in Leningrad who were really close to Vavilov, two others were brought to the NKVD's prison. One was from Kiev—Professor Panshin, director of the All-Union Institute of Sugar Beet, of whom Vavilov was not very fond; the other, from near Moscow, was a man called Zaporozhets, director of a fertilizer institute, whom Vavilov scarcely knew. Why the investigator decided to bring these five people together into one single case is a mystery. It was probably for purely personal reasons: Khvat's superiors rated the discovery of a *group* of criminals more highly than the exposure of a single, independently operating "enemy of the people." But whatever the reason, in March 1941 Vavilov was forced to halt his work on the book. He once again had to go through the grim process of interrogation.

It seems to me that the purpose behind the second round of the interrogation was simply to pin as many more charges as possible on Vavilov. The actual nature of the charges and whether they could be proved were of no importance to Khvat. In the bureaucratic task he was performing, the only thing that mattered was the *quantity* of secret police reports, records of questionings, and confrontations, not whether they were genuine. Khvat had to show that Vavilov was a really terrible criminal, whose hostility to the Soviet regime went back almost to 1917, and he strained his limited imagination to the full to think up what "crimes" had been committed. He forced Govorov and Karpechenko to confess that Vavilov had drawn them into an anti-Soviet organization. Panshin "testified" that Vavilov had opposed the government's decision about liquidating the so-called white patch in agriculture. (This matter concerned the sowing of wheat in the traditionally difficult regions of central Russia. Vavilov and his colleague Pisarev had in fact been the principal organizers of this important scientific and economic undertaking, which resulted in the production of millions of tons of additional grain for the nation.)[10] But Lieutenant Khvat was not interested in facts. He was loading the ship to make it sink and making up stories to give the appearance of legitimacy to the forthcoming murder.

Khvat's imagination was especially productive when it came to espionage and Vavilov's alleged contacts with foreign intelligence services. All he had at his disposal was a list of the countries that Vavilov had visited and the names of the European and American geneticists, plant breeders, and agronomists he had met. Since Vavilov *must* have handed over state secrets to someone somewhere, the case history gives names of numerous "messengers," including a French intelligence officer, the leaders of a German farmers' organization, and Danish diplomats.

This was not enough for Lieutenant Khvat. One day he presented Vavilov with the charge that as director of the Institute of Plant Breeding he had "damaged the landing grounds in the Leningrad Military Region by sowing the airports with seeds containing weeds." With his keen sense of humor, Vavilov must have smiled as he read such rubbish. But it was no laughing matter for Lieutenant Khvat. On June 22, 1941, because of the outbreak of war, interrogators received instructions to speed up the transfer of their cases to the court. There arose a real danger that anyone who did a bad job might be sent to the front. Khvat became anxious and an element of hysteria crept into his entries in the case. On June 29 he entered in the file as "damning material in the Vavilov case" a manifesto of the counterrevolutionary "Byelorussian Alliance," allegedly found during the search of Vavilov's apartment, as well as a photograph of Alexander Kerensky. The new documents purported to expose contacts between Vavilov, the Trotskyist, with extreme monarchists, at the same time as he was supposed to be a supporter of the Provisional Government, which had brought down the monarchy. Lieutenant Khvat's knowledge of history was on a level with his knowledge of botany. But that did not matter. The Military Collegium of the Supreme Court of the USSR, sentencing on the same day both Vavilov, the great botanist, and Academician Luppol, the well-known Soviet philosopher, founder and director of the Institute of World Literature of the Soviet Academy, found nothing wrong with the indictment that Khvat and his colleagues had concocted.

The course of the second stage of the investigation was de-

scribed in 1968 by Grigori Fillipovsky, an artist and illustrator and a
member of the Soviet Artists' Union, who in the spring of 1941
spent several months in the Butyrki prison in Moscow, in cell 27 on
the second floor of the old prison building.[11] There were more than
two hundred prisoners in a cell intended to accommodate twenty-
five. Practically no air could get in through the little window; the
atmosphere and the overcrowding were indescribable. The prisoners were continually being changed—some being taken off to be
executed, others being transferred to a camp. But some of them
stayed there quite a long time—Kozhevnikov, the famous military
commander in the Civil War, Manyan, the builder of the Monche-
gor mining complex, and Bzhezinsky, the designer of Soviet battle-
ships. When Fillipovsky was thrust into the cell, he noticed immediately a strange figure among the prisoners who were lying, sitting,
and standing around—an elderly man lying on a bunk with his
swollen legs raised up. It was Academician Vavilov. He had only
recently returned from a night-long interrogation during which the
interrogator had kept him standing for more than ten hours. His
face was swollen, there were bags beneath his eyes indicating heart
trouble, and the soles of his feet were swollen and looked to
Fillipovsky to be huge and gray in color. Every night Vavilov was
taken off for questioning. At dawn a warder would drag him back
and throw him down at the cell door. Vavilov was no longer able to
stand and had to crawl on all fours to his place on the bunk. Once
there his neighbors would somehow remove his boots from his
swollen feet and he would lie still on his back in his strange position
for several hours.

Vavilov, who had always been sociable and cheerful, changed
completely after the second round of interrogation and retired into
himself, practically never exchanging any words with his cell-mates
or telling them what went on in Khvat's office. But once, when
Vavilov was not present, they told Fillipovsky about the sort of
"dialogues" that were taking place between the vice-president of the
Academy of Agriculture and his interrogator. Every time he was
brought in, Khvat asked him the same question:

"Who are you?"

"I am Academician Vavilov."

"You're a load of shit and not an academician," the valiant
lieutenant would say and then, eyeing his humiliated "enemy" in

triumph, he would proceed to interrogate him. Fillipovsky observed Vavilov for about six weeks. Then Vavilov disappeared. We now know that he was returned to the Lubyanka prison until his trial.

The trial took place on July 9, 1941. Before handing the indictment over to the court, Khvat reviewed once again the material he had manufactured and decided to guard against all eventualities by obtaining one further document—an expert opinion regarding Vavilov's scientific work.

Fourteen years later, in June 1955, as he was checking through case no. 1,500, the prosecutor, Major of Justice Kolesnikov, invited Professor Yakushkin of the Timiryazev Academy to call on him. Yakushkin was not in the least reticent and spoke quite frankly about being recruited by the OGPU in 1930 and the slanderous secret reports he had written. He had a lot to say about the "expert" opinion provided in 1941. The commission of experts had been carefully chosen:

> Apparently I was specially selected, as a secret collaborator with the NKVD who would have no difficulty in reaching the necessary conclusion about Vavilov. To be quite honest, the members of the expert commission—Vodkov, Chuyenkov, Mosolov and Zubarev—were all very hostile to Vavilov. Vodkov simply hated him. Chuyenkov was very much under Lysenko's influence and was a natural opponent of Vavilov. Zubarev was a colleague of Lysenko's and also much under his influence. And Mosolov, being Lysenko's assistant, was also an opponent of Vavilov. The expert commission was formed with the specific purpose of providing a deliberately prejudiced and negative opinion of Vavilov's work.[12]

One of the other members of the "expert" commission, Aleksei Zubarev, told Prosecutor Kolesnikov:

> The expert opinion was arrived at in this way: in 1941, after the outbreak of war with the Germans, Major Shundenko of the NKVD summoned me and Chuyenkov and told us that we had to provide an opinion in the Vavilov case. I no longer remember the details. . . . But I

do remember that our commission never met together as a whole and did not make any special inquiries. . . . However, when we were presented with the final text of the opinion (who drew it up I don't know), I, like the other experts, signed it. At that time I was unable not to sign it, because circumstances made it difficult not to do so.[13]

The "circumstances" were indeed not the best. The so-called opinion of the expert commission repeated practically word for word the charges that filled the other ten volumes of the Vavilov case. It included "arguments in defense of metaphysical and anti-Darwinistic ideas," "lack of attention to local varieties," and an unwillingness to engage in practical plant selection. Perhaps for the sake of variety, someone added that Vavilov had filled his Institute of Plant Breeding with "alien elements," because among the scientists were no fewer than twenty-one who came from titled families, eight whose fathers had been in holy orders, twelve children of men honored by the tsarist regime, ten descendants of merchants, and fourteen of middle-class extraction. Already identified as a Trotskyist and a monarchist, Vavilov was in addition denounced for not liking the working class.

Zubarev's testimony throws some light on the person who was most closely involved in the actual composition of the shameful "expert opinion": "I have to say in addition that the Major Shundenko who interrogated me and Chuyenkov at the offices of the State Security in 1941 concerning the preparation of an opinion about Vavilov's work had previously worked—in particular in 1938—in the All-Union Institute of Plant Breeding as a scientist, basing his work on the Michurin-Lyseno views." Who was this scientific worker who changed the white coat of a research worker for the uniform of an employee of the State Security?

Stepan Nikolayevich Shundenko is well remembered by the older members of the institute. "You felt there was something dangerous about him, in his rather frail, restless body and his dark eyes, which had a penetrating, furtive look," Professor Sinskaya wrote. "He quickly became friendly with another equally repulsive type, a graduate student by the name of Grigori Shlykov, and between them they set about disorganizing the life of the institute."[14] Geneticist Mikhail Khadzhinov summed up Shundenko:

In 1937 I was working in the Institute of Plant Breeding. On one occasion I received a reprimand from the party committee because my student Shundenko had not submitted his thesis to the examiners. I replied that Shundenko was simply not capable of writing a thesis and that he had neither the necessary theoretical knowledge nor the experimental data. "Nevertheless he must receive a degree," I was told. "If you can't teach him, write it for him yourself." And, however ashamed I am to admit it now, I did in fact dictate a thesis for Shundenko for which he very soon received his doctorate.

In 1937 Khadzhinov, who did not belong to the Communist party and was close to Vavilov, could do nothing else. The institute was shaken by internal and external storms. Graduate students, including Shundenko, made all sorts of difficulties for their scientific supervisors, the older professors, demanding that they teach not the "bourgeois fabrications" of Mendel and Morgan but Lysenko's "people's agrobiology." Prezent, the *éminence grise* of the Lysenko clique, made special visits to the institute to set the young people against their teaching staff. Vavilov and other leading scientists in the institute realized, of course, that the provocative impudence of Shundenko and other equally illiterate young people was being stoked up from outside, but Shundenko's actual role remained for a long time a secret.

In the spring of 1938, despite Vavilov's vigorous protest, Shundenko was appointed deputy director of the institute on the scientific side. As soon as he took up his new position, the former graduate student announced that he did not share Academician Vavilov's mistaken views on genetics and plant breeding, and he began talking about the "enemies" who had concealed themselves in the institute and who would sooner or later be exposed by Academician Lysenko. Immediately after Vavilov's arrest Shundenko disappeared from the institute altogether. Dr. Nina Bazilevskaya, the biologist, remembers coming across him again in Moscow in 1941: "It was in a café opposite the GUM department store. Shundenko was in the uniform of the NKVD. He smiled but did not come across to talk to me. I could not make out what rank he had, but it was said that he was promoted several ranks for his part in the Vavilov operation. In any case, it is quite clear that he had been working for the secret police previously, when he was a student."[15]

There can be no doubt that Major Shundenko of the State Security provided indispensable services to the interrogator Lieutenant Khvat. He knew who was who and what was what at the institute and which charges to make against which people. Nobody else could pick out as quickly as he the experts the prosecutor needed or compose the text of the experts' opinion as competently, and nobody could provide the interrogator with such excellent scientific-sounding statements better than Dr. Stepan Shundenko. "An amazingly ignorant man, Shundenko was incapable of speaking in public and was completely helpless in a laboratory or an experimental farm, but he was a virtuoso when it came to organizing Vavilov's opponents and he was a real master of intrigue," said Academician Khadzhinov.

The story of the "expert opinion" includes another little episode worthy of note. Having drawn up a list of the experts serving on the commission, Khvat sent it to the president of the Academy of Agriculture so that he might "acquaint himself with the list and give his opinion of its composition." President Lysenko did so. The document still bears his comment, written in a bold hand: "Agreed, Lysenko."

We do not know whether Vavilov succeeded in finishing his work on the history of agriculture by the beginning of July. But there is no doubt at all that on July 5, 1941, Lieutenant Khvat had completed *his* work, which had demanded of him no little effort and skill. In eleven months Vavilov had been subjected to interrogation no less than four hundred times, taking up seventeen hundred hours of the interrogator's waking hours. And there were four other participants in the conspiracy to be questioned. But Khvat's task was at last over, the case was complete, the indictment had been confirmed by his superiors, and the portrait of Kerensky and the manifesto of the Great Russian Alliance all accepted and approved. Now it was up to the court to do its work.

What took place on July 9, 1941, and was described officially as a closed session of the Military Collegium of the Supreme Court of the USSR, did not bear the slightest relationship to judicial proceedings. The collegium consisted of three generals (chairman: divisional military advocate Suslin; members: divisional military advocate Dmitriev and brigade military advocate Klimin) and a secretary. The generals passed sentence without calling any witnesses or lawyers. In a matter of minutes they determined that former member of the Soviet Academy of Science N. I. Vavilov had indeed committed offenses covered by articles 58-1a, 58-7, 58-9, and 58-11 of the Criminal Code of the Russian republic. Describing the procedure later, Vavilov wrote: "At the trial, which lasted a few minutes in a military atmosphere, I declared categorically that the charges were based on hearsay, untruths and slanders which had not been confirmed to any degree by the investigation." But the judges had no need to hear the defendant. The sentence had already been drawn up and was in the chairman's briefcase.

> In the name of the Union of Soviet Socialist Republics . . . it has been established in the course of a preliminary and judicial inquiry that from 1925 Vavilov was one of the leaders of an anti-Soviet organization known as the "Party of the Working Peasantry," and from 1930 was an active participant in an anti-Soviet organization of right-wingers operating within the Commissariat for Agriculture and several scientific institutions in the USSR. . . . In the interests of these anti-Soviet organizations he carried on widespread wrecking activity aimed at disrupting and destroying the collective farm system and the collapse and decline of socialist agriculture in the USSR. . . . Pursuing anti-Soviet aims he maintained contacts with White émigré circles abroad and transmitted to them information containing state secrets of the Soviet Union.
>
> Declaring Vavilov to be guilty of the offenses covered by articles 58-1a, 58-7, 58-9, and 58-11 of the Criminal Code of the RSFSR, the Military Collegium of the Supreme Court of the USSR sentences Vavilov, Nikolai Ivanovich, to suffer the supreme penalty—to be shot and all his personal property to be confiscated. The sentence is final and is not open to appeal.

Only one other body could stop the sentence being carried out—the Presidium of the Supreme Soviet of the USSR, which was headed at the time by the much-loved and respected elder statesman Mikhail Kalinin. On the evening of July 9, Vavilov wrote on a small sheet of paper in ink (specially issued for such purposes) the following request for a pardon:

> To the Presidium of the Supreme Soviet of the USSR.
>
> Appeal by Vavilov, Nikolai Ivanovich, former member of the Academy of Science of the USSR, Vice-President of the Academy of Agriculture and Director of the All-Union Institute of Plant Breeding, sentenced to the supreme penalty of death by shooting:
>
> I humbly entreat the Presidium of the Supreme Soviet to grant me a pardon and to give me the opportunity to atone by my work for my guilt in the eyes of the Soviet regime and the Soviet people.
>
> Having devoted 30 years to research work in the field of plant breeding (recognized by the award of the Lenin Prize, etc.) I pray that I may be granted the most minimal possibility of completing work for the benefit of the socialist agriculture of my Motherland.
>
> As an experienced educator I pledge myself to give myself over entirely to the training of Soviet specialists. I am 53.
>
> 20.00 hours.
> 9.VII.1941.
>
> > Person under sentence:
> > N. Vavilov.
> > former Academician, doctor of biology and agronomy.

Vavilov waited seventeen days for a reply to his request. Not until July 26 was it made known that the Presidium of the Supreme Soviet had refused to pardon Vavilov. He was transferred to the Butyrki prison for the sentence to be carried out.

7   In Search of Justice

*Where is Vavilov, one of the greatest Russian
scholars and one of the greatest geneticists in the world?
Vavilov was elected President of the International
Congress in Edinburgh in 1939. But he didn't turn up
there and from then on we have heard nothing of him.*
                    Karl Saks, Science, December 21, 1945

*When that great, intelligent and happy man, who
had borne with so little fuss and with such apparent
ease the burden of a tremendous amount of scientific
and public work, went out of our lives, we were left
with a terrible feeling of emptiness.*
                            Lidia Breslavets

The news that its director had been arrested reached the
Institute of Plant Breeding on August 12, 1940, when Bakhteyev,
Vavilov's favorite pupil, returned to Leningrad from the Ukraine.
His story about the black automobile, whose passengers were so
determined to seek out Academician Vavilov in the Carpathian
foothills, and about the visitors who came in the night to
Chernovitsy to collect Vavilov's things, spread quickly around the
laboratories. The last note that Vavilov wrote was passed from hand
to hand. Everybody understood that Vavilov's arrest and the political character of the case would mean the end of Vavilov's teaching,
the end of the institute, and possibly the end of Soviet biology. But
people were so reluctant to believe such a frightful thing had
happened that for several weeks members of the institute staff tried
to convince themselves and others that it was nothing more than a
misunderstanding. In their conversations with one another they
kept repeating, as a sort of incantation, that in a day or two
everything would be explained—the officers of the secret police
would talk with Vavilov and would see at once what a transparently
honest and decent man he was.

If this sounds rather naive, it must be remembered that in August 1940 not a single truthful word had yet been uttered about Stalin's victims, about the millions of people who had come under the heading, as under a shroud, of "enemies of the people." A great country was still passing through a period of great naiveté, and the scientists at the Institute of Plant Breeding were not an exception. They believed, or they wanted to believe, what they said: they were incapable of imagining the institute without Vavilov, for until then it had lived and moved by virtue of his ideas, his energy, and his enthusiasm.

For some weeks confusion reigned in the institute. Earlier in August, the organizers of the All-Union Agricultural Exhibition had announced their decision to award Vavilov their gold medal for his services to the country's agriculture. Then, suddenly, came his arrest. Another six months went by before, in December 1940, Lysenko's deputy, Academician Mosolov, signed a decree excluding Vavilov from membership of the Lenin Academy of Agriculture. Then the deputy commissar for Agriculture, Dorogov, ordered that Vavilov be dismissed from his position as vice-president of the Academy and director of the Institute of Plant Breeding.[1] From August to December, people at the institute continued to cherish the faint hope that things would still turn out all right, imagining that one day the door of the laboratory would open and Nikolai Vavilov, smiling and full of life, would walk in. But events of a quite different kind began to take place. Vavilov's office in the institute and his apartments in Moscow and Leningrad were subjected to elaborate searches by the police. Plainclothes police pulled up the floorboards and searched the attics and the cellars. They were said to be looking for some bombs, according to Professor Sinskaya, and rumor said they found some. Soon after that the "official" version of Vavilov's arrest began to circulate—he was said to have undertaken the expedition to the western Ukraine deliberately with a view to escaping abroad but to have been caught crossing the frontier. Nobody in the institute believed that story. But the people who had put the story around were not concerned about the views of the students and colleagues of the man they had arrested. The fate of Vavilov's friends and colleagues had already been decided in advance.

Professor Sinskaya described the events:

Then began the brutal dispersal of the institute. Conferences and party meetings became quite unbearable.
Every one of us was in real danger of suffering a heart
attack or something similar. . . . One of the first victims of
the reign of terror was the head of the biochemical department of the institute, the elderly professor N. N. Ivanov.
He became so excited at a meeting of one of the learned
councils that he carried on the argument in his office,
which they wanted to take away from him, then went
home and said: "It's no good going on living like that." He
lay down and an hour later they found him dead.

Specialists with the sort of unique qualifications that Ivanov
had became the objects of real persecution. Even in 1937, agents of
the security police and the new director, J. H. Eikhfeld (an able
agronomist with a good knowledge of biology but a faithful follower of Lysenko), appeared to vie with each other to see who
could knock out more of the "intellectuals." One after the other
leading scholars, geneticists, biologists, and plant breeders, some of
them with international reputations, were put under arrest. Any
scientists employed at the institute who had ever voiced unfavorable
opinions about Lysenko were ordered to be "transferred to productive work," which meant that they were transported by force to
work on the collective and state farms.

The mass deportation of scholars was not an invention of the
new bosses of the institute. It was an "undertaking" planned on a
nationwide scale by Benediktov, the commissar for agriculture. He
ordered that one-third of all scientists specializing in biology and
agriculture should be sent to work on a collective farm, a state farm,
or some local land office to "strengthen" them. The order was
issued on January 2, 1940, and only five days later Lysenko,
president of the Lenin Academy, gave instructions to "review the
structure of the administration of the academy and the institutes
with a view to reducing the number of separate units."[2] So long as
Vavilov remained director of the Institute of Plant Breeding he had
resisted as best he could the destruction of the "units"—the laboratories and departments. But in the autumn of 1940, Eikhfeld used
the commissar's order as a legitimate basis for deporting a great
many scientists from Leningrad.

The "destruction of Babylon," which had been planned by
Lysenko's people back in 1938 and 1939, reached its climax in the
autumn of 1940. Lysenko sent to the institute a man close to him,
by the name of Zubarev, with a special investigation commission.
The commission was supposed to confirm that in its present form
the institute was not only failing to bring any benefit to agriculture
but was even interfering with the work of the collective and state
farms. Aided by the general atmosphere of terror and fear, members
of the commission had no difficulty in performing the tasks set
them. Zubarev carried out a series of crudely conducted interviews,
insulted and ridiculed the older members of the teaching staff, and
forced some of them to resign and others to accept his unlawful
actions. Even people who were not directly affected by the commission's activities realized that Lysenko would not rest until he had
razed Vavilov's creation to the very foundations.

Although the Soviet press did not print a line about what was
going on within the walls of the institute, and the radio said nothing
about the destruction of the finest scientific plant-breeding institution in the world, the news that the institute would inevitably be
destroyed spread quickly around the country. In Uzbekistan, the
Crimea, and the northern Caucasus the local government and land
authorities began seizing farms and other property belonging to the
Leningrad institute. The network of experimental stations covering
all the soil and climatic zones of the USSR, which Vavilov had set up
over decades, began to be torn to pieces. The local authorities
reorganized the whole of the scientific work in their newly acquired
institutions and, of course, halted all research work initiated by
Vavilov.

On November 25, 1940, the Presidium of the Lenin Academy
of Agriculture assembled on Bolshoi Kharitonov Street in Moscow,
in an old building that had once been the home of the princely
family of the Yusupovs and had elaborately decorated walls, doors
padded with velvet, and a gilded sculpture of a lion standing in the
front vestibule. It was not long since such gatherings had contained
the most distinguished figures in Russian agricultural sciences—
Academicians Vavilov, Tulaikov, Meister, Koltsov, Serebrovsky,
Lisitsyn, and Konstantinov. Now the only people round the table
were Lysenko's creatures—Prezent, Polyachenko, Mosolov, Tsit-
sin, and Zubarev. They had also invited the people who had in

recent years been directing the fifth column inside the institute—Eikhfeld, Sizov, Teterev, and Shlykov. The day of their triumph had come at last. Vavilov was in prison and the whole institute was holding its breath, waiting to learn its fate.

Protocol no. 18 of the Presidium of the Lenin Academy, dated November 25, 1940, set out in plain terms why the meeting had been called. After listening to Eikhfeld's report the Presidium resolved:

> The All-Union Institute of Plant Breeding has not dealt satisfactorily with the tasks before it, as is apparent from the material in the hands of the [Zubarev] commission that examined the institute's affairs:
>
> a. Although the institute assembled large collections of cultivated plants, it was not invariably governed by the usefulness of the material being collected and it is now difficult to establish the scientific or practical value of each sample in the collection;
>
> b. The study of the collections obtained was wrongly organized and did not produce results of any practical or scientific value. Careless handling of the collections resulted in the loss of some of the samples;
>
> c. The institute did not do sufficient work on the development of varieties likely to result in increased crop yields.

This resolution was all untrue. Shlykov and Eikhfeld knew very well what tremendous scientific and practical value the 360,000 samples of cultivated plants collected by Vavilov and his team represented. Vavilov himself had collected 60,000 of them during his expeditions. The specimens were carefully preserved and had been studied so seriously and in such detail as to evoke the envy of Western biologists. Lysenko also knew the truth, but he had brought the Presidium of the academy together not to establish the truth about the institute but to put an end to it; that is what he did. The Presidium passed a series of resolutions transferring sections of the institute to other bodies or suppressing them altogether. The resolutions were signed by Lysenko.

Everyone who described later the way the institute was broken up invariably talked about the fear that prevailed. The new people put in charge of the institute thought nothing of depriving uncooperative members of the staff of their degrees or their laboratories, of having them sent to some remote corner of the country, or even of having them arrested. Sheer fright took hold of all the employees, especially the older ones and those with families. Nobody felt safe. Vavilov had taught people to be bold in their defense of scientific principles when confronted with an honest opponent. But the situation that developed after Lysenko's people took over bore little relation to a genuine scientific debate. Eikhfeld and his gang (Sizov, Shlykov, Pereverzev, Teterev, Orel, Khoroshailov, Ponomarev, and Sidorov) were united primarily by a desire to acquire the good things that followed from appointment to a high position and a professorial chair. The so-called teaching of Michurin and Lysenko was for them a password to the receipt of a high salary, and Vavilov's arrest made it possible for them to grab whatever they wanted.

A scientist who survived the wartime blockade of Leningrad said he found the situation in the institute in the autumn of 1940 similar to that of the winter of 1942. Abandoned in Leningrad during the blockade, the institute's collection attracted thousands of starving rats. At night the rodents would invade the laboratories by the thousands, hurl the metal boxes containing priceless specimens from the shelves, and gobble up indiscriminately the fruits, seeds, nuts, and other items that had been collected with such difficulty on Vavilov's expeditions. Members of the staff, themselves weak from lack of food, would arm themselves with metal rods and try to beat off the invaders. At first the rats were afraid of humans and retreated from flashlights, but as the blockade continued through the winter, the rats became ever more brazen and eventually turned into dangerous predators ready to attack human beings.

Despite the prevailing atmosphere of fear, however, in 1940 Vavilov's remaining supporters suppressed their fears and came to the defense of their director. At the end of August members of the institute's staff—N. A. Bazilevskaya, N. V. Kovalev, M. A. Rozanova, and E. A. Stoletova—drew up a letter to the Central Committee of the Communist party, the government, and the NKVD. They said that they had known Vavilov for many years and were absolutely convinced of his loyalty to the Soviet regime and the Communist party; they therefore requested that, as a leading scientist and organizer of scientific work, he should be released. Nine people signed the letter. But when the Kovalevs showed it to a relation who worked for the NKVD, he warned them that, if their complaint went forward in that form, all nine of them would be arrested; he thought it would be better if only one of them signed it.

It was Nina Aleksandrova Bazilevskaya who took the risk, since all the others had small children. She was soon summoned to appear at the headquarters of the Communist party in Leningrad, where she again tried to demonstrate Vavilov's innocence. She even went so far as to say that, if Vavilov were to be banished, then most of the people at the institute would follow him into exile, whether it was to Siberia or even Kamchatka. The reply she received from a party official was: "Nonsense. We don't make mistakes when it comes to arresting people. Get on with your work quietly and don't bother leading officials with trifles." Three days later Bazilevskaya was dismissed from the institute.

The search for justice continued. Professor Sinskaya turned for support to L. O. Orbeli, vice-president of the Academy of Science. A forthright and honest man, Obeli wrote to some official, but a few days he later informed Sinskaya that it was impossible to help Vavilov and that his influence, at any rate, was not sufficient. Other efforts to intervene were made in great secrecy. Vavilov's closest friend, Professor Leonid Govorov, slipped off on the quiet to Moscow in the hope of obtaining an audience in the Kremlin.

Maria Shebalina, from the department of fodder crops, went to see Vavilov's younger brother, Sergei. A senior member of the institute's staff and the chair of its trade union, Shebalin took Sergei Vavilov a specially prepared memorandum of several dozen pages (typed in secret by the institute's typists), setting forth in great detail all the material benefits that the Soviet Union had derived from the expeditions, experimental work, and research carried out by Nikolai Vavilov. Twenty-five years later Maria Shebalina told me, "We thought that Nikolai Ivanovich's persecutors would be horrified to see the tremendous loss his arrest would inflict on the state." But Academician Sergei Vavilov, director of the state optical institute, apparently did not share the naive hopes of the people from Vavilov's Institute of Plant Breeding. He received Shebalina on Vasilevsky Island, in a fine building in which all the apartments had long been occupied by members of the Russian Academy of

Science. "It was at the end of August," Maria Shebalina said. "Sergei Vavilov sat in his study at a large desk and I sat opposite him. I well remember his indistinct, colorless manner of speaking and his seemingly empty, tired eyes. He didn't even bother to read the memorandum that we had put together with such effort. Stroking his graying hair rather absently, he said: 'There is no misunderstanding here. My brother has been arrested on the orders, or at least with the knowledge, of the first person in the land. We can hardly hope to do anything about it.' "[3]

Sergei Vavilov was apparently right. All attempts to save his brother came to grief against an invisible but very solid wall. Vavilov's tragic fate soon became a forbidden topic of conversation. The grindstones of governmental repression reduced to dust anyone who tried even to mention it. Professors Kovalev and Govorov were arrested, and Bazilevskaya, Sinskaya, and Shebalina were driven out of the institute.

Still there smoldered on among the people working at the institute a belief, perhaps not in the justice of the powers that be, but in what might be called their wisdom. The authorities might well be cruel and unjust, but it made no sense for them to inflict losses on their own country and ruin its agriculture. It was obvious that the members of the Central Committee of the party simply did not realize that breaking up the institute and Vavilov's arrest would result in the collapse of Russian agricultural science and later in a lowering of crop yields and a crisis in agriculture. If the Central Committee could be told the truth about the scandalous actions of Lysenko and the secret police, then the institute and Vavilov would be saved. Once again Bazilevskaya assumed the role of messenger.

Bazilevskaya left Leningrad, where no one would give her a job, and called on Sergei Vavilov in Moscow to ask him to help her to meet someone in the Central Committee of the party. The younger Vavilov promised to arrange a meeting with Andrei Andreyev, a member of the committee and the person in charge of agricultural matters. The meeting eventually took place in February 1941. Bazilevskaya had prepared a long speech explaining Lysenko's dictatorial behavior and describing what was going on in the Institute of Plant Breeding and other scientific departments of the Academy of Agriculture. Andreyev was in a position to obtain a fairly complete and objective account of what was happening to

Soviet biology and agricultural science. Though Bazilevskaya had been warned that Andreyev was extremely busy and would give her only a few minutes, the meeting lasted less time than she had imagined. She had hardly started to explain the fatal mistake that had been committed in Vavilov's case when Andreyev interrupted her with one sentence, which she repeated to me later: "There could be no fatal mistake; there are facts of which you are not aware." With that the audience came to an end.

It was not only the Institute of Plant Breeding that was thrown into confusion in the autumn of 1940. According to reports received by agents of the secret police, Vavilov's arrest had a disastrous effect throughout the Soviet Academy of Science. Reports at the time said that the academicians were convinced that the arrest had been carried out at Lysenko's insistence. Academician Luzin described the arrest as "the latest horror"; he said that Vavilov could not have committed any crime and that he was a victim of slander and intrigue. "What have they done! They've put a citizen of the world behind bars!" exclaimed Academician Pryanishnikov when he heard the details of the arrest in Chernovitsy. Even the president of the academy, Vladimir Komarov, was not unmoved: he told Academician Zavadovsky that Vavilov had been sent to prison like a rogue, a gangster, or a murderer "because he had the courage not to agree with Lysenko."[4]

Komarov's opinion, recorded by such responsible people as the secret agents of the State Security,[5] is of special interest because the part he played in Vavilov's fate varied greatly. Academician Komarov (1869–1945), a distinguished botanist and authority on flora, naturally despised Lysenko. He can have derived very little pleasure from the comedy of the "election" of Stalin's favorite to membership of the academy in January 1939. But Komarov was also jealous of Vavilov's worldwide reputation. It did no good that on every suitable occasion Vavilov declared, in speeches and in writing, that pride of place in Russian botany belonged to Komarov, because Komarov knew perfectly well that he was not, in fact, the first person in that branch of science. For several years Komarov had to play a double game, maneuvering between the two opposing forces in biology, and his maneuvers did not always do him credit.

The wife of Doncho Kostov recalled an episode that took place at a meeting in the academy in 1939. Lysenko had made a speech in his usual threatening, aggressive tone. He was followed by Komarov, president of the academy, who agreed with what he had said. When the meeting was over, Komarov invited Vavilov and Kostov to join him in his office, where he took Lysenko's book out of a drawer and started to criticize it and to ridicule its author for his lack of education. Vavilov frowned, made a few ironic comments, and abruptly took his leave. He made it quite clear to everyone by his manner that he found Komarov's duplicity disagreeable. When they left Komarov's room, Vavilov nodded in the direction of the huge presidential doorway and asked Kostov, "Did you see that? How do you like our Vasili Shuisky [the sly courtier made famous by Pushkin]?"[6]

Something else set the two botanists apart. In the field of general biological teaching Komarov was closer to Lysenko than to Vavilov, rejecting the works of Morgan, Bateson, and Nilson-Ele and the conclusions drawn by modern science about the gene as the carrier of an organism's hereditary characteristics. Vavilov's views on the gene, he said in one of his books, "evokes in us a strong desire to contradict him."

Vavilov's arrest did not, however, make life any easier for the "sly courtier." Rather the reverse. When he found he was not meeting any serious resistance in the scientific world, Lysenko threw aside all restraint. Within the Academy of Agriculture he made himself an absolute autocrat.[7] In the Academy of Science he behaved with a little more restraint, but even there he let it be known that henceforward he intended to be the real master in the field of biology. It is not difficult to imagine the mixture of shame, fear, and helpless rage experienced by Komarov as he watched a semiliterate agronomist do as he pleased in the academy's Institute of Genetics.

The Institute of Genetics had been the pride of the academy. Founded in 1934 on Vavilov's initiative, it had in six years come to be recognized as one of the most important centers of scientific research in the world. Geneticists who worked there included Sapegin, Shmuk, Navashin, Lepin, Herman Muller, and Doncho Kostov. Well-known scientists came from Britain, the United States, and Germany to lecture there. But with the disappearance of Vavilov, the Institute of Genetics suffered the same fate as the

Institute of Plant Breeding. In March 1941 Academician Dmitri Nikolayevich Pryanishnikov wrote to Beria:

> Following the appointment of T. D. Lysenko as director of the Institute of Genetics of the Soviet academy (the manner of his appointment deserves separate treatment) practically all the really able scientists (Navashin, Shmuk, Sapegin, Medvedev, etc.) have been dismissed from the institute (or have left of their own accord). The program of work drawn up by the new director of the Institute of Genetics reveals a striking poverty of thought; it contains no genetics but only elementary farming technology, the same insistence on the late planting of potatoes over 300,000 hectares, the same "experiments" with the autumn sowing of clover, the same cutting up of the roots of kok-sarghyz—a mere repetition of the work done by the Commissariat for Agriculture on farm technology.[8]

The disruption of the Institute of Genetics soon brought about a state of paralysis in genetics research throughout the country. "I consider it a great and incomprehensible mistake that work on genetics, a science with a great future, has come to a stop in our country," wrote Academician V. I. Vernadsky in 1944. In another letter he wrote: "Unfortunately all the centers of scientific work on genetics in our country have been destroyed. I can tell by the appointment of scientists in the academy how disastrous are the consequences of that mistake on the part of the state."[9]

The invasion of vandalism into science forced Komarov to reconsider his attitude to Vavilov. On several occasions he voiced his sympathy for Nikolai Ivanovich, though not too loudly, and later even made certain representations in his defense. To tell the truth, the moves he made cost him a great deal. Komarov was afraid to act and tried to avoid doing anything, but Pryanishnikov and some of Vavilov's students were so insistent that on each occasion the head of the Academy of Science was forced to behave with greater decency and determination.

The most important person among those who had the courage to speak out publicly in defense of Vavilov was Dmitri Nikolayevich Pryanishnikov, who in 1940 was already seventy-five years of age. A most distinguished agrochemist, he had been awarded the title of hero of socialist labor as well as a Stalin Prize. But none of these "favors" altered the elderly scholar's sense of justice or his determined character. The disaster that had taken place in Chernovitsy affected him deeply. Quite unconcerned about being overheard, everywhere he went, in the Academy of Science, the Academy of Agriculture, the Timiryazev Academy, in conversation with students, with his scientific colleagues and with officials of the Commissariat for Agriculture, Pryanishnikov kept on asserting that Vavilov was not guilty of anything. In the spring of 1941 he wrote a letter to Beria criticizing Lysenko as a scientist and as leader of the Academy of Agriculture. He hoped in this way to undermine the confidence that Lysenko enjoyed among the top people so that Fortune might smile on Vavilov once again. But Beria refused to engage in scientific polemics, and Pryanishnikov's letter remained unanswered. From Samarkand, where he had been evacuated early in 1942, Pryanishnikov sent a telegram to Moscow submitting Vavilov's works for the award of a Stalin Prize. Such impudence might have cost him his life, since Stalin did not permit anybody to defend "state criminals." But Pryanishnikov got away with that breach of the rules on that occasion. Perhaps he was saved by the confusion of the war years, or perhaps the telegram from a seventy-five-year-old academician was simply regarded as the eccentricity of an old man.

In the autumn of 1942, as the country at war was celebrating its twenty-fifth anniversary, a special session of the Academy of Science was held in Sverdlovsk, attended by Russian academicians who were then scattered around the towns and villages of the Soviet Union. Pryanishnikov also arrived and was received politely by Komarov in his office. Lysenko, on the other hand, was refused an audience. During their conversation Pryanishnikov told Komarov frankly that Lysenko had murdered Vavilov so that he could grab his appointments and his position in the world of science. He appealed to Komarov to complain immediately to the Central Committee about the actions of the secret police. "What can I do?" Komarov said with a gesture of despair. "But Vyshinsky's coming here—ask him to help." Andrei Vyshinsky, academician, prosecutor general of the USSR, and organizer of the famous Stalin trials of the late 1930s, did in fact arrive in Sverdlovsk a little later. With all the tact he could summon, Komarov requested him to look into

Vavilov's case, to bear in mind . . . to take account of past merits. . . . But his pleading had no success. In his official and personal relations, Andrei Vyshinsky knew only one precept: "Always kick a man when he's down."

Pryanishnikov learned of the failure but did not call off his assault on Komarov. Six months later he found Komarov in Alma-Ata and again insisted that Komarov send a letter from the Academy of Science to the Central Committee of the party. "Our country will not forgive us Vavilov's premature death," Pryanishnikov repeated over and over. "You must understand, Vladimir Leontievich, it won't forgive us." But Komarov did not write: in such circumstances he preferred oral communications. When Pryanishnikov next approached him, in Moscow, after the academy had returned from evacuation, Komarov agreed to speak to Molotov about Vavilov's fate. The conversation actually took place, but Molotov had scarcely heard Vavilov's name mentioned when he said crossly: "I am not going to bother myself with that now, I've no time." It is possible that the all-powerful Vyacheslav Mikhailov really was very busy that day with urgent matters of state. But even if he had had eternity at his disposal, it is most unlikely that he would have done anything to help an academician in disgrace, whose arrest he had sanctioned personally only three years previously.

By the beginning of 1943 not only Komarov but also Pryanishnikov realized that Moloch had no intention of yielding up his victim, and anyone else in Pryanishnikov's place would have considered that he had done his duty: the weakest go to the wall. But Vavilov's teacher was a man of a very special kind. With his limp and his walking stick he would appear again and again in the office of the president of the academy, begging, arguing, insisting. His next idea was to draw up a letter and address it personally to Comrade Stalin.

In the winter of 1943, when Pryanishnikov was persuading Komarov to write about Vavilov to the Kremlin, another petitioner—Sergei Vavilov—called on the president. He had learned by some roundabout means that his brother Nikolai was suffering cruelly from lack of food in prison, that his health had been severely undermined, and that his very life was in danger. The conversation between the two academicians took place without witnesses, but the president's assistant saw Sergei Vavilov leave the office in tears. Komarov also appeared very upset. Something that had hitherto been a state secret was now apparent: Nikolai Vavilov, a man who had given his country millions of tons of grain, was dying of hunger in a prison cell. Sergei Vavilov was asking for the same action as Pryanishnikov—for the Academy of Science to inform Stalin immediately about everything. He even drafted a letter himself, saying that the greatest botanist of our time, Nikolai Ivanovich Vavilov, was in prison and his health had been undermined. The president of the Soviet Academy of Science was ready to make himself responsible for Vavilov. If it did not appear possible for Vavilov to be released, the president requested that he should be allowed to carry on his research into plant breeding.

A letter to Stalin was the last resort in the life of Soviet society in the 1930s and 1940s. In a country in which all laws were flouted, a citizen looked to the authorities not for respect for his rights but only for indulgence, not for justice but for mercy. At the time of the Stalinist terror the general atmosphere of fear and helplessness generated a blind faith in miracles, a faith in the power of letters to the all-highest to bring salvation. A sort of nationwide postal epidemic arose. Tens of *millions* of complaints were dispatched, addressed to "Stalin, the Kremlin." It was not just the backward inhabitants of the provinces who were gripped by this elemental faith in Stalin's mercy. The educated people in the capital appealed to the "last resort" just as devoutly and with the same faith.

Months passed. As usual, Stalin's office remained silent. In the autumn of 1943 Pryanishnikov again reminded the Presidium of the academy about the unsuccessful appeal. Komarov got busy and immediately ordered his assistant to speak to Stalin's personal secretary Poskrebyshev by private line. Poskrebyshev's reply was brief—the letter had been sent on to Beria. The circle was closed.

Accounts of the further developments reached me in several different versions. But Pryanishnikov's daughters, Komarov's assistant Chernov, and some of Vavilov's students agree about one thing—at the end of 1943 Pryanishnikov succeeded in obtaining an interview with Beria. It was apparently Beria's wife, who had worked with Pryanishnikov in the Timiryazev Academy, who helped to arrange the meeting. Beria received the elderly academician in his magnificent office in the building on Dzerzhinsky

Square. The commissar for state security and deputy prime minister was extremely amiable, even courteous. On his desk lay several volumes recording the investigation into Vavilov's case, and Pryanishnikov was given the opportunity of reading the testimony of Vavilov himself and of witnesses. "So there you are," Beria is supposed to have said as he turned the pages of the files. "There he writes in his own hand that he sold himself to the British intelligence service."[10] Pryanishnikov glanced through the documents, then pushed the big volumes away from him and declared that he did not believe what was written. He said he had known his student for nearly forty years and was convinced that he could be neither a spy nor a "wrecker." "I shall believe it only if he tells me it himself," the old man said in conclusion and, without taking his leave, moved toward the door. He wandered around for half an hour, not knowing where he was going and not seeing what was in front of him, until someone helped him to turn in his pass and leave the building.

Professor Alexsandr Kuptsov, another student of Pryanishnikov, recalled that in January 1944 he heard Pryanishnikov's own account of his unsuccessful attempts to help Vavilov. "Beria went along with those people who wanted to capitalize on the decline of our agriculture and the poverty of our peasants. Vavilov got in their way. He is no more. And we don't have the strength to do anything against them," Pryanishnikov said. Kuptsov remarked, "As he said this Dmitri Nikolayevich started to cry and he was still wiping his tired eyes with a handkerchief for a long time, although we had turned to other subjects of conversation."[11]

8 Into the Flames

We will go into the fire and we shall burn, but we shall not renounce our convictions.

N. I. Vavilov, March 15, 1939

In 1927 members of the staff of the Timiryazev Academy paid their last respects to their colleague Sergei Zhegalov, a talented plant selector and one of Professor Rudzinsky's most gifted students, who died before reaching the age of forty-five. Vavilov followed the coffin along with his schoolfriend Lidia Breslavets. It was a sad moment for both of them: Zhegalov reminded them of their youth, their happy student days, and their first scientific inquiries. Lidia Breslavets was in tears, because Zhegalov had died so young and because a scientist of such great promise had died without having achieved even a small part of what he had planned.

"Suddenly, to my surprise," Breslavets told me, "Nikolai Ivanovich said: 'A scholar has to die young. No scholar and no man of great ability ought to live too long.' "

"What about Darwin?" Breslavets inquired.

"Look, my dear, Darwin's a different question altogether—there cannot be anyone else like Darwin," Vavilov replied with a sad smile.

In 1927 Vavilov was still under forty. Did he really believe that a scientist produces everything of value only in his early years and that old age brings only rigidity, emptiness, and the painful approach of death? It seems to me that Vavilov's paradox conceals a different idea. A man of emotion and enthusiasms, Vavilov probably imagined for a moment what life would be like for him as an old man—life with a cold heart and mind. And he was horrified. It would not suit him at all. When, on another occasion, he returned to the same subject in conversation with another close friend, Vavilov expressed the hope that his death would be sudden. But his wish was not granted. Although Vavilov did in fact die a relatively young man, he died slowly, painfully, and agonizingly.

They did not execute him in the cellars of the Butyrki prison: his death sentence was postponed for a year and a half, a very long time for so diligent a person as Vavilov. If he had been at liberty, he could have read a pile of books, written several, organized expeditions, and initiated a whole series of experiments; he could have given speeches, held conversations with friends and students, and spent time with his family. But in prison the postponement meant simply that sudden death from a bullet was replaced by an agonizing death, utterly humiliating and interminably slow. And though it is possible with some degree of certainty to point to the people who landed Vavilov in prison and to those who sentenced him so unjustly, it is quite impossible to identify the people responsible for his slow murder over the following eighteen months. It was the work of the Stalin regime, the Stalin-Beria machine of destruction.

At first, however, a ray of hope shone into the death cell in which Vavilov was held, about which he wrote to Beria:

> On August 1, 1941, i.e. three weeks after I was sentenced, I was informed in the Butyrki prison by your agent in your name that you had petitioned the Presidium of the Supreme Soviet of the USSR for the sentence in my case to be set aside and that my life was to be spared. On October 4, 1941, I was transferred on your instructions from the Butyrki prison to the internal prison of the NKVD and on October 5 and 15 I had conversations with your agent about my attitude to the war and to fascism and about my employment as a scientist with long experience. I was informed on October 15 that I would be offered every possibility of carrying out scientific work as an academician and that the matter would be settled finally in the course of the next two or three days.[1]

There can have been only one purpose behind those conversations—to repeat with Vavilov the "Tupolev version."[2] In the late 1920s a new form of penal institution, which came to be known to the inmates as *sharashki*, had begun to take form in the Soviet Union. In such institutions at first tens and later hundreds of engineers, technicians, and scientists did scientific work for the

government. Aircraft were planned and built and military weapons
were designed. The scientists under arrest carried out mathematical
and engineering calculations connected with the expansion of industry, and chemists, physicists, and bacteriologists conducted experiments in the prison laboratories on orders of the secret police.
Though they were in prison, such highly qualified specialists as
Academicians Kapitsa and Tupolev directed the work of whole
groups of research workers who were themselves also prisoners.
The *sharashki* continued into the 1950s. Discoveries of tremendous
scientific importance were sometimes made in the greatest secrecy
in those secret laboratories, though they had no more chance of
becoming part of generally known scientific knowledge than did
most of the scientists of regaining their freedom.

It appears that at the beginning of the war it had been decided
to put Vavilov in one of those *sharashki*. Beria's agents were
probably given the job of assessing, not so much Vavilov's own
attitude, as the true value of the work that might be extracted from
him if he were allowed to live. It would not have been difficult for
Vavilov to guess what was in the mind of the authorities. At that
time he could not have wished for anything better—for his life to be
spared and for him to carry on with the work to which he was
devoted. What more could a man sentenced to death ask for? On
August 8, 1941, Vavilov addressed the following appeal to Beria:

> With reference to the petition you have made to the
> Military Collegium regarding my pardon and the setting
> aside of my sentence, and also bearing in mind the enor-
> mous demands being placed on all citizens of the Soviet
> Union as a result of the war, I am taking the liberty of
> appealing for me to be given the possibility of concentrat-
> ing my work on tasks of the most immediate importance
> at the present time in my speciality—*plant breeding*.
>
> 1. I could complete in six months the writing of a
> *Practical Handbook for the cultivation of varieties of crop
> plants resistant to the principal diseases*.
>
> 2. By intensive work over six or eight months I could
> complete a "Practical Handbook on the selection of bread
> grains" dealing with conditions in the various regions of
> the USSR.
>
> I am also well acquainted with questions of subtropi-

cal plant breeding, including crops of importance for the country's *defense*, such as the tung-oil tree, the quinine plant and others, as well as plants rich in vitamins.

All my experience in the field of plant breeding and all my knowledge and strength I would like to devote entirely to the Soviet regime and my native land wherever I can be of maximum use.

8.8.1941.

Butyrki prison, Cell No. 49.

Nikolai Vavilov

August passed, and September, and half of October. The cumbersome, slow-moving bureaucratic machinery in the Lubyanka prison was still not able finally to decide whether to do away with Vavilov at once or whether he might still be of some use. It is possible that the machine might in the end have arrived at a reasonable decision, but unforeseen circumstances intervened.

On October 15, 1941, when Beria's messenger appeared once again at Vavilov's cell to continue the talk about war and fascism, the Nazi tanks were moving to the outskirts of Moscow and the position of the Soviet capital became critical. The official press continued to conceal the true state of affairs, although rumors about the proximity of the Germans had filtered through to the city. On the morning of October 16 panic broke out in Moscow, and the population rushed to escape from the city and make for the east. By the middle of the day the public transport system had broken down and shops were being looted. People became even more alarmed when they learned that government offices had been ordered to burn their documents. At this point detachments of the secret police started the mass evacuation of prisoners, and Vavilov was among the thousands of inmates of the NKVD's internal prison and of the Butyrki, Taganka, Lefortovo prisons who were taken to the rail terminals for transportation to prisons in Saratov, Orenburg, and Kuibyshev.

I succeeded in finding several people who were prisoners at the time and who spent that autumn night on railway station platforms. Dr. Andrei Ivanovich Sukhno told me:

We were transported from the Butyrki to the Kursk station somewhere around midnight. Guards with dogs surrounded the whole of the square in front of the station and we were ordered to go down on all fours. The first snow had fallen in Moscow the previous day and had quickly melted so that the asphalt was covered with a cold, dirty slush. People tried to crawl away from the bigger puddles, but they were prevented by the crush of people and by the guards, who took stern measures whenever they noticed a movement in the crowd. How many of us were there? I reckon not less than ten thousand, maybe more. To judge from their clothes and their outward appearance, all the people I saw that night and with whom I later traveled by train were educated people from Moscow. We were forced to remain on all fours for six hours. When daylight came people started to appear on the streets. We were strictly forbidden to raise our heads, but we clearly heard people who saw us exclaiming: "Spies! Traitors!"

At last the trucks were formed up—those "Stolypin" trucks which every Russian knows from Yaroshenko's famous painting. You will remember that in the picture the prisoners are throwing bread crumbs through the bars of the trucks to the pigeons strutting around the platform. We who were prisoners in 1941 could not conceive of doing anything like that, for the good reason that in the "compartment" in which the tsar's policemen had put five prisoners, the Communist guards squeezed in between twenty and twenty-five people. We had to take turns to sit down. Some of us lost consciousness because of lack of air and fatigue.[3]

Vavilov's journey took two weeks: his ordeal by train came to an end on October 29.

At Saratov the prisoners were again made to go down on all fours. Then they had to strip naked, were searched, and after a medical examination and a cold shower, were led off to their cells. Vavilov was put into block 3, used for the most important political and public figures. A few individuals were transferred from this block to special interrogation cells where they were questioned by officials from Moscow. Throughout the day and night the sound of blows and the groans of people being beaten came from those cells.

At the beginning Vavilov was kept in solitary confinement. By January 1942 his health had already been undermined but, according to people who saw him then, he still appeared to be an impressive figure crushed by hunger and the prison regime. That was how he seemed to Irina Piotrovskaya, a sixteen-year-old schoolgirl from Saratov sentenced for "trying to organize an attempt on the life of Comrade Stalin." She told me:

> I cannot fix the exact date, but I well recall that it was in January, 1942. I saw him, or rather he made himself known to me, not in the Saratov prison hospital but in the courtyard of the Saratov prison [in the third block, the so-called special block for political prisoners]. We were taken one by one from different cells and brought together in the courtyard before being sent, as it later turned out, to the prison hospital. I say "as it later turned out" because the system was that none of the prisoners should know where he was being taken. The guard would simply open the little window in the cell door [through which meals were pushed in] and say: "Get yourself ready with your things." That would strike horror into you, because such a summons could mean that most awful fate.
>
> When they led me out, there were already people standing in the yard with their faces to the wall and their hands behind their backs. I was pushed across to join the group and found myself next to Nikolai Ivanovich. Of course at that moment I didn't know who was standing next to me and I didn't try to find out, being taken up with my own sufferings, fear of the unknown, my tears and sobbing. Suddenly I heard a very calm voice say: "Why are you crying?" and I turned to look at him. A man in a black overcoat, very thin, with a little beard and an intelligent face took two steps toward me. I replied that I was very scared, that I didn't know where they were taking me, that I had pains everywhere, and that I wanted to go home. He asked me how old I was and what I was in prison for. I told him and he said, "Listen to me carefully and, since you will almost certainly survive this, try to remember my name. I am Vavilov, Nikolai Ivanovich, an academician. Now don't cry and don't be afraid, we are

being taken to the hospital. They have decided to treat even me before they shoot me. I am being held alone in a death cell. Don't forget my name."

Then he went on to tell me a story about some Jews who, when they had excessive taxes imposed on them, started to cry, but then, when they no longer had any means of paying, started to laugh. Shortly after that we were all hustled into a "Black Maria" and driven off. The journey lasted only a few minutes, since the prison hospital was in the prison grounds, only in another block, but it could be reached only by crossing the public street. We were taken out of the prison van one by one, and I never saw Nikolai Ivanovich again.

They didn't keep me long in the hospital and after I had returned to the cell I heard a little later over the prison radio [the various devices prisoners have for communicating with each other] that Academician Vavilov had died in the prison hospital. It may be, of course, that the prison radio was not the most reliable source of information, but that I met him in January 1942 I am absolutely certain.

In fact the "prison radio" *was* mistaken on that occasion. Vavilov returned from the hospital. But then he was no longer on his own. Saratov prison no. 1, despite its many blocks and many floors, was impossibly overcrowded in the war years. Angelina Karlovna Rohr, a journalist and doctor, told me that in the winter of 1942 prisoners could sleep only on their sides on account of the overcrowding.[4] At night no one lying on the wooden bunks could turn over unless the whole row did the same. In that airless, stifling atmosphere the prisoners kept losing consciousness, not only in the general blocks but also in the special one.

It was in the cellar, in a narrow stone cell, apparently used in peacetime for solitary confinement, but now used as a death cell, that Vavilov met up with two inmates: Academician Ivan Luppol and an engineer from Saratov, Ivan Filatov, both of whom had been sentenced to death. The story of how Filatov landed in prison is not without interest. Everyone who remembers him says it would be difficult to imagine a more modest or hardworking person. The job he had could not have been humbler or worse paid, but from the point of view of the authorities he had one serious fault—before the

Revolution his uncle had had his own timber wharf in Saratov. The fact that his family had been relatively well-off before the Revolution was sufficient grounds for the nephew to be arrested in the first month of the war as a secret enemy of the Soviet regime. Thirteen people were arrested in the same trumped-up affair, including a young truck driver, Georgi Lozovsky. Most of the "conspirators" had never set eyes on each other before, but that did not worry the interrogators. Week after week they dragged the prisoners out to confront them with each other, trying at all costs to put together a group affair. Lozovsky refused, despite all the beating and torturing, to sign the records of the interrogations, and so he was sent off to the front to fight. But Filatov, weaker in willpower and physical strength, agreed to sign the false testimony, and in February 1942 he was sentenced to death. During the several months it took for his appeal to go to Moscow and back, Ivan Filatov was held in the death cell. His death sentence was finally commuted to ten years in a prison camp, but by then the unfortunate engineer was so weak and emaciated that he was sent home to die.

By the spring of 1944 not one of the three inmates of the death cell remained alive. Filatov did not survive longer out of prison than did Luppol, who was sent to the camp complex in Mordovia (in his last letter the academician begged his wife to send him a few crusts of bread). Vavilov died even sooner. With the three of them in their graves, it was unlikely that anyone would ever hear an account of their life in the underground cell, their sufferings, or their conversations as they waited to be taken out and shot. But shortly before his death, when he was already out of prison, Filatov happened by chance to meet up with Lozovsky, the truck driver, to whom he told everything. As a private in the Soviet army Lozovsky could very well have been killed at the front, but in fact he survived and forgot nothing of what he was told. And so, on February 12, 1967, Georgi Matveyevich Lozovsky, then a mechanic at the Saratov taxi garage, was interviewed in his little house on the outskirts of Saratov by representatives of the Soviet Academy of Science. At their request he recorded on tape what he had been told twenty-three years previously by Filatov:

> It was in 1944, in January or February. I had returned from the front to Saratov for a short leave. My house was cold—there was nothing to heat it with. The

whole family, all five of them, were in one room. I went down to the Volka-Kama timber base to try and get some wood for burning. In the office there I saw a man whom I did not recognize at first. He was sitting at a desk and with his right hand kept reaching into the drawer for a piece of black bread which he chewed greedily. It was Ivan Filatov, or rather just his shadow. I sat down near him and we started to talk. I was so shaken by what he had to say that I quite forgot my family at home in a cold room—there was a sharp frost outside. I sat there with him for something like five hours and then accompanied him home after his work.

Filatov described what life had been life for the condemned men.

It was a very narrow cell without windows and with a single bedstead fixed to the wall. It was in the cellar beneath the prison. The prisoners called the prison with its many floors the *Titanic* because of its resemblance to the famour liner that went down in the Atlantic. An electric light bulb burned in the cell night and day. It was hot and stuffy. The temperature went sometimes as high as 30 degrees [centigrade]. They sat there covered in sweat. Their clothes consisted of a canvas sack with holes cut for the head and arms, and on their feet they wore slippers made from the bark of the lime tree. Luppol said that the slaves in ancient Rome had been similarly dressed. They received food three times a day: two spoons of *kasha* [groats] and a tin of soup made from rotten salted tomatoes with a piece of bad salt fish for the midday meal and a spoonful of *kasha* for supper. Apart from that they were supposed to have three or four hundred grams of black bread made from barley flour. That category of prisoner was not allowed to receive parcels or make outside purchases. All the efforts that Filatov's wife made to help him were unsuccessful.

But man does not live by bread along. Intelligent, educated people needed something more to occupy them through the long days and nights in the prison cell, which was so small that two of them had to squeeze up against the wall to allow the third to walk a few paces. Georgi Lozovsky described Vavilov's life in the cell:

> Vavilov brought a measure of discipline into things. He tried to cheer up his companions. To take their minds off grim reality he arranged a series of lectures on history, biology and the timber industry. Each of them delivered a lecture in turn. They had to speak in a very low voice because if the guard heard them he would order them to talk only in a whisper. Two of them would take turns to sleep on the bed while the third would doze at the table that was fixed to the wall and floor of the cell. So it went on, day after day—lectures in the morning after breakfast, then rest and the midday meal, then lectures again until supper and sleep. In those conditions Vavilov remained very steadfast, as though the cruel reality had no effect on him.

Another acquaintance of Filatov's, an agonomist from Saratov, N. I. Oppokov, confirmed that Vavilov delivered more than a hundred hours of lectures on biology, genetics, and plant breeding while he was in the cell. An accountant from Moscow, N. S. Puchkov, who spent some time in the Saratov prison during the war, also heard from a prisoner who was with Vavilov for a few days in the winter of 1941 that he had found him in an optimistic mood, that he was looking to the future hopefully, and that he had told a lot of interesting stories about his journeys in distant lands. Moreover, he named Lysenko as the man responsible for his arrest.

Lozovsky told the Academy of Science:

> Nikolai Ivanovich was very worried about what would happen to his students. Four of them were outstanding, he said, but I forget their names. He said they would do great things for our country. When he talked about Trofim Lysenko he described him as a speculator in the world of science, that he was leading our government astray for the sake of his own career and his lust for power. In his lectures in the cell, Vavilov explained his theory of homologous lines and compared it with Lysenko's unscientific experiments which could cause untold harm to Soviet agriculture, plant breeding and stock

breeding. Nikolai Ivanovich was convinced that he had fallen victim to Lysenko.

Lozovsky also recalled some of the stories Vavilov had told Filatov about the past:

> In 1936 and 1937, when Stalin put forward the slogan about raising the total grain harvest to 5,000 or 6,000 million poods, Vavilov had published an article in which he recalled that prerevolutionary Russia had harvested between 10,000 and 13,000 million poods of grain. Vavilov had reckoned that with up-to-date technology the harvest should not be less than that. After his article appeared, Molotov summoned him, as vice-president of the Lenin Academy, to the Kremlin. During the interview Stalin came into the office through a side door and, without a word of greeting, said: "Academician Vavilov, why do you have to have these empty dreams? Just help us to get a dependable harvest of 5,000–6,000 million poods. That's enough for us." And, puffing at his pipe, Stalin left Molotov's office without another word.

Just before his arrest in 1940, Vavilov had again been summoned to the Kremlin. He had no idea who had summoned him and he waited ten or twelve hours without being seen by anyone. Putting the first and second Kremlin visits together, he understood that had been the beginning of the end.

"Vavilov spent altogether about a year in the death cell," Lozovsky said. "During that time he and his cell-mates were not once taken out for exercise. They were not permitted to correspond with their families or to receive parcels. They were not allowed to visit the bathhouse or even to have soap for washing in the cell. There was of course no question of their having any books."

Vavilov made several applications to the governor of the prison, begging him to modify the regime and to make inquiries about his fate, since Beria had through his agents promised to petition for his pardon. Lieutenant Irashin had a short answer to all his requests: "If we get a paper from Moscow telling us to shoot you, we shall shoot you; if they tell us to pardon you, we shall pardon you." The prison governor was not lying: according to the documents, the academician who had been sentenced to death remained "Moscow's business" and Moscow alone could decide what was to be done with him. By the spring of 1942, however, Vavilov's condition—he was suffering badly from scurvy—had declined to such an extent that even the obedient Irashin took pity on him and allowed the condemned man to write a letter to Beria.

I saw that letter in the first volume of the police record of Vavilov's case. It was closely written by hand on both sides of a large sheet of paper and dated April 25, 1942. Next to it was entered a typewritten copy especially for Beria. In that appeal to the "deeply respected Lavrenti Pavlovich" Vavilov went through the story of his arrest and recalled that "at the trial which lasted only a few minutes in wartime conditions" he had declared categorically that the treason and espionage charges against him were "based on pure invention, lies and slanders that had not been proved in the slightest degree during the investigation." Vavilov went on to recall the talks he had had with Beria's officers in the Butyrki and the NKVD internal prison. But the most important point in his letter was the plea to be allowed to work. Even if he were not to be released, even if he had to be behind bars, it made no difference, so long as he could work:

> I am 54, with a vast experience and knowledge in the field of plant breeding, with a good command of the principal European languages, and I would be happy to devote myself entirely to the service of my country, even to die for it. Since I am quite strong physically and morally I would be glad at this difficult time to be used to improve the country's defenses in my speciality as a plant breeder, increasing the output of plants, foodstuffs and industrial crops. . . . I request and beg you to make my lot easier, to decide on my future and to allow me to work in my special field even at the lowest level.

Vavilov said very little, just three lines, about what he was having to endure in the death cell, although in the spring of 1942 his sufferings appear to have reached the limit of what a human being could bear. The prison was swept by an epidemic of dysentery, which carried off several hundred people, including Steklov, the former editor-in-chief of *Izvestia,* and Ryanzanov, the director of the Marx-Engels Institute. Vavilov also came down repeatedly with dysentery, but he had still other sufferings ahead.

A. I. Sukhno, who was also a prisoner, wrote:

> Our cell was just opposite the death cell. I had already learned from a friendly guard that Academicians Vavilov and Luppol were in it. I also knew that people sentenced to death were not usually taken out for questioning or beaten up. But every morning we would hear frightful screams coming from the cell opposite. It was obvious that somebody was being very brutally treated there. The guard did not want to tell me what the reason for the screams was but I managed to find out what was going on. A certain Nesvitsky, a teacher of the history of the Far East who had been sentenced to death, was put in our cell. Nesvitsky, who had been accused of having "depicted the pharaohs of Egypt in an un-Marxist way," had spent several days in the same cell as Vavilov, and he told us that they had put into the cell with the two academicians a madman who took their ration of bread from them every day. To be without bread in those conditions meant certain death. Luppol and Vavilov naturally tried to deal with the madman, but he would then get to work with his fists and teeth and often came out on top in the battle for the bread.[5]

Vavilov's letter was delivered by the NKVD's secret postal service from the prison in Saratov to the central office of the State Security Organization on Dzerzhinsky Square in Moscow at the end of April or the beginning of May 1942. Unlike hundreds of thousands of similar communications addressed to Beria as commissar for internal affairs, Vavilov's letter quickly reached him personally. Nobody but Beria had the power to countermand Vavilov's death sentence. His orders were sufficient to make the slow-moving bureaucratic machine work at full speed. On June 13 Beria's deputy Merkulov sent a special letter to Ulbrikh, the chairman of the Military Collegium of the Soviet Supreme Court. Referring to the cases of Luppol and Vavilov, he wrote: "In view of the fact that the men under sentence referred to above *might be used on work of importance for the country's defense*, the NKVD of the USSR petitions for the sentence of death to be commuted to detention in the corrective labor camps of the NKVD for a period of 20 years each" (emphasis added).[6]

The Presidium of the Supreme Soviet sprang immediately into action. In June 1941 it had been adamant in its refusal to grant Academician Vavilov his life; now, with the same firmness, it took the completely opposite decision. The question of whether Academician Vavilov was to be murdered or not was item 325 on the agenda of a meeting of the Presidium of the Supreme Soviet on June 23, 1942. It took the powers that be scarcely a minute to reach their decision—a minute for which Vavilov had waited in prison eleven months and fifteen days.

One can only imagine what the two academicians felt in the death cell on that summer morning when they received at last the news that their lives had been spared. For the first time in a year the nightmare of waiting for the end had been dispersed. They would no longer suffer that secret dread of every unusual noise in the prison corridor and of every turn of a key in a lock. A born optimist such as Vavilov must have laughed for joy when he read the contents of the paper from Moscow, with the same wonderfully cheerful Vavilov laugh that hundreds of his friends and students cannot forget to this day. He must have been full of the highest hopes as, with a hand that had grown weak and unused to holding a pen, he wrote on the back of the official document: "This decision was communicated to me on July 4, 1942."

At a fateful moment for his country Vavilov felt he had been called on to help his native land as a plant breeder, as a scholar. They would probably send him to one of the NKVD's agricultural camps. It did not matter where, but he hoped he could be sent to the famous state farm–cum–prison camp called Dolinsky, near Karaganda. That was where, from the early 1930s, they had sent thousands of agronomists, physiologists, agrochemists, and plant breeders. In the steppe lands of Kazakhstan

there was plenty of room for a scientist and plant breeder
to develop his work and a good base to work on.

In the summer of 1942 it really seemed as though the dreams of
the man who had been so recently in the death cell were destined to
come true. Vavilov and Luppol were transferred from the cellar to
the common cell on the ground floor. They were just as hungry and
just as crowded there, but at least prisoners were taken out for
exercise, they were allowed a bath, and those who had any money
could even go to the prison shop and buy a bunch of onions or a
packet of cheap tobacco. Luppol was soon sent off to a prison
camp, and that also seemed to be a good sign—the prison inmates
considered a camp a place where you would get more food and
stand less chance of dying. Vavilov was expecting that he would also
be sent off somewhere any day. But weeks and months went by.
Summer came to an end and so did the autumn, and he still
remained in the cell.

What had happened? Why was the plan, so useful for the state
and so beneficial for Vavilov, not carried out? Had Beria forgotten
what he had proposed, or had some powers who hated Vavilov
interfered again? The answer remains a secret for the time being.
Among the dozens of people who saw Vavilov in the Saratov prison
or heard about him from other prisoners, I did not come across
anyone who was with him between July 1942 and January 1943.
Cell 57 is not very large (it now holds three prisoners), but during
the war there were never fewer than ten or fifteen people in it. If any
of Vavilov's cell-mates are still alive, I hope they will make themselves known and tell the final chapter in the tragic biography of
their comrade. The only thing that is known up to now is that
Nikolai Ivanovich Vavilov died in the Saratov prison hospital on
January 26, 1943. The official death certificate, of which there is a
copy in the police file, reads as follows:

> CERTIFICATE concerning the death of a prisoner.
> I, Doctor N. L. Stepanova, with nurse M. N. Skri-
> pina, examined the corpse of the prisoner Vavilov, Nikolai
> Ivanovich, born in 1887, sentenced under article 58 to 20
> years, who died in the hospital of prison No. 1 in Saratov
> on January 26, 1943, at 7 hours — minutes.
> Result of examination: habitus normal, nutritional

state very poor, skin and mucosa pale, skeletal and muscular system unchanged.

According to the history of his illness Vavilov, Nikolai Ivanovich, had been under treatment in the prison hospital since January 24, 1943, for lobar pneumonia. Death came as a result of cardiovascular failure.

> Duty doctor: Stepanova.
> Duty nurse: Skripina.

At first reading this document seems like a record of nothing more than an accident. A man, apparently not well clothed, had caught cold, probably during the exercise period, and contracted pneumonia. In the age before antibiotics, pneumonia was rightly considered dangerous, and especially so in the case of a man who had spent two and a half years in prison.

But the longer I study the bare words of that document, the stranger its contents appear to me. It is not that I had heard rumors that Vavilov had been executed in August 1942 when, following the fall of Stalingrad, the more famous people being held in prison were executed "just in case." Rumor cannot provide the historian with grounds for serious speculation. But aspects of the death certificate itself give rise to doubts. Vavilov is said to have been "under treatment in the prison hospital since January 24, 1943," suggesting that the fatal illness lasted only two days. The explorer who had covered forty miles a day on foot and on horseback, the mountaineer who had without difficulty ascended the sixteen-thousand-foot summits of the Hindukush and the Andes, the man who, when crossing the bare desert, had lived a whole week on dried locusts—surely a man with such a constitution could not be brought down by pneumonia in a couple of days? True, the people who drew up the certificate did not conceal the fact that Vavilov was emaciated ("nutritional state very poor"). Even so, I had doubts.

I decided to write to Saratov to try and make contact with Stepanova and Skripina. In the meantime I succeeded in finding in Moscow a mining engineer by the name of Viktor Vikentievich Shiffer, who had been imprisoned from 1941 to 1955. On October 15, 1941, like Vavilov, he had been sent straight from the Lubyanka by train to Saratov. It took a long time and they were short of food but in very good company. Of the sixteen men in the compartment,

eleven were air force generals, and well-known generals at that—
Smushkevich, Klenov, Gaiursky, and Ptuyin, a double hero of the
Soviet Union. The other passengers included the director of the
Dinamo factory in Moscow and the director of the Kovrov aircraft
factory. Shiffer endured the same sufferings as Vavilov, though he
was put not in the death cell but in the common cell. In January
1943 he landed in the hospital in the bed next to old Professor
Artsybashev, the specialist on southern flora, who was dying. From
the nurses' talk, Artsybashev had discovered that Vavilov was in the
next ward. In Leningrad in the 1930s the two professors had not
gotten along very well together, but there, on the brink of death,
Professor Artsybashev was delighted to hear a familiar name. He
started to question the nurses about what was wrong with Vavilov,
and Shiffer heard from his lips a short but impressive account of the
last days of the great explorer.

Vavilov was in the same ward as Steklov, the former editor of
Izvestia. They both had dysentery, or probably simply diarrhea
resulting from lack of food. When the man in charge of the prison
made his rounds of the ward, Vavilov asked that he and Steklov
might be given each a glass of rice water. The man flared up: "What
on earth are you asking for! There isn't enough rice for wounded
soldiers at the front, and you think I'm going to feed it to enemies
of the state!"

That was the last that Shiffer ever heard about Vavilov. Artsybashev died the next day, and Vavilov apparently died at the same
time.

Then I received a letter from nurse Skripina in Saratov. It was
long and contradictory. But one thing she made quite clear: she had
never known anybody called Vavilov. She had worked as a nurse,
not in the prison hospital, but in its polyclinic; on the night in
question she had been standing in for someone else as duty nurse,
and she had been forced to sign the death certificate. But, she
added, Dr. Stepanova would doubtless have known Vavilov, and
she was now living in retirement at Number 10 Gorky Street in
Saratov.

I wrote to Dr. Natalia Stepanova. Her reply was the shortest
postal communication I have every received. "Don't remember
nothing. Stepanova." It was a sad thought: if a doctor did not
remember a patient who died under her care, then who would?

All the same Professor Bakhteyev and I decided to go to Saratov in the hope of finding a witness or some evidence concerning Vavilov's last days. Our trip was authorized by the commission set up to preserve and organize Vavilov's works at the Department of General Biology in the Soviet Academy of Science. The chairman of the commission, Academician Sukachev, defined its task with extreme precision: to establish how Vavilov died and where he is buried, in connection with the forthcoming celebration of the eightieth anniversary of his birth.

The head of the office for the preservation of public order in the Saratov region, Commissar of Police (third class) Demyan Gavrilovich Degtyarev, received the members of the academic commission very politely in his huge office. He was a handsome, even majestic general, with a radiant smile. Yes, he had heard of Vavilov—he had been a great scholar. The commission could count on the full support of his office. The necessary searches would be made in the archives and members of the commission would be able to meet all the members of the prison staff who were connected with this prisoner.

But even in Degtyarev's office we had our first disappointment. We learned that Vavilov's personal case file had been destroyed when the period for preserving it had expired. Our faces dropped. But perhaps the history of his illness had been preserved? After all, if one were to believe the death certificate, Vavilov had died in the hospital. The general promised that the history of his illness should be sought out.

The next day we visited Colonel A. M. Gvozdev, who had been instructed to carry out the search. The colonel said he thought our trip to Saratov was quite pointless. Since, as we had been told, the personal file had been burned, it was impossible to establish the date and cause of Academician Vavilov's death. And it was hopeless to try and find his grave. The colonel then proceeded to describe at length how carelessly the deaths of prisoners were recorded in the past and how well the matter was dealt with now that he was in charge of the records. Having heard him through, we understood only one thing—that, in spite of the instructions from his superiors, Gvozdev did not intend to reveal to us the truth about Vavilov's death. The reason became clear a few days later. The only important fact that we succeeded in obtaining from the conversation was that

Vavilov had not been shot. In the records of people who had been executed, going back for many years, his name did not appear. As we took our leave Gvozdev again advised us to go back to Moscow. But since we were insistent, he agreed to summon to his office the members of his staff who had worked in the prison in 1942 and 1943 and to ask them what they knew about Vavilov.

Three more days passed. We had time to record what Lozovsky, the truck driver, had to say, to visit Filatov's family and friends, and to call on Yelena Barulina's sister. Still there was no word from the public order office. It was obvious that the arrival of the members of the commission had alarmed the "Gery House." On the one hand there was the Academy of Science and a special letter signed by the minister for public order, Shchelokov, but on the other hand. . . . On the fourth day we received a telephone call inviting us to call on Colonel Gvozdev. He now looked even grimmer than before. But we could now afford to ignore his bad mood altogether, because on the green cloth of the colonel's desk lay what we had come to Saratov to see—the documents about Vavilov's death. A few faded pages from the records of the prison's medical room were sufficient to establish in detail the tragic events that had taken place a quarter of a century previously.

The first document, no bigger than a cigarette paper, was the report made by the prison nurse. On the morning of January 24, 1943, she informed the man in charge of the prison that N. I. Vavilov, from cell 57 of the third block, was ill. The head of the prison gave permission for the sick man to be moved to the infirmary. The next document, bearing a three-cornered stamp and signatures, was an extract from Protocol no. 137:

> On January 25th, 1943, a commission of doctors at the N. K. Z. hospital attached to the solitary confinement section of the Saratov prison consisting of: Chairman— the officer in charge of the prison, Senior Lieutenant Comrade Irashin; members—Senior medical inspector Turetsky; the head of the medical section, Tveritin, and Dr. Talyanker.
>
> *Patient examined:* Vavilov, Nikolai Ivanovich, born in 1887.
>
> *Examined person's complaint:* Complains of general weakness.

Observed symptoms: Exhaustion, skin and mucosa
pale, edema on legs. Hospitalized.
Diagnosis: Dystrophy, edema.
Decision of the Commission: Covered by item No. 1
of the list of illnesses.[7]

The members of the commission had not gone against their
consciences. They had recorded what they saw—a prisoner who
was utterly exhausted and dying from dystrophy. Their decision
meant that a person in such a condition certainly had the right to be
treated in the hospital. The very fact that the document was drawn
up meant that Vavilov was dying when he was admitted. The only
point that is not clear is what swellings the Saratov prison doctors
discovered. As every doctor and even every nurse must know,
lengthy albumin starvation results in the formation of hunger
edemas on the body of the patient. In the final stage of dystrophy
the patient is no longer able to digest food and profuse diarrhea
produces even greater dehydration and emaciation. The picture of
Vavilov's illness is quite clear.

All the same, in the third document the diagnosis suddenly
undergoes a strange metamorphosis. In the history of Vavilov's
illness, under the heading "Final Diagnosis," written in Dr. Stepanova's handwriting we find: "Lobar pneumonia and enteritis."
Here at last is the explanation of Dr. Stepanova's "bad memory"
and Colonel Gvozdev's gloomy mood. Stepanova falsified the
history of the illness; it was apparently not the first or the last time
she had done so. And Gvozdev's superiors had ordered him to
reveal this piece of forgery to outsiders.

Four days after Vavilov's death a postmortem examination was
carried out. It was performed "in accordance with oral instructions
by the head of the medical department of Saratov prison no. 1" by a
forensic expert Zoya Fyodorovna Rezayeva. She wrote in the
postmortem certificate: "Corpse of man of about 65, medium
height, average build, badly undernourished, skin pale, subcutane-
ous cellular tissue absent." Though the true cause of death of this
victim of starvation should not have been difficult to establish,
Rezayeva, the expert, knew what her superiors expected of her. She
wrote, in full agreement with Stepanova's "diagnosis": "Vavilov's
death was the result of bronchial pneumonia."

All the time Professor Bakhteyev and I were reading the

documents and comparing the strangely conflicting statements, Colonel Gvozdev looked as if he were sitting on needles. The next day, however, he was to have even more unpleasant experiences. At ten in the morning members of the academy's commission gathered in his office to meet Dr. Natalia Stepanova and nurse Maria Skripina. We approached this encounter in a state of some excitement, since they were the last people to have seen Vavilov alive and the last people he saw. Perhaps as he was dying Nikolai Ivanovich had wanted to make some statement? Had he whispered someone's name on his deathbed or made a last request?

Gvozdev introduced us. The little old women, rather plump, their faces clumsily made up, in expensive dresses, extended their hands as if by word of command. Stepanova rested her hand on the nurse's arm for support. Finally they sat down on the very edges of their chairs along one side of the table. Professor Bakhteyev and I sat opposite. Gvozdev was at his desk to one side.

At first there was just general talk: the two sides were summing each other up, trying to assess what to expect from their opponents, since that we *were* in fact opponents became clear from the first words spoken. The doctor and the nurse revealed a mixture of self-assurance and fright, which was not difficult to understand. This was their home, the place in which they had spent their lives. This was where they had earned their ample pensions and their positions of respect in society. To get so far they had had to do many things that it would be better now not to recall. Why on earth had those dangerous documents suddenly been dragged out into the light of day? Why was Comrade Gvozdev allowing outsiders to poke their noses into such secret places, into prison affairs, and into subjects that should have been closed for ever?

Dr. Stepanova bestowed some rather forced smiles upon us, but her puffy countenance told us that she was worried and frightened. Academician Vavilov? No, she did not recall anyone of that name: "There were so many of them!" But it was her signature on the history of the illness. Yes, but she did not draw up the document. Who did? Dr. Olga Veniaminovna Pichugina, whose name was now Kuznetsova. Why had one person drawn up the history of the illness and another signed it? She shrugged her shoulders. "It's a long time ago." I asked Stepanova why, in the history of Vavilov's illness, the diagnosis was given as lobar pneu-

monia, whereas in Protocol no. 137 which was drawn up *one day
later* it was clearly shown as *dystrophy*. I asked her what sense there
was in taking samples of blood and urine for analysis from a man at
the end of his strength and dying? Perhaps they did not in fact take
any blood or urine and simply entered the tests on the report for
appearances' sake? Her replies were unintelligible and confused.

Stepanova did not have a command of medical terminology.
Was she really a doctor? From 1923 she had worked in the prison as
a medical orderly and from 1936 as a doctor. "How and where did
you complete your higher education?" Reply: "By correspondence." Another lie. In the 1930s there were no correspondence
courses organized by medical colleges. Stepanova's little black eyes
turned pleadingly to Colonel Gvozdev, but Gvozdev remained
silent, frowning. His whole appearance seemed to be saying, "You
must get out of it yourselves. I have nothing to do with your affairs
of the past." A few more questions, which again produced a mixture
of lies and professional ignorance. There was nothing more to be
said. Professor Bakhteyev tried to take a photograph of Stepanova
and Skripina, but the old women covered their faces with their
hands. They were not so vain as to want to leave their portraits for
posterity.

There were two other interviews, which added little, however,
to the picture we already had. We called on Olga Veniaminovna
Kuznetsova (formerly Pichugina) in a well-built prerevolutionary
house on Volskaya Street. It was she who on January 24, 1943, had
started to draw up the history of Vavilov's illness. We found her, by
no means an old woman, smart and well dressed, in a spacious,
well-furnished room. She did not remember Vavilov but knew there
had been someone of that name in the prison. She had recalled the
name recently when she had read in the magazine *Novy Mir* an
article entitled "Russian Wheat." "It's terrible to think what sort of
people perished!" Kuznetsova remembered what prisoners were fed
on in the war years: for months they had only a sort of mash made
from flour and frozen cabbage. She had been able to save the lives of
some prisoners, but the less fortunate ones mostly arrived in the
hospital in such a state that they died a few hours later from heart
failure. Dr. Kuznetsova confirmed that Vavilov's death had been the
direct result of dystrophy.

At another address we visited the forensic expert Zoya

Fyodorovna Rezayeva, who was obliged to receive us in bed because she was suffering from inflammation of the lungs. She did not remember Vavilov and seemed to regard our visit as an attempt to cast a shadow over the faultless service she had rendered her country during the war. Suddenly she sat up in bed and, forgetting her weak state, hurled upon us a stream of what sounded like abuse: "You are going round checking up on people? You think we didn't earn our keep back here during the war? Only when you're young can you carry out such work! Fifteen or twenty corpses a day! There was no time to register them!" We said nothing, but simply noted down that Dr. Rezayeva said that in Saratov prison no. 1 between 1941 and 1945, the forensic experts wrote down their pathological and anatomical notes from memory, sometimes several days after the postmortem. I asked her: "Why was Vavilov's body not examined until four days after his death and the document recording the conclusions of the forensic experts drawn up another five days later—on February 4?" Rezayeva's reply was again an indignant roar: "I've already told you in plain language—there was a lot of work, we couldn't cope."

The commission could not complain that the people of Saratov were indifferent to their work—we came across quite a few voluntary helpers. The tragedy of Academician Vavilov was causing much concern among the students and teaching staff of the university, agronomists, and the police. One of our most active friends turned out to be Major Vasili Andreyev, the man in charge of the remand prison—formerly prison no. 1. The good Vasili Andreyev took the fate of the long-deceased prisoner very much to heart. This relatively young man, not involved in any way with the evil things done in the past, seemed to feel responsible for the crimes that other people had committed at another time in *his* institution. It was thanks to Major Andreyev's efforts that the history of Vavilov's illness was discovered, and it was he who showed Professor Bakhteyev cell 57 and ward 12 in the prison hospital, which was Vavilov's last refuge. Finally, it was to him we were obliged for discovering the place where Vavilov was buried.

In the course of twenty-four years several people had searched for that grave, and more than once. But Andreyev pointed to the most likely line of inquiry—he spoke with some old folks who had worked in the prison. They suggested a former storekeeper, now a

pensioner, Aleksei Ivanovich Novichkov, who had in earlier days
not scorned the trade of undertaker. We found the old man, with a
face suggesting a mixture of cunning and stupidity, very ready to
talk. He was eager to take us to the cemetery where in 1942 and
1943 he had buried the prisoners. On the way he told us that
burying prisoners was not part of his official duties, but he had been
glad to do it. For one thing, he used to receive some spirits—"to
clean his hands"—for doing it, and, for another, he was paid
something. As he recalled the good old days, Novichkov muttered,
with a chuckle, "I mean to say—who would want to waste spirits
on his hands?"

The burial of prisoners in wartime was not a particularly
elaborate affair. A couple of dozen naked corpses with metal
nametags attached to their legs were simply loaded into a big
wooden container, which was then put onto a sledge and under
cover of darkness dragged to the cemetery. There, without any
unnecessary fuss, the load was tipped out into a common grave and
covered with earth. The grave-diggers marked the nameless grave
with only a small metal spike, which they stuck into the gound so as
not to dig up again a part that had already been "acquired." Twenty-
four years later, on February 16, 1967, Novichkov led us through
the deep snow to the spikes. In the war years this most distant part
of the cemetery, close to the surrounding wall, had been quite
deserted. Only the prison grave-diggers had the right to perform
their simple ritual. Novichkov indicated an area roughly a hundred
yards square where he had buried corpses in the winter of 1943.[8]

We asked Novichkov whether he remembered anything about
Academician Vavilov. The old man did not in fact recall the name of
Vavilov, but he told us about one incident. Sometime in January
1943 he had arrived with his sleigh for the usual load of corpses and
was kept waiting longer than usual. When he went into the mortu-
ary to find out the reason for the delay, he was told that some
famous prisoner had died who, unlike the others, was going to be
buried in clean underwear. While the body was being prepared,
Novichkov examined the famous person and found him very much
like all the other corpses, just as thin and emaciated. The prisoner
was put into a special box and Novichkov was instructed to bury
him separately. Never before or after was such an honor bestowed
on a prisoner.

I do not know whether Novichkov was telling the truth or whether it was just the fruit of his imagination. Even if it were true, could one say with certainty that the body was really Vavilov's? We shall probably never know. Nor is it so important to know whether the bones of the long-suffering academician rotted in one hole or another. It is much more important that posterity should not forget the terrible sufferings that Russia's intellectuals went through in Stalin's torture chambers.

Epilogue

In the autumn of 1967, after the approximate place of Vavilov's burial had been found in the Voskresensky cemetery, the members of the commission on Vavilov's legacy decided to erect a memorial to him in Saratov. The commission asked the Department of General Biology of the Soviet Academy of Science who would be responsible for the cost of erecting the memorial: ought we invite voluntary subscriptions from private people, or would the academy erect the monument at its own expense? A year passed without a word from the department, and in August 1968 two members of the commission—Professor Bakhteyev and I—addressed a similar inquiry to the president of the Academy of Science. Again there was silence for many months.

Citizens of our country, so vast and rich in administration, learned long ago that silence on the part of an official is a sign that he does not approve your plan but prefers not to leave any written trace of his disapproval. So, having wasted two years, the commission appealed to everyone who treasured the memory of Nikolai Vavilov to contribute to the memorial. Yuri Vavilov made his bank account available for that purpose, and at the outset everything went very well. Being free of any bureaucratic attention, the undertaking began to make rapid and easy progress. Money flowed in from all over the country—the hard-earned wages of people engaged in scientific work. A sculptor, Konstantin Suminov, was found in Saratov, and in Leningrad we managed to buy a huge block of gray granite. We planned to unveil the memorial in September 1970 to coincide with the fiftieth anniversary of the publication of Vavilov's law of homologous lines. Many of the country's biologists expressed a desire to take part in the celebrations.

At last the memorial was finished, and it seemed as though nothing could prevent a group of private people, who had erected a memorial to their much-loved teacher, from performing quietly and unobtrusively the ceremony of unveiling it. But it was not to be. The regional and city committees of the Communist party in Saratov decided to appoint an organization committee for the unveiling of the memorial to Academician Vavilov. The committee was appointed on August 22 and announced that the unveiling would take place on August 25. Their idea was quite simple: there would not be time for most of Vavilov's friends to learn about the ceremony and come to Saratov. From the very beginning the main object of the Saratov party bosses was to ensure that as few people as possible attended the ceremony and that the ceremony itself attracted a minimum of attention. The plan worked well. Many of the people who had longed to meet up with their colleagues and friends in Saratov only learned about the occasion a couple of weeks after it had taken place.

But official interference did not stop there. On August 23 and 24 the Soviet Academy of Science and the Academy of Agriculture, which had remained silent for two years, suddenly burst into life. In great haste, fearing they would be too late, they started dispatching their representatives to Saratov. From Leningrad came the deputy director of the Institute of Plant Breeding and two party officials. The Academy of Science sent its representative off only a few hours before the ceremony was due to take place. Quite uninvited, all these officials, who a year or two previously had been afraid to say Vavilov's name aloud, were now rushing to be at his grave. Their presence had only one purpose—to demonstrate that the academies had not stood aside from the affair.

Now, at last, Vavilov's friends and the rest of them were crowded around the memorial, still covered, in the Voskresensky cemetery. "When the covering fell away we, the older members of Vavilov's institute, simply gasped," Klavdia Ivanova said. "The face carved out of the granite bore no relation to Vavilov's features." It came as a great shock. Several hundred people stood around the gray granite obelisk topped by a huge head unlike the man they had known. Only by looking at the monument from the side was it possible to detect a certain resemblance. People started muttering that the sculptor lacked talent, that his first model in clay had been very good and he had spoiled the portrait when he transferred it into granite. But the truth turned out to be much sadder than what had been imagined.

When the sculptor, Konstantin Suminov, had finished the work and was about to move the monument to the cemetery, he was visited in his studio by representatives of the Saratov Glavlit. These "art experts" did not approve the sculptor's work. The censors were not interested in whether the monument was a good likeness or not; they demanded that Suminov remove all the wrinkles from the granite features of Vavilov, on the grounds that they suggested the poor nourishment he had received in the Saratov prison. They also found undesirable the way Vavilov was screwing up his eyes, especially the right one, which clearly implied that he had been beaten while in prison. To settle once and for all with Vavilov's unhappy past, the censors demanded that the sculptor carve a happy smile on Vavilov's granite features.

Notes

Drafts of this MS, notes and personal papers were smuggled out of the Soviet Union in various ways, over a period of time. It has been impossible to verify references to material that remains in Moscow, Leningrad, or elsewhere in the USSR, so while compiling these notes the author has had to rely on those limited files available to him.

Prologue

1. *Prostor*, (1966), nos. 7 and 8.

1. The Making of a Scientist

1. V. Keler, *Sergei Vavilov* (Moscow: Molodaya Gvardiya, 1961), 15.

2. Lidia Petrovna Breslavets, *Next to Vavilov; A Collection of Reminiscences* (Moscow: Sovetskaya Rossiya, 1962), 36-37.

3. Mark Popovsky, *We Must Hurry!* (Moscow: Detskaya Literatura, 1968), 21-22; Lidia Petrovna Breslavets, *Next to Vavilov;* 89-91.

4. Nikolai Vavilov to Ekaterina Sakharova, circa 1911-12. (Ekaterina Sakharova's sister, Vera Nikolaevna Sakharova, showed the original letters to the author in the late 1960s).

5. Ekaterina Sakharova to Nikolai Vavilov, circa 1911-12.

6. Nikolai I. Vavilov, "The Law of Homological Series in Hereditary Variables." Lecture presented at the Third All-Russian Selection Congress, Saratov, June 4, 1920.

7. Mark Popovsky, *We Must Hurry!* 54.

8. Obituary written by Vavilov upon the death of Professor R. Regel. It was printed as the foreward to Regel's book *Grains in Russia*, Petrograd, 1920.

9. M. Gorky to H. G. Wells, Mar. 1921. *Gorky and Science* (Moscow, 1964).

10. N. I. Vavilov to P. P. Podyapolsky, spring 1912, Petrograd. The (unpublished) originals are in the author's Moscow archive.

11. N. I. Vavilov to the People's Commissariat of Agriculture, May 1922, Petrograd, the Leningrad State Archive of the October Revolution and Socialist Construction (LGA).

12. N. Vavilov to Professor Zalensky, fall 1922, Petrograd, LGA.

13. William Sumner Harwood, *The New Earth: A Recital of the Triumphs of Modern Agriculture in America* (New York, 1906).

14. N. Vavilov to Podyapolsky, winter 1925, Petrograd, LGA.

2. Michurin, Lysenko, and the Birth of "Progressive Biology"

1. N. I. Vavilov, "Exploit," *Pravda,* June 8, 1935.

2. Archives of VIR (All-Union N. I. Vavilov Research Institute of Plant Breeding), op. 2, case 15, list 4, LGA.

3. N. I. Vavilov, "Introduction" in *Michurin: Achievements of His Work in Hybridization* (Krasnaya Derevnya, 1924).

4. S. P. Lebedeva, "Recollections." Original ms. with Yuri N. Vavilov, son of Nikolai Vavilov.

5. *I. V. Michurin in the Recollections of His Contemporaries* (Tambov, 1963), 195-98.

6. Ibid.

7. R. A. Gregory, *Discoveries, Goals, and the Meaning of Science,* translated from the English under the editorship of N. I. Vavilov (Petrograd, 1923).

8. Vavilov to G. D. Karpechenko, Dec. 30, 1925, VIR, case 81, list 181, LGA.

9. N. I. Vavilov, *Novy mir,* mo. 11, (1934).

10. Ibid.

11. Ibid.

12. VIR, case 647, lists 18-19, LGA.

13. Tape recorded by A. G. Khvalina, a reporter for Moscow Radio, Saratov, Mar. 1965.

14. N. V. Timofeyev-Resovsky, private conversation with author, May 15, 1966.

15. Yuri A. Dolgushin, *At the Source of a New Biology* (Moscow: Goskultporsvetizdat, 1949), 10-11. (The author is the brother of D. A. Dolgushin.)

16. Ibid.

17. Ibid.

18. Federley, interview with *Smena*, Leningrad newspaper, Jan. 11, 1929.

19. Dolgushin, *Source of Biology.*

20. Op. 141, fasc. 17, case 35, list 18 (136), All-Union Academy of Agricultural Sciences (VASKHNIL).

21. Vavilov to N. V. Kovalev, May 28, 1932, Odessa, VIR, no. 9708, case 469, lists 24-25, LGA.

22. Robert Cook, letter in *Scientific Monthly,* June 1949.

23. Vavilov to Eikhfeld, Nov. 11, 1931, VIR, no. 9708, case 409, list 155, LGA.

24. VIR, no. 9708, case 620, list 3, LGA.

25. Vavilov to commission, Mar. 16, 1933, VIR, no. 9708, case 620, list 12, LGA.

26. Vavilov to the Biology Section of the Soviet Academy of Science, Feb. 8, 1934, VIR, no. 9708, case 667, list 28, LGA.

27. L. P. Breslavets, "Memoirs," ms.

28. Ibid.

29. Op. 450, fasc. 192, case 3, VASKHNIL.

30. Op. 450, fasc. 196, case 43, list 100, VASKHNIL.

31. Transcript of Lysenko's report, VIR, case 686, list 34, LGA.

32. Lysenko, speech at the Second Congress of Kolkhoz Shock-Workers, in *Pravda*, Feb. 15, 1935.

3. A Strange Debate

1. A. I. Kuptsov, "In Memory of Nikolai Ivanovich Vavilov," (1958), manuscript.

2. N. I. Vavilov, testimony, investigation case no. 1,500.

3. Vavilov, speech at a conference preparing for the institute's anniversary, Sept. 29, 1934, VIR, no. 9708, case 646, list 42, LGA.

4. Muller, letter, Feb. 28, 1935, no. 9708, op. 1, case 654, lists 140-142, LGA.

5. N. V. Timofeyev-Resovsky, private conversation with author, Feb. 25, 1971.

6. N. I. Vavilov, "Increasing Productivity," *Collected Words,* 5: 707.

7. A. N. Shekhurdin, in *Selection and Seed Growing,* (1937), no. 2.

8. Konstantinov, in *Socialist Reconstruction of Agriculture* (1937), no. 2.

9. Lysenko, speech at a conference of shock-workers in seed production, tractor drivers, and party and government leaders, in *Pravda,* Nov. 2, 1936.

10. Transcript of VASKHNIL session, op. 450, fasc. 473, case 48, VASKHNIL.

11. A. A. Zaitseva, conversation with All-Union Radio correspondent, July 21, 1968, tape recording.

12. N. I. Vavilov, Afterword, in *Socialist Reconstruction of Agriculture,* no. 2 (1937), 49.

13. Vavilov to Muller, May 8, 1937, VIR, no. 9708, case 1436, list 104, LGA.

14. E. N. Sinskaya, "Recollections of Nikolai I. Vavilov," manuscript.

15. Details of this experiment were told to the author in a private conversation with M. I. Khadzhinov, winner of the Lenin Prize and member of the Academy of Agricultural Science (Krasnodar), and Professor A. N. Lutkov, doctor of sciences, head of the polyploid laboratory of the Academy of Sciences (Novosibirsk). Lutkov died in 1971, Khadzhinov in 1981.

16. Transcripts of scientific council of VIR, July 27, 1935, VIR, case 828, LGA.

17. Ibid.

18. N. I. Vavilov, *Plant Selection as a Science* (Moscow-Leningrad, 1934).

19. Vavilov to Harland, Sept. 13, 1938. A copy was graciously sent to the author by Professor Harland in 1966.

20. Lysenko, speech at the Second Congress of Kolkhoz Shock-Workers.

21. Francis Darwin, *The Life and Letters of Charles Darwin* (London, 1887).

22. Lysenko, *Under the Banner of Marxism* (1939), no. 11: 147.

23. Sinskaya, "N. I. Vavilov."

24. VIR, no. 9708, 1377, lists 15-16, 23, LGA.

25. Ibid., list 23.

26. Sinskaya, "N. I. Vavilov."

27. Lysenko, "Creator of Soviety Agrobiology," *Vernalization* (1939), no. 3: 18-20.

28. P. Yakovlev, "On the Theories of True Geneticists," *Socialist Reconstruction of Agriculture* (1936), no. 12: 55-56.

29. Lysenko, *Under the Banner of Marxism*, 186.

30. I. Prezent, "Pseudoscientific Theories in Genetics," *Vernalization* (1939), no. 2.

31. G. Shlykov, "In the Shackles of Pseudoscience," *Soviet Subtropics* (1939), no. 6: 57-61.

32. A. V. Gursky, "In Memory of a Teacher and Friend," in *Next to Vavilov* (Moscow: Sovetskaya Rossiya, 1962).

4. The Destruction of "Babylon"

1. Sinskaya, "Memoirs," MS.

2. No. 9708, case 175, list 52, LGA.

3. Ibid., list 5.

4. Benediktov at an all-union conference of selection and seed growing, held Feb. 27 to Mar. 4, 1939 in Narkonseme. The citation is from *Vernalization* (1939), no. 2.

5. V. S. Lekhnovich to author, Feb. 14, 1965.

6. S. K. Chayanov, "Academician Nikolai Ivanovich Vavilov" (1962), MS.

7. A. V. Gursky, "In Memory of a Teacher and Friend."

8. Vavilov to Lysenko, Sept. 12, 1938, VIR, no. 9708, case 1572, list 32, LGA.

9. Lysenko, *Under the Banner of Marxism*, 151.

10. V. S. Lekhnovich, private conversation with author.

11. Editorial, *Vernalization* (1940), no. 2: 22.

12. Professor Robert Andrews Millikan (1869-1953), physi-

cist, Nobel laureate, president of the U. S. National Academy of Sciences.

13. Vavilov to G. D. Karpechenko, Jan. 7, 1930, VIR, LGA.

14. VIR, no. 9708, 1372, LGA.

15. Vavilov to Karpechenko, Jan. 7, 1930, VIR, LGA.

16. VIR, no. 9708, case 1192 and 1187, LGA.

17. Vavilov, "The Seventh International Congress of Geneticists in the USSR," *Izvestia*, March 29, 1936.

18. F. Crew, in *Proceedings of the Seventh International Congress of Genetics*, Edinburgh, 1939.

19. Sinskaya, "Memoirs," MS.

20. Lysenko to deputy commissar for education, Apr. 8, 1940, VASKHNIL, op. 1, fasc. 2, case 11, list 164.

21. Vavilov, "Report note." Copy is in possession of Yuri N. Vavilov.

22. Ibid.

23. I. Prezent, "Pseudoscientific Theories in Genetics," *Vernalization*, No. 2, 1939.

5. Nineteen Forty

1. K. I. Pangalo, "Vavilov: The Man and Scientist," MS.

2. Sinskaya, "Memoirs," MS.

3. The "notes" in the wall newspapers speak primarily of the "wreckers" protected by N. I. Vavilov. VIR, no. 9708, list 3, LGA.

4. Vavilov to Doncho Kosto, May 25, 1940. Photocopy.

5. P. Pomerantsev. "Nikolai Ivanovich Vavilov in the Geographical Society," MS.

6. VIR, no. 9708, case 1705, list 35, LGA.

7. Vavilov to D. Kostov, May 25, 1940, Bulgaria. A photocopy was given to the author by A. A. Kostova-Marinova, who died in 1967.

8. Minutes of meeting, VASKHNIL, op. 1, fasc. 2, archive no. 4, list 146.

9. Charles Nodin (1815-99), French botanist.

10. VIR, no. 9708, case 1735, list 102, LGA.

11. Professor Atabekova feels that Vavilov had visited A. A. Zhdanov during those days.

12. L. P. Breslavets, "Memoirs," MS.
13. V. S. Lekhnovich, private conversation with author.
14. F. K. Bakhteyev, "The Last Decade," speech presented at the Moscow Society of Natural Researchers, Nov. 24, 1965.
15. Notes in possession of V. S. Lekhnovich (Leningrad).
16. Bakhteyev, "The Last Decade."

6. State Prisoner

1. Investigation case no. 1,500, 6:4.
2. Investigation case no. 1,500, vol. 4.
3. Investigation case no. 1,500, vol. 10.
4. Investigation case no. 1,500, vol. 4.
5. Investigation case no. 1,500, 5:247 ff.
6. Shlykov to Malinin, chief of the secret division of the Oktyabr Regional Committee of the party of Leningrad, Mar. 7, 1938.
7. Investigation case no. 1,500, 11:100-101.
8. Investigation case no. 1,500, 4: lists 1-15.
9. Nikolai Vavilov to Lavrentii Beria, head of the NKVD (now the KGB). Investigation case no. 1,500.
10. This matter is described in detail in Mark Popovsky, *White Spot* (Moscow: Znanie Publishers, 1962).
11. Grigori Fillipovsky, private conversation with author, Dec. 9, 1968.
12. Investigation case no. 1,500, vol. 10.
13. Ibid.
14. Sinskaya, "Recollections."
15. N. A. Bazilevskaya, private conversation with author, Dec. 1966.

7. In Search of Justice

1. Personal file on N. I. Vavilov, VASKHNIL, no. 67, fasc. 7.
2. Minutes of the meeting of the Presidium of VASKHNIL, Jan. 7, 1940, Archives of VIR.

3. VIR, case 1833, list 110, LGA.

4. Archival file on N. I. Vavilov, no. 300669, in 3 vols. Begun Dec. 13, 1938.

5. One agent signed his denunciations with the code name "Academician."

6. Anna Kostova-Marinova, "The Story of a Friendship: Academician Kostov and Academician N. I. Vavilov, Sofia-Moscow, 1965-1967." MS.

7. In a letter to Beria in March 1941, Academician D. N. Pryanishnikov wrote: "As president of the Lenin Academy, T. D. Lysenko disorganized its work; the academy, in effect, does not exist—there is only the president-commander and the apparatus that obeys him. There are never any meetings of academicians to discuss scientific questions, academicians are no longer elected. . . . The president says: "What do I need new academicians for, when I don't know what to do with the ones I have?"

8. Ibid.

9. V. I. Vernadsky to his son, Oct. 6, 1944. Archives of the Academy of Sciences of the USSR, 518, op. 2, 61, list 162.

10. The author did not find this in the investigation case for N. I. Vavilov.

11. A. I. Kuptsov, "In Memory of Nikolai Ivanovich Vavilov" (Moscow, June 22, 1958). MS.

8. Into the Flames

1. Vavilov to Beria, Apr. 25, 1942, from prison no. 1 in Saratov. Investigation case no. 1,500, vol. 1.

2. See Alexander Solzhenitsyn's novel, *The First Circle* (New York: Harper and Row, 1968).

3. A. I. Sukhno was a member of the CPSU from August 1917. He taught the history of the CPSU at Moscow University in the 1960s.

4. Private conversation with author.

5. Putting a crazy man into a cell with political prisoners who beat them and took away their food is not a new trick. In the magazine *Hard Labor and Exile*, published in the 1920s, the author

read reports of tsarist gendarmes who treated revolutionaries in the same way. The gendarmes called it "contenting" the prisoners.

6. Letter no. 52/8996, June 13, 1942. Copy in the investigation case no. 1,500, vol. 1.

7. A copy of the document was signed on Feb. 16, 1967 by Dolnikov, the head of the medical unit of the Investigation Isolator no. 1 with the round seal of the prison.

8. A document on the burial site of Academician Vavilov was later drawn up and signed by members of the commission and by Novichkov, the head of the Investigation Isolator Major Andreyev, and Professor S. S. Khokhlov of Saratov University.

Index

Shiffer, Viktor Vikentienvich, 188
Shlykov, Grigori Nikolayevich,
    95, 140–41, 152
Shundenko, Stepan Nikolayevich,
    152, 153–54
Sidorov, Fyodor Fyodorovich,
    139–40
Simirenko, V. L., 50
Sinskaya, E. N., 84, 92, 93, 98,
    110, 117, 119, 152, 158–59,
    164
Skripina, Maria N., 186, 188, 192
Socialist Agriculture, 77
Soviet Academy of Science, 3, 4:
    effect of Vavilov's arrest on
    the, 164; Lysenko and the, 9,
    58–59; Michurin and the, 49
Soviet Subtropics, 95
Spangenberg, G. E., 97
Speransky, A., 75
Stalin, Yosif Vissarionovich: Ly-
    senko and, 66, 79, 80; Prya-
    nishnikov and, 168; Tulaikov
    and, 71; Vavilov and 74,
    99–100
Steklov, 183
Stepanenko, 54–55
Stepanova, Natalia L., 186, 188,
    191, 192
Stoletova, E. A., 162
Stromin, 143
Sukachev, 189
Sukhno, Andrei Ivanovich,
    175–76, 184
Suminov, Konstantin, 197, 199

Talanov, 101, 134, 135
Talyanker, 190
*Theoretical Foundations of Plant
    Selection, The,* 88, 108, 111
Third All-Russian Plant Selection
    Congress, 27
Times (London), 10
Timiryazev, K. A., 24, 34
Timofeyev-Resovsky, Nikolai Vla-
    dimirovich, 50, 75
Tulaikov, I. M., 71, 132

Tulaikov, N. M., 142
Turetsky, 190
Tveritin, 190
Tyumyakov, Nikolai Ananevich,
    49

Ukrainian Academy of Science, 3,
    58
"Uses of Foreign Agricultural Ex-
    perience, the Latest Foreign
    Inventions, and Improved
    Seeds and Plants, The," 112

Vavilov, Nikolai Ivanovich: arrest
    of, 103, 127–29; arrest of his
    supporters, 71, 83, 96–97,
    123; awarded Lenin Prize, 3,
    67; ban on foreign literature
    and, 112–13; burial site of,
    195, 196; in Butyrki prison,
    150, 156; childhood of, 13–15;
    confessions of, 132, 135–36,
    146; cyclical crossings and,
    117; death of, 173, 186–87,
    188, 193; death sentence com-
    muted, 184–85; declining
    health of, 119; as director of
    the All-Union Institute of Ap-
    plied Botany, 34; education
    of, 15, 19; establishment of
    the All-Union Institute of
    Plant Breeding, 4, 67; evacua-
    tion of prisoners in 1941 and,
    175–76; expeditions of, 2, 24,
    35, 67, 68, 70, 123, 124–25;
    forced to resign the presidency
    of the Academy of Agricul-
    ture, 100; hybridization and,
    101–2; informers against,
    137–41, 147; law of homolo-
    gous lines and, 27, 29, 94; Ly-
    senko helped by, 52–53, 54,
    57, 58–60, 65; as member of
    the Academy of Science of the
    USSR, 34; Michurin and,
    42–49; Molotov and, 100, 105,
    145–46, 169; patriotic feelings

of, 70; petitions to Beria,
174–75, 182–83, 184–85; in
Petrograd, 30–33; political
views of, 68; as president of
the Academy of Agriculture,
67; as a prisoner, 130–35, 146;
publications of, 111; relations
with the West, 106–7; restrictions imposed on, 122; in Saratov prison, 176–86; in Saratov prison hospital, 186, 188,
190–91; Seventh International
Congress of Geneticists and,
108–9; sons of, 24, 38, 196;
Stalin and, 74, 99–100; as a
teacher, 24, 25; treatment
from Lysenko, 122, 125; trial
of, 149–51, 154–55; vernalization and, 53–54, 56, 58–59;
views on plant selection, 87;
views on student defectors,
118; wife (first), of, 22, 23, 38;
wife (second), of, 38–40; at
Zhegalov's funeral, 172
Vavilov, Oleg, 24, 38
Vavilov, Sergei, 1, 13, 15, 163, 169
Vavilov, Yuri N., 197
Vernadsky, V. I., 167
Vernalization, 53–54, 56, 58–59, 76
Vernalization, 91, 102, 110

Volf, 132
Vyshinsky, Andrei, 167

Wallace, Henry, 103
White émigrés, 71, 136, 155
"World Resources of Varieties of
Grain Crops and Their Use in
Plant Selection," 112
"Wrecking Activities within the In-
stitute of Plant Breed-
ing . . . ," 133

Yakovlev, P., 59, 62, 73, 93, 132,
135
Yakushevsky, Yefrem, 106
Yakushkin, Ivan Vyacheslavoch,
96, 137, 151

Zaitseva, Aleksandra Alekseyevna,
83
Zalensky, 27
Zaporozhets, 148
Zarubailo, T. Y., 99
Zavadovsky, Mikhail M., 55,
63–64
Zdorodvsky, P., 75
Zhegalov, Sergei, 172
Zirkl, Conway, 79
Zubarev, Aleksei, 151, 160